To Bob Lauer
With Best Wishes
Jim Thompson
January 12, 1998

ENTREPRENEURSHIP AND PRODUCTIVITY

ENTREPRENEURSHIP AND PRODUCTIVITY

Edward E. Williams
and
James R. Thompson

University Press of America,® Inc.
Lanham • New York • Oxford

University Press of America,® Inc.
4720 Boston Way
Lanham, Maryland 20706

12 Hid's Copse Rd.
Cummor Hill, Oxford OX2 9JJ

Printed in the United States of America
British Library Cataloging in Publication Information Available

Library of Congress Cataloging-in-Publication Data

Williams, Edward E.
Entrepreneurship and productivity / Edward E. Williams and James R. Thompson
p. cm.
1. Entrepreneurship. 2. Industrial productivity. I. Thompson, James R. (James Robert), 1938— II. Title.
HB615.W55 1997 338'.04—dc21 97—37314 CIP

ISBN 0-7618-0938-4 (cloth: alk. ppr.)
ISBN 0-7618-0939-2 (pbk: alk. ppr.)

™ The paper used in this publication meets the minimum requirements of American National Standard for information Sciences—Permanence of Paper for Printed Library Materials, ANSI Z39.48—1984

To my wife, Susan Horowitz Williams
Edward E. Williams

To my wife, Ewa Majewska Thompson
James R. Thompson

Contents

LIST OF TABLES

LIST OF FIGURES

Preface

The purpose of this book is to examine a number of the issues affecting entrepreneurship and productivity. Since the advent of the industrial revolution, productivity growth has been far greater than in prior human history. Indeed, growth over the past hundred or so years for the sixteen leading industrial countries of the world has averaged an increase of about 1,150 percent. In the prior fifteen centuries, there was little significant growth. Yet, between 1870 and 1980, output per work-hour increased five-fold in Australia, twelve-fold in the United States, and twenty six-fold in Japan.

Huge increases in productivity have resulted in tremendous improvements in living standards as expressed in terms of per capita income. But we must ask: What factors contribute to enhanced productivity and substantially higher income levels? Has world-wide productivity peaked and is the United States doomed to lower growth rates in future production? What role do entrepreneurship and quality play in productivity and production decisions? The purpose of this book is to address these questions and provide guidance to enhance the chances for continued growth in productivity and improved quality production.

In our view, when discussing "productivity," one should avoid the insistence of most authorities on dealing simply with labor productivity. The real issue is the productivity of all the factors of production. We want to know about productivity because of its intimate relationship to the production of quality goods and services competitively. A principal task of this book is to show how technological progress can be translated into gain for an individual, a company, and a nation. Some view an economy as a kind of zero sum game where the gain of someone represents a loss for somebody else. Such an outlook might be appropriate for a primative society devoid of innovation. It certainly has no basis in the First World, including the new technological tigers in Japan, South Korea, Taiwan, and Singapore. A treatise which neglects the importance of a constantly increasing level of productivity might be appropriate for the Twelfth Century, but is hardly so for the Twenty-First.

Input/output analysis addresses the issue of maximizing production given a certain level of inputs or minimizing inputs usage given a certain output. Unfortunately, the issue of quality is often lost in the analysis. An aggregate economy may produce lots of goods and services, but these outputs may provide little consumer satisfaction if they are of inferior quality. Similarly, an enterprise may maximize its production of output given input usage; but if the product is shoddily made, it will not provide utility to consumers and ultimately will not sell in the market place. Hence, quality control is also an integral part of any analysis of production and productivity.

It is our hope that this book will find an attractive home as a textbook for students of business administration, economics and engineering. It is written with the market decision-maker (entrepreneur) as its focus, and it is intended to give the decision-maker insights into issues affecting enterprise production and productivity as well as the macroeconomic aspects of aggregate output. The book should be effective at the undergraduate and graduate levels in management, economics, and engineering courses where there is an emphasis on production and productivity. Students who have not had any introductory courses in economics should be able to handle the material without much difficulty, and many of the important ingredients of both microeconomics and macroeconomics are revealed in the context of production analysis. The book could also be useful as a supplement in mathematical sciences and statistics courses. Students in these areas will find the mathematics relatively simple, but the issues addressed are seldom found in standard texts used by these students. One of the authors has used the material in the book quite successfully as a supplement in first year MBA courses in both managerial economics and entrepreneurship.

The genesis of this book was in a course taught jointly by the authors to MBA students at Rice University several years ago. Since then, the manuscript has been revised extensively and used subsequently in several courses. The book is organized along topical lines with introductory and philosophical material coming first and more difficult and application material coming later. The manuscript was typeset using the Textures package of Blue Sky Software.

This book is divided into eleven chapters and three distinct areas of analysis. The first chapter serves as an over all introduction to the nature of productivity and production. The measurement of productivity is analyzed and production functions are discussed in this chapter. In Chapters 2 and 3, we provide an analysis of aggregate production for an economy. In Chapters 4 through 7, we consider production at the enterprise level and provide an entrepreneurial and planning model for the entrepreneurial enterprise. Chapters 8 through 11 are concerned with modern statistical techniques useful for the analysis and utilization of time indexed economic and production oriented data.

The authors would like to thank Diane Brown, Jagdish Chandra, Katherine Ensor, Thomas Eubank, Jacek Koronacki, Robert Launer, Ewa Thompson, and Susan Williams. Thanks are due to the Army Research Office (Durham) which has supported, in part, Thompson's research for this book under ARO-DAAH04-95-1-0665.

E.E.W. Houston, Texas
J.R.T. January, 1998

Chapter 1

Productivity and Production

1.1 Introduction

Since the advent of the industrial revolution, productivity growth has been far greater than in prior human history. Indeed, growth over the past hundred or so years for the sixteen leading industrial countries of the world has averaged an increase of about 1,150 percent. In the prior fifteen centuries, there was little significant growth. Yet, between 1870 and 1980, output per work-hour increased five-fold in Australia, twelve-fold in the United States, and twenty six-fold in Japan [see 1].

Huge increases in productivity have resulted in tremendous improvements in living standards as expressed in terms of per capita income. But we must ask: What factors contributed to enhanced productivity and substantially higher income levels? Has world-wide productivity peaked and is the United States doomed to lower growth rates in future production? What role do entrepreneurshp and quality play in productivity and production decisions? The purpose of this book is to answer these questions and provide guidance to enhance the chances for continued growth in productivity and improved quality production.

1.2 What Is Productivity?

Most experts define productivity in labor efficiency terms. At the aggregate level, the Bureau of Labor Statistics, the primary source of productivity information, focuses its attention on output per hour of labor input. Suppose we let gross domestic product be 100 (in "units of output") and it takes fifty hours of labor to produce the 100 units of output. The productivity of labor might thus be determined as $100/50 = 2$. This number may not mean much in and of itself, but over time it can be quite meaningful as an efficiency measure. We have data going back a number of years tracing gross domestic product per work hour (see Figure 1.1). There is a trend in these data with major increases taking place between 1947 and 1973, with productivity reaching a plateau and with *relative* productivity (the rate of growth in gains) beginning to decline. This decline in relative productivity appears to have been reversed during the early 1980s, only to begin its decline once again by the late 1980s (See Figure 1.2).

The data in Figures 1.1 and 1.2 are compiled using a simple equation:

$$\text{Productivity} = \frac{\text{Gross Domestic Product}}{\text{Total Hours Worked}} \tag{1.1}$$

This is essentially an engineering relationship of physical phenomena wherein we take gross domestic product (the sum of all final goods and services produced within an economy) and divide that figure by the number of hours worked in a year. This gives us production per work hour. Of course, gross domestic product must have some numeraire of measurement. Dollars (or yen or pounds, etc.) help us to count apples and oranges (literally) so that we can sum aggregate output. The data in Figures 1.1 and 1.2 trace out the efficiency of American labor since 1947. First, the data are calculated as per equation (1.1). They are then indexed, using 1982 as a base year. For example, if workers could produce \$50 worth of goods per hour in 1982 and \$60 worth in 1990, then the nominal dollar value of output per hour may be indexed as: \$50 = 100 and \$60 = 60/50 = 120. The data on growth in labor productivity (Figure 1.2) simply take the percentage change from one year to the next.

Notice there is also an apparent cyclical element in these data. There is a tendency for productivity to fall during recessions and to rebound during periods of expansion. During the 1974 recession, for example, productivity fell by 1.8%, but then grew by 2.3% and 2.9% in the following two years. Similarly, during 1979 and 1980, productivity declined during recession and then increased in 1983 and 1984. (There was a slight recession in 1981, causing the 1982 number to be weak as well.) Meager real economic growth after 1988 caused productivity to be essentially flat over the period 1989-1991. With the end of the 1990-1991 recession, productivity rebounded in 1992. Interestingly, in periods prior to 1974, the rate of increase in productivity merely slowed during recessions but still remained positive. From 1974 onward, the rate has actually become negative during economic recessions.

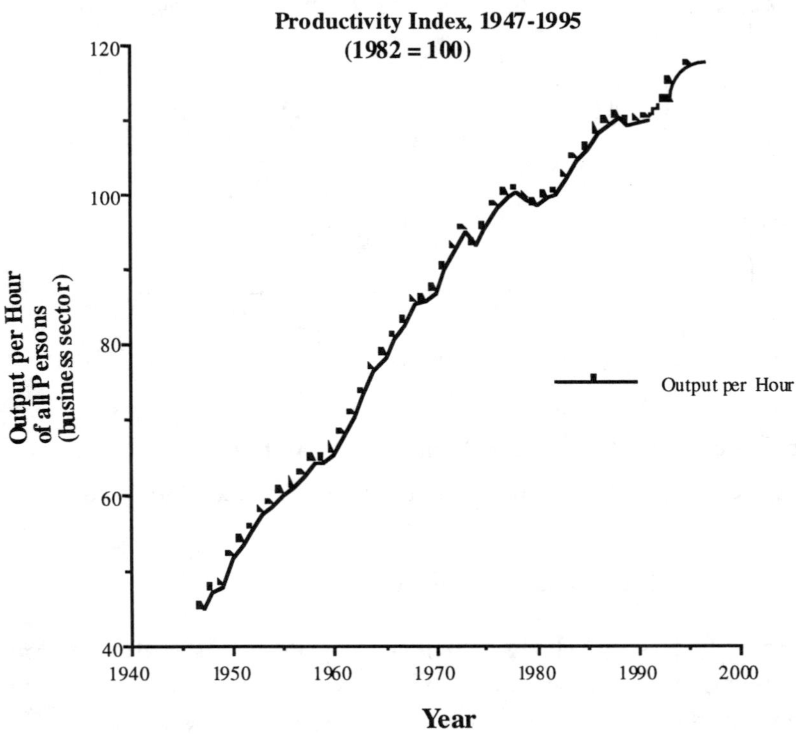

Source: ***Economic Report of the President*, 1994 and 1996**

Figure 1.1 Productivity Index, 1947-1995.

There is an economic explanation for the apparent cyclicality of productivity: During recessions, workers are laid-off. As prosperity returns, businesses do not normally rehire until they are convinced the upturn is not transitory. Hence, during the early stages of growth out of a recession, a given work force does more work. Of course, this enhances the relative productivity of that work force.

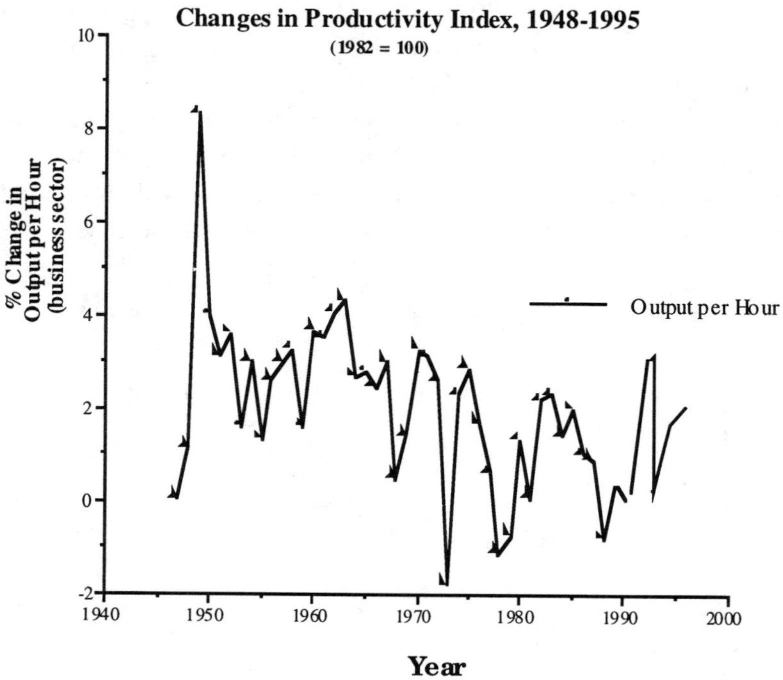

Source: *Economic Report of the President*, 1994 and 1996

Figure 1.2 Changes in Productivity Index, 1948-1995.

1.3 Beyond Labor Efficiency

Equation (1.1) is clearly an efficiency measure. It certainly does tell us whether or not we have had to expend less (or more) hours of labor to get a "unit" of output. Nevertheless, many authorities question the use of productivity measures that focus on labor alone in assessing productivity. Professor W.B. Chew of Harvard University, for example, relates the following: "A few years ago, a major manufacturing-based conglomerate asked a gifted mathematician to join its corporate staff. One of his first assignments was to design a system that senior managers could use to evaluate the operating efficiency of the company's various divisions. He devoted many months to the assignment and also tapped the knowledge of several academic experts. The result was a truly sophisticated model that combined historical performance data with economic forecasts to set target productivity levels for each business unit. "Much to management's dismay, however, when the results were in, the model suggested that not one unit was performing up to snuff. So headquarters asked the obvious question — Why? Why was an organization that was generating handsome profits and cash flows showing such disappointing productivity? The expert could not answer the question, nor was his model designed to do so. Not surprisingly, executives saw little value in the new system and scrapped it." [3, p. 110].

The mathematician in Chew's example had a highly complex model, but it simply did not apply. The reason was that the model ignored other very important factors besides labor inputs. "Productivity measurement should focus on overall capabilities, not on one set of costs. How good is your company at taking a pile of raw materials, a bunch of machines, stacks of paperwork, and groups of employees, and turning out useful goods or services? That's what a productivity index should address" [3, p. 111]. A simple formula to measure productivity, according to Professor Chew, would be:

$$\text{Productivity} = \frac{\text{Units of Output}}{\text{Units of Input}} \,. \tag{1.2}$$

Getting more output for a given amount of input would result in higher productivity by this measure. Alternatively, obtaining the same amount of output for less input would result in enhanced productivity.

1.4 Beyond Efficiency

Although Chew is quite correct in pointing out that there are other factors besides labor that influence productivity, it should also be recognized that the whole reason we want to know something about *productivity* is because we really want to find out about *production*, i.e., the volume of goods and services that we can ultimately produce and consume (in the aggregate case) or bring to the market place and sell (in the enterprise level case). Unfortunately, we often confuse productivity with production, and the lay (non-economist) reader might be forgiven for being alarmed when told that the rate of growth of productivity is falling even though he can see that production (in the form of gross domestic product) and standards of living are rising. Because of this confusion between the words "productivity" and "production," the reader should be aware that we shall be concerned with *both* notions in this book. Our primary concern, however, will be with production (how a society or a firm can produce more), although we shall not lose sight of the importance of efficiency (the economists "productivity") in abetting production. We shall also be concerned with the quality of production. Quality has to do with the ability of an economy or an enterprise to produce goods and/or services that are relatively free of defects. Finally, we shall be interested in getting as much output as possible given the inputs with which we have to work (available inputs). A side issue here relates to idle inputs, or insufficiently utilized inputs. Particularly in the case of an aggregate economy, these potential inputs may be significant and may contribute substantially to increasing output. Idle inputs would include unwillingly unemployed labor and insufficiently utilized capital.

1.5 The Factors of Production

At the aggregate level, an economy's inputs may be broadly categorized as land, labor, and capital; or, in the parlance of the economist, as the *factors of production.* Land is a general term used to signify the natural resources of an economy and is essentially a fixed factor, although it can be freshly discovered, improved in quality and reclaimed. Land is thus essentially inelastic in supply. Labor may increase with population growth, and labor utilization may vary depending on the condition and preferences of laborers. (There are 8,760 hours in a year, but the average American only works about 2,000 of them. The rest are spent sleeping, relaxing, and performing non-work activities). Thus, labor is somewhat more elastic (than land) in supply. Capital results from an economy electing not to consume all of its output. When participants in an economy choose to save (i.e. not consume), that part of the economy's output may take the form of new structures (plant), new producer durables (equipment), and changes in inventory levels (raw materials, goods in process, or finished goods). The supply of capital over the long-run may be highly elastic, depending on the willingness of economic participants to sacrifice consuming today for more consumption tomorrow, although in the short-run the stock of capital is essentially given (inelastic) since it takes time to produce plant, equipment, and inventories.

Although economists often think of land, labor and capital as the only factors of production, other less tangible factors such as technology and the creative use of factors (called entrepreneurship) may be even more important as determinants of production. Professor Robert Solow, for example, has found only a small fraction of the growth in real output over the first half of the twentieth century can be accounted for using the traditional economic inputs [see 8]. Nevertheless, it is difficult to discover what causes technological improvement and entrepreneurial successes. These are very important factors in any discussion of productivity, however, and we shall return to them later in this book.

1.6 Enterprise Level Factors

At the enterprise level, the same inputs are employed (land, labor, and capital) although the firm may also purchase another firm's outputs (called materials). Thus, the firm may use varying combinations of inputs like an economy. The firm "saves" just like an economy as a whole (by retaining earnings) and it may finance its acquisition of capital by saving. The problem with using labor productivity measurements alone is even better illustrated when we consider the productivity decisions of an individual company, however. The trouble with single-factor productivity measures (whether output per labor hour, output per machine, or output per ton of material) is that it is easy to increase the productivity of one factor by replacing it with another. Labor, capital, and materials are all potential substitutes for each other.

Effective productivity measurement requires the development of an index that identifies the contribution of each factor of production and then tracks and combines them. "Take a hypothetical plant that machines purchased castings as one step in its production of motors.

Now the company decides to purchase this component pre machined. The pre machined parts cost 20% more than standard castings, but buying them allows the company to lay off skilled workers and sell its machine tools. What happens to productivity? Output has remained constant, but the number of workers has fallen, so labor productivity is up. So too is capital productivity, by virtue of the lower asset base. But materials productivity has declined by 20% since output is unchanged, while the value of purchased materials has gone up" [3, pp. 111-114]. We may call the phenomenon referred to above as the *fallacy of mistaken productivity measurement.* Given the substitutability of all input factors, it is possible, for example, to substitute materials for labor and capital and get constant output. Labor and capital productivity might be enhanced as a result, but materials productivity would fall. Has the firm become more or less productive as a result? The answer can only be obtained with additional data: the price of labor inputs, the price of capital inputs, and the price of materials inputs. If the dollar savings in labor and capital were greater than the extra costs of materials, the firm would be more productive. If the dollar savings were less than the costs, the firm would be less productive. Thus, it is a mistake to attempt to measure productivity unless all input factors (and their relative costs) are taken into account with total output [see 5].

1.7 Productivity Correctly Considered

We have seen above that it is incorrect to focus on only one input factor to measure productivity. Also, it is wrong to look just at input factors without also considering their respective costs in determining optimal production levels. Efficient production takes place where all factor outputs, given their relative costs, are set equal to each other. It is clear that this formulation results in efficiency since if output resulting from the use of any input, given its cost, were greater than another, it would pay to substitute that factor for a more expensive (less efficient) factor.

For example, suppose three units of output could be produced by one unit of resources, five units could be produced by one unit of labor, and ten by one unit of capital. Suppose further that one unit of resources costs $3, a unit of labor costs $5, and a unit of capital costs \$8. It follows that by spending \$3 on resources we can get three units of output (\$1 per unit), by spending \$5 on labor we can get five units of output (\$1 per unit), and by spending \$8 on capital we can get ten units of output (\$.80 per unit). Here resources and labor would be said to be less efficient (less productive) than capital. As a consequence, it would make economic sense to substitute capital for resources and labor until either the efficiency (output) of capital fell and/or that of labor and resources rose. Later in this chapter, we shall discuss factors that would cause one or both of these events to occur. From the example above, we may posit a formula to attain efficient production, given costs, as follows:

$$\frac{R_0}{P_R} = \frac{L_0}{P_L} = \frac{K_0}{P_K} \; . \qquad (1.3)$$

where:

R_0 = Units of output produced by one unit of resources (land, natural resources, and for the enterprise, materials).
L_0 = Units of output produced by one unit of labor.
K_0 = Units of output produced by one unit of capital.
P_R = The cost of a unit of resources.
P_L = The cost of a unit of labor.
P_K = The cost of a unit of capital.

Given our example above, we would find:

$$\frac{3}{\$3} = \frac{5}{\$5} < \frac{10}{\$8}$$

Equation (1.3) describes the efficient use of all available inputs. It does not address the issue of how more inputs may be created (discussed later in this book), and it does not consider what may be done with under- or unutilized inputs. In a sense, these are "free" inputs if a way can be thought of to use them. For an aggregate economy, it is often true that insufficient aggregate demand (say, a recession) will cause unemployment of labor or underutilization of plant capacity, and a goal of aggregate economic policy might be to figure out how to employ these resources.

1.8 Production Functions

Like all efficiency equations, (1.3) does not tell us how (or whether) we should increase production, only how to minimize the cost of a given production level. A more broad-based equation would take total output (Q) into account and would relate output to inputs. Such an equation, called a *production function*, would be of the form:

$$Q = f(R, L, K). \tag{1.4}$$

and would show what would happen to total output (Q) whenever resources (R), labor (L), or capital (K) were changed. Of course, for any level of Q, we could invoke (1.3) to assure that an efficient mix of inputs were utilized.

Economists assume given shapes for production functions. Short-run functions are defined as those where the time period is too short to vary the amount of plant and equipment with which they operate. If we were to simplify (1.4) by ignoring R, labor would be the only variable factor in the short-run. In this case, we might find the production function shown in Figure 1.3. In this function, there is an increasing portion between zero and A. This increasing portion suggests that production may increase at a faster rate than the use of labor inputs as more labor inputs are employed. Such an event may happen as certain labor efficiencies are achieved when more people are hired. Specialization of tasks may make it possible, for example, for two people to produce more than twice as much as any one individual could produce on his or her own. Between A and B, there is a linear portion. The linear portion may be said to indicate "constant returns" because it indicates that output varies proportionally with labor. Eventually, as we see in Figure 1.3, as more and more labor is employed with a fixed amount of plant and equipment, however, inefficiencies may result. When this occurs, the proportional relationship between the output of product and the input of labor will be succeeded by one that is less than proportional. Thus we see that, beyond B, the increment to total output that results from each increment of labor input becomes smaller and smaller. The decreasing portion of the total product curve, starting at B, illustrates this stage of diminishing or decreasing returns to further labor input. Finally, beyond C, further labor input will not increase total output at all (Q is constant between C and D); in fact, at some even higher level of labor input (beyond D), output will begin to decrease as more workers are hired.

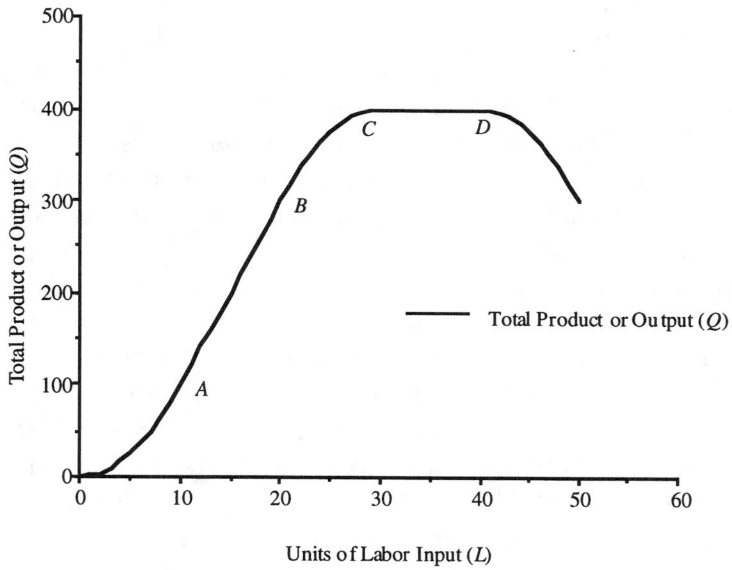

Figure 1.3 The Short-Run Production Function.

1.9 Return Economies

A similar analysis would apply if we were to ignore L and let R vary in the short-run. This is illustrated in Figure 1.4, which looks very much like Figure 1.3 except output Q is related to any input (R, L, and K), holding the other two constant. In the case of the increasing portion, (zero to A), Q rises by more than the utilization of the variable input (F). This is called a case of *increasing returns to the variable input.* We discussed reasons for this to occur for labor above. In the case of resources, we might achieve economies of combination whereby the utilization of additional inputs (say raw materials) could be more productive at higher levels of use than lower. In the case of capital, certain equipment may operate more efficiently with heavier than lighter use. The linear portion (A to B) illustrates *constant returns to the variable input* where there are neither efficiencies or inefficiencies of utilization. Increasing inputs by a factor of X raises output by a constant factor of Y. Anywhere along F, any ΔF will produce a given ΔQ depending on the slope of the production function over its linear span. The decreasing portion (B to C) suggests a case of *diminishing or decreasing returns to the variable input* where Q rises at a slower rate than the utilization of the variable input. The reasons for decreasing returns for labor were alluded to above but may be amplified. One explanation is that more efficient workers are typically hired first. As more labor is added, new workers produce less per hour than their previously hired counterparts. Also, diminishing returns may occur when extra inputs come from working a given labor force more intensely. Overtime hours are notoriously less efficient than hours worked by fresh labor early in the shift, for example. Capital equipment may be less efficient the more intensely it is employed. Breakdowns and downtiming frequently occur for machines that are operated over long time spans. These clearly reduce the output of such equipment per unit of input (say hours operated). At some point (C to D), output may not increase at all even if more inputs are added. Generally speaking, economists regard capital and resources as fixed in the short run. Hence, the diagram in Figure 1.4 becomes identical to that in Figure 1.3.

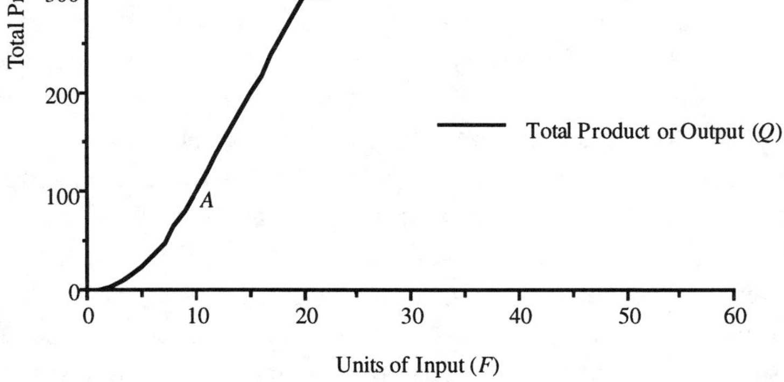

Figure 1.4. Production with One Variable and Two Fixed Components.

1.10 Absolutely Diminishing Returns

An interesting phenomenon occurs at D in Figure 1.4. Total production actually declines as additional units of input are added. In Figure 1.4, this causes the Q function to turn down from its peak and the marginal product of the additional unit would become negative. Table 1.1 portrays a discrete production function with an increasing portion (F=0 to F=10), a constant portion (F = 11 to F=20), and a decreasing portion F = 21 to F=30). *Zero returns* is the term applied to a case where added inputs result in producing the same quality of inputs (F = 31 to F = 40), and *absolutely diminishing returns* is the term applied to a case where added inputs actually cause output to fall (F = 41 to F = 50).

It is undoubtedly an engineering (and sociological) possibility for an economy or an enterprise to continue adding inputs until output declines, but such an occurrence would never make economic sense. There are some nations (and even possibly a number of American businesses) where objectives other than efficiency may dominate. After the 1949 Communist Revolution in China, for example, providing a job for every worker was clearly a goal which received priority over maximizing output. As a consequence, there were many years where Chinese gross domestic product could have been higher if *fewer* workers were assigned to the nation's various government owned plants. Workers would get in each other's way and, in an attempt to "look busy," might actually undo the positive work of others! In the very long-run, the sorts of policies that reduce output will become politically unacceptable. This has happened in a number of formerly socialist countries [see 9, 10, 11]. Also, even though some companies in capitalist countries may attempt to "provide jobs" rather than maximize profits, these policies will become unacceptable as well: in the very long-run, these enterprises will go bankrupt unless they are subsidized.

1.11 Scale Economies and Optimal Production

Economists generally admit complete variability in all the factors of production in the long run (where R, L, and K are freely variable

Table 1.1. A Short-Run Production Function.

F	Q	ΔQ
0	0	0
1	1	1
2	4	3
3	9	5
4	16	7
5	25	9
6	36	11
7	49	13
8	64	15
9	81	17
10	100	19
11	120	20
12	140	20
13	160	20
14	180	20
15	200	20
16	220	20
17	240	20
18	260	20
19	280	20
20	300	20
21	319	19
22	336	17
23	351	15
24	364	13
25	375	11
26	384	9
27	391	7
28	396	5
29	399	3
30	400	1
31	400	0
32	400	0
33	400	0
34	400	0
35	400	0
36	400	0
37	400	0
38	400	0
39	400	0
40	400	0
41	399	-1
42	396	-3
43	391	-5
44	384	-7
45	375	-9
46	364	-11
47	351	-13
48	336	-15
49	319	-17
50	300	-19

and substitutable). Figure 1.5 illustrates total production from varying all inputs. Generally, when we are considering varying all inputs, we think in terms of total, or scale, production. If total output increases more than proportionally to total inputs (zero to A in Figure 1.5), we say that we are enjoying *increasing returns to scale.* If total output increases proportionately with total inputs ($A$to B in Figure 1.5), we say that we are experiencing *constant returns to scale.* If total output increases less than proportionally to total inputs (B to C in Figure 1.5), we say that we are suffering *decreasing returns to scale.* If total output does not increase as inputs we added (C to D in Figure 1.5), we say we have a case of *zero returns to scale*; and, if total output actually falls as inputs are added (beyond D in Figure 1.5), we say we have a case of *absolute decreasing returns to scale.*

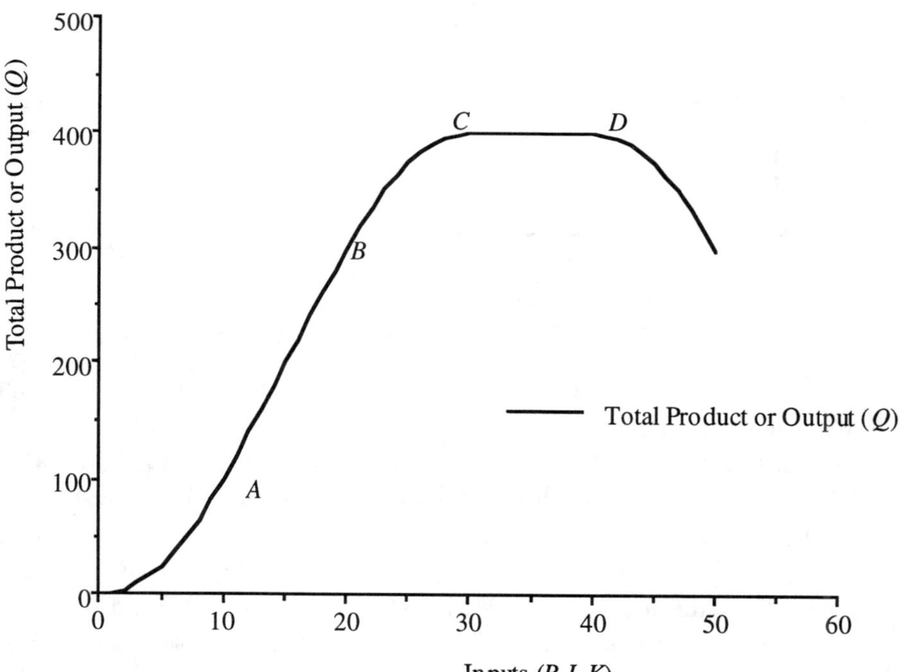

Figure 1.5 The Long-Run Production Function.

Figure 1.6 illustrates the *marginal (or extra) product* associated with the total product of Figure 1.5. As we move from zero to A, Q rises by more than the utilization of inputs and the marginal product is increasing. From A to B, marginal product is constant; from B to C, marginal productivity is falling; from C to D, marginal product is zero; and beyond D, marginal product is negative. Letting Q be production (output) and I represent all inputs, $\Delta Q/\Delta I$ would be the marginal product or marginal production resulting from employing I inputs.

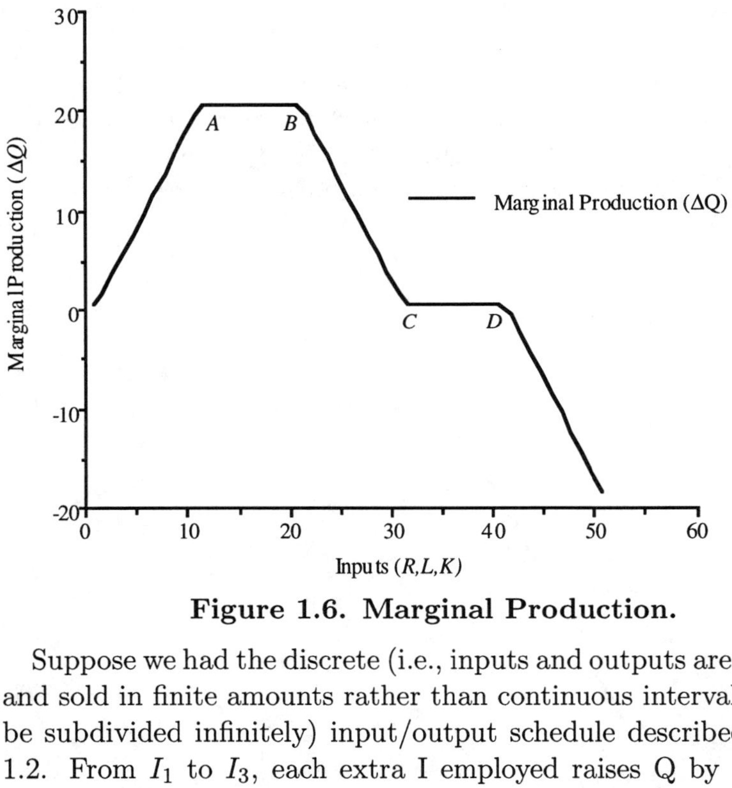

Figure 1.6. Marginal Production.

Suppose we had the discrete (i.e., inputs and outputs are purchased and sold in finite amounts rather than continuous intervals that can be subdivided infinitely) input/output schedule described in Table 1.2. From I_1 to I_3, each extra I employed raises Q by more than each prior extra unit. This is the area of increasing returns. For I_4 and I_5, each extra I added increases Q by an equal quantity (constant returns), while for I_6 to I_8, each extra I employed raises Q by less than each prior extra unit (decreasing returns). Given the shapes of the input/output (production) functions posited above, we might return to equation (1.3) and reformulate it to take into account the possibilities of increasing, constant, and decreasing returns. It should be obvious that the principal issue here is one of substitutability; that is, can (or should) resources, labor, and capital be switched, and if so, what is the optimal (best) combination.

Table 1.2. A Long-Run Production Function.

I_n	R	L	K	Q	$\frac{I_n}{I_{n-1}}$	$\frac{Q_n}{Q_{n-1}}$
I_1	10	10	10	10	–	–
I_2	20	20	20	30	2.00	3.00
I_3	40	40	40	75	2.00	2.50
I_4	80	80	80	150	2.00	2.00
I_5	160	160	160	300	2.00	2.00
I_6	320	320	320	450	2.00	1.50
I_7	640	640	640	600	2.00	1.33
I_8	1280	1280	1280	600	2.00	1.00

1.12 Factor Switching

The issue of *can* resources be switched (substituted for each other) depends on the facts. Certain tasks may be performed *only* by labor. If this is true, there is no question of substitution. In this case, the marginal product of labor would always exceed that of capital and resources since the latter would essentially have zero productivity. Similarly, other tasks may *only* be handled by machines. Here the marginal product of capital would always exceed that of labor ($= 0$) and resources ($= 0$). Some output can only be made with a combination of inputs.

Without raw materials, all the labor and capital in the world might not be able to produce output. In this case, we would have required joint inputs, where only certain combinations of R, L, and K could be employed. For example, the production of a tank car may require so much steel, period. It simply cannot be made out of thin air (although other materials, such as aluminum, might be substituted). Although joint inputs requiring R, L, and/or K may seem to be the most common case, there is more substitutability in many production processes than one might think. Take the tank car example above. Although some steel might be required, varying amounts could be used depending on the efficiency of the labor producing the car and the quality of the machinery being employed to fabricate it. New equipment and a highly trained labor force might be able to produce the same car with less steel than old equipment and less skilled labor that caused material wastage. Similarly, there is probably a good deal of substitutability between capital and labor. Modern equipment might be employed to produce a car with less labor required than older equipment.

Table 1.3. Inputs, Outputs.

R	L	K	Q	$C(R,L,K)$	$\frac{C}{Q}$
0	0	0	0	\$0	\$0.000
0	0	1	14	12	0.857
0	0	2	26	24	0.923
0	0	3	36	36	1.000
0	1	0	12	11	0.917
0	1	1	26	23	0.885
0	1	2	38	35	0.921
0	1	3	48	47	0.979
0	2	0	23	22	0.957
0	2	1	37	34	0.919
0	2	2	49	46	0.939
0	2	3	59	58	0.983
0	3	0	33	33	1.000
0	3	1	47	45	0.957
0	3	2	59	57	0.966
0	3	3	69	69	1.000
1	0	0	10	10	1.000
1	0	1	24	22	0.917
1	0	2	36	34	0.944
1	0	3	46	46	1.000
1	1	0	22	21	0.955
1	1	1	36	33	0.917
1	1	2	48	45	0.938
1	1	3	58	57	0.983
1	2	0	33	32	0.970
1	2	1	47	44	0.936
1	2	2	59	56	0.949
1	2	3	69	68	0.986
1	3	0	43	43	1.000
1	3	1	57	55	0.965
1	3	2	69	67	0.971
1	3	3	79	79	1.000
2	0	0	18	20	1.111
2	0	1	32	32	1.000
2	0	2	44	44	1.000
2	0	3	54	56	1.037
2	1	0	30	31	1.033
2	1	1	44	43	0.977
2	1	2	56	55	0.982
2	1	3	66	67	1.015
2	2	0	41	42	1.024
2	2	1	55	54	0.982
2	2	2	67	66	0.985
2	2	3	77	78	1.013
2	3	0	51	53	1.039
2	3	1	65	65	1.000
2	3	2	77	77	1.000
2	3	3	87	89	1.023
3	0	0	24	30	1.250
3	0	1	38	42	1.105
3	0	2	50	54	1.080
3	0	3	60	66	1.100
3	1	0	36	41	1.139
3	1	1	50	53	1.060
3	1	2	62	65	1.048
3	1	3	72	77	1.069
3	2	0	47	52	1.106
3	2	1	61	64	1.049
3	2	2	73	76	1.041
3	2	3	83	88	1.060
3	3	0	57	63	1.105
3	3	1	71	75	1.056
3	3	2	83	87	1.048
3	3	3	93	99	1.065

1.13 Optimal Inputs

In general, we shall assume there is some degree of substitutability for most production processes. Thus, we can invoke an equation similar to equation (1.3) to determine least cost and efficient inputs. Let us assume the data provided in Table 1.3. It is clear from these data that maximum output would occur when $R = L = K = 3$ where 93 units would be produced. However, is this necessarily efficient? The answer would depend on the costs of each R, L, and K. Suppose R costs \$10, L costs \$11, and Kcosts \$12. Given these facts, we could work out column $C(R, L, K)$, which is the cost of each factor unit times the number units employed.

Dividing that by Q, we could calculate the least unit cost production level. This would occur at $R = 0$, $L = 0$, $K = 1$, where $Q = 14$ and C/Q =\$.857. However, the least cost combination is not necessarily an efficient combination, as we shall see.

Lurking behind the data in Table 1.3 are production functions for R, L, and K. The production functions assumed in Table 1.3 are:

Table 1.3a. Subproduction Functions.

R	Q		L	Q		K	Q
0	0		0	0		0	0
1	10		1	12		1	14
2	18		2	23		2	26
3	24		3	33		3	36

The extra physical production of each unit of each factor (called *marginal physical products* or MPPs) would thus be:

Table 1.3b. Marginal Physical Products.

Units	MPP_R	MPP_L	MPP_K
1	10	12	14
2	8	11	12
3	6	10	10

Comparing the efficiency of each input, we might reformulate equation (1.3) as:

$$\frac{MPP_R}{P_R} = \frac{MPP_L}{P_L} = \frac{MPP_K}{P_K} \tag{1.5}$$

where:

MPP_R = The marginal physical product of one unit of resources.
MPP_L = The marginal physical product of one unit of labor.
MPP_K = The marginal physical product of one unit of capital.
P_R = The cost of a unit of resources.
P_L = The cost of a unit of labor.
P_K = The cost of a unit of capital.

Applying (1.5) to our example, we find the following:

Table 1.3c. An Efficient Solution.

Units	Resources	Labor	Capital
0	0	0	0
1	10/10 = 1.00	12/11 = 1.09	14/12 = 1.17
2	8/10 = .80	11/11 = 1.00	12/12 = 1.00
3	6/10 = .60	10/11 = .91	10/12 = .83

Thus, invoking equation (1.5), an efficient solution could be determined as: $R = 1$, $L = 2$, $K = 2$, producing $Q = 59$.

1.14 Optimal Output

At this point, the thoughtful reader might observe: It is true that the least unit cost solution is $R = 0$, $L = 0$, $K = 1$ and an efficient solution is $R = 1$,$L = 2$, $K = 2$, but total efficiency surely must take into account what output could be sold for as well as its cost. Thus, at the enterprise level, the key to the question would be: How much can be obtained from selling each unit of output. If we are in the widget business and widgets can be sold for \$2 a piece, it might pay to use as much resources, labor, and capital as possible until unit costs exceeded \$2. Of course, we would still have to decide optimal inputs, but the question could not even be addressed properly until we knew at what price we could sell our product. Competitive conditions in the marketplace might thus also influence the result. If our participation in the market could influence price, the \$2 unit selling price might change depending on the quantity we supplied. We shall ignore this complexity for now, but we shall return to a discussion of price/quantity decisions in imperfect markets. Similarly, at the aggregate level, it is impossible to make correct statements about the efficient use of resources, labor and capital until we know something about optimal output levels. This critical issue will occupy much of Chapters 2 and 3 of this book.

Table 1.4. Output and Costs.

Q	C	$\frac{C}{Q}$	Combinations (R, L, K)
0	\$0	\$0.000	0,0,0
10	10	1.000	1,0,0
12	11	0.917	0,1,0
14	12	0.857	0,0,1
18	20	1.111	2,0,0
22	21	0.955	1,1,0
23	22	0.957	0,2,0
24	22	0.917	1,0,1
24	30	1.250	3,0,0
26	23	0.885	0,1,1
26	24	0.923	0,0,2
30	31	1.033	2,1,0
32	32	1.000	2,0,1
33	32	.970	1,2,0
33	33	1.000	0,3,0
36	33	0.917	1,1,1
36	34	0.944	1,0,2
36	36	1.000	0,0,3
36	41	1.139	3,1,0
37	34	0.919	0,2,1
38	35	0.921	0,1,2
38	42	1.105	3,0,1
41	42	1.024	2,2,0
43	43	1.000	1,3,0
44	43	0.977	2,1,1
44	44	1.000	2,0,2
46	46	1.000	1,0,3
47	44	0.936	1,2,1
47	45	0.957	0,3,1
47	52	1.169	3,2,0
48	45	0.938	1,1,2
48	47	0.979	0,1,3
49	46	0.939	0,2,2
50	53	1.060	3,1,1
50	54	1.080	3,0,2
51	53	1.039	2,3,0
54	56	1.037	2,0,3
55	54	0.982	2,2,1
56	55	0.982	2,1,2
57	55	0.965	1,3,1
57	63	1.105	3,3,0
58	57	0.983	1,1,3
59	56	0.949	1,2,2
59	57	0.966	0,3,2
59	58	0.983	0,2,3
60	66	1.100	3,0,3
61	64	1.049	3,2,1
62	65	1.048	3,1,2
65	65	1.000	2,3,1
66	67	1.015	2,1,3
67	66	0.985	2,2,2
69	67	0.971	1,3,2
69	68	0.986	1,2,3
69	69	1.000	0,3,3
71	75	1.056	3,3,1
72	77	1.069	3,1,3
73	76	1.041	3,2,2
77	77	1.000	2,3,2
77	78	1.013	2,2,3
79	79	1.000	1,3,3
83	87	1.048	3,3,2
83	88	1.060	3,2,3
87	89	1.023	2,3,3
93	99	1.065	3,3,3

Let us examine Table 1.3 again. Suppose we can sell our output for $1.00. How much should we produce? The answer would be determined by reflecting on two things: 1) What are our goals as an enterprise, and 2) What choices do we have?

Table 1.5. Output, Costs, and Profits.

Combination	Revenue= (P × Q)	C	Profit = (P × Q) - C
0,0,0	$1 x 0 = $ 0	$0	$0
1,0,0	1 x 10 = 10	10	0
0,1,0	1 x 12 = 12	11	1
0,0,1	1 x 14 = 14	12	2
2,0,0	1 x 18 = 18	20	- 2
1,1,0	1 x 22 = 22	21	1
0,2,0	1 x 23 = 23	22	1
1,0,1	1 x 24 = 24	22	2
3,0,0	1 x 24 = 24	30	- 6
0,1,1	1 x 26 = 26	23	3
0,0,2	1 x 26 = 26	24	2
2,1,0	1 x 30 = 30	31	- 1
2,0,1	1 x 32 = 32	32	0
1,2,0	1 x 33 = 33	32	1
0,3,0	1 x 33 = 33	33	0
1,1,1	1 x 36 = 36	33	3
1,0,2	1 x 36 = 36	34	2
0,0,3	1 x 36 = 36	36	0
3,1,0	1 x 36 = 36	41	- 5
0,2,1	1 x 37 = 37	34	3
0,1,2	1 x 38 = 38	35	3
3,0,1	1 x 38 = 38	42	- 4
2,2,0	1 x 41 = 41	42	- 1
1,3,0	1 x 43 = 43	43	0
2,1,1	1 x 44 = 44	43	1
2,0,2	1 x 44 = 44	44	0
1,0,3	1 x 46 = 46	46	0
1,2,1	1 x 47 = 47	44	3
0,3,1	1 x 47 = 47	45	2
3,2,0	1 x 47 = 47	52	-5
1,1,2	1 x 48 = 48	45	3
0,1,3	1 x 48 = 48	47	1
0,2,2	1 x 49 = 49	46	3
3,1,1	1 x 50 = 50	53	-3
3,0,2	1 x 50 = 50	54	-4
2,3,0	1 x 51 = 51	53	-2
2,0,3	1 x 54 = 54	56	-2
2,2,1	1 x 55 = 55	54	1
2,1,2	1 x 56 = 56	55	1
1,3,1	1 x 57 = 57	55	2
3,3,0	1 x 57 = 57	63	-6
1,1,3	1 x 58 = 58	57	1
1,2,2	1 x 59 = 59	56	3
0,3,2	1 x 59 = 59	57	2
0,2,3	1 x 59 = 59	58	1
3,0,3	1 x 60 = 60	66	-6
3,2,1	1 x 61 = 61	64	-3
3,1,2	1 x 62 = 62	65	-3
2,3,1	1 x 65 = 65	65	0
2,1,3	1 x 66 = 66	67	-1
2,2,2	1 x 67 = 67	66	1
1,3,2	1 x 69 = 69	67	2
1,2,3	1 x 69 = 69	68	1
0,3,3	1 x 69 = 69	69	0
3,3,1	1 x 71 = 71	75	-4
3,1,3	1 x 72 = 72	77	-5
3,2,2	1 x 73 = 73	76	-3
2,3,2	1 x 77 = 77	77	0
2,2,3	1 x 77 = 77	78	-1
1,3,3	1 x 79 = 79	79	0
3,3,2	1 x 83 = 83	87	-4
3,2,3	1 x 83 = 83	88	-5
2,3,3	1 x 87 = 87	89	-2
3,3,3	1 x 93 = 93	99	-6

Suppose our goal is simply to be "big." If that is the case, we should produce all we can (combination 3,3,3). Suppose our goal is to provide as many jobs as possible. Here, any combination that would use three units of L would be acceptable. Unfortunately, pursuing either of these goals may put us out of business in the long-run! We also must cover our expenses. We may also need to make a profit for those who have invested in our business. At what output levels do we cover our expenses and make a profit? Table 1.3 can be reformulated as Table 1.4 to see costs in relation to increasing output. Output may then be multiplied by price to obtain total revenue which, when costs are subtracted, equals profit (see Table 1.5). A number of combinations yield a profit. Some are even consistent with providing as many jobs as possible. In the sense that providing jobs subject to a "profit constraint" (so as not to go out of business) is deemed "efficient," these could be deemed to be "optimal solutions."

What if the enterprise wants to maximize its profits? A number of combinations (0,1,1; 1,1,1; 0,2,1; 0,1,2; 1,2,1; 1,1,2; 0,2,2; and 1,2,2) all produce \$3 of profits. These would all be "efficient" and "optimal" given this objective.

Let us re-examine these possibilities by considering the MRPs, or marginal revenue products (i.e., the marginal physical products times price) and costs of each profit maximizing combination in Table 1.6. This will enable us to establish a rule for both profit maximization and cost minimization (by using the most efficient combinations of inputs).

Table 1.6. Marginal Revenue Products, Factors Costs, Optimal Production.

Combination	$\frac{MRP_R}{P_R}$	$\frac{MRP_L}{P_L}$	$\frac{MRP_K}{P_K}$
0,1,1	—	12/11	14/12
1,1,1	10/10	12/11	14/12
0,2,1	—	11/11	14/12
0,1,2	—	12/11	12/12
1,2,1	10/10	11/11	14/12
1,1,2	10/10	12/11	12/12
0,2,2	—	11/11	12/12
1,2,2	10/10	11/11	12/12

What do you notice about all of the combinations? Clearly, in every instance the marginal revenue product of each factor equals or exceeds its cost. For example, in combination $R = 0$, $L = 1$, $K = 1$, no resources are used, but one unit each of capital and labor is used. One unit of labor produces twelve units of output which sell at \$1 each. The marginal revenue product is 12x\$1=\$12. The cost of a unit of labor is \$11. Since \$12 > \$11, it pays to use the unit of labor. Similarly, one unit of capital produces fourteen units of output, which at \$1 each produces \$14 of marginal revenue product. This exceeds the \$12 cost of a unit of capital. Combined profit is \$0+\$1+\$2=\$3. In combination $R = 1$, $L = 1$, and $K = 1$, the marginal revenue products are, respectively, \$10, \$12, and \$14 and the costs are \$10, \$11, and \$12, yielding \$3 in profit. In combination $R = 1$, $L = 2$, and $K = 2$, the marginal revenue products are \$10,\$11, and \$12 which just exactly equal their costs. This is the combination where both profit and output together are maximized. It is also the point beyond which any additional input units will reduce profits.

At ($R = 1$, L=2, $K = 2$), we find:

$$\frac{MRP_R}{P_R} = \frac{MRP_L}{P_L} = \frac{MRP_K}{P_K} \tag{1.6}$$

where:

MRP_R = The marginal revenue product of resources.
MRP_L = The marginal revenue product of labor.
MRP_K = The marginal revenue product of capital.
P_R = The cost of a unit of resources.
R_L = The cost of a unit of labor.
P_K = The cost of a unit of capital.

1.15 Choice and Output

A major conclusion we may reach from the above exercise is that optimal output decisions depend upon a careful analysis of the benefits (revenues) and costs of production. The example is pursued at the enterprise level, but a similar problem exists in the aggregate. At the macroeconomic level, we cannot simply assume that greater output is necessarily optimal. The factors of production must be used to generate output, and these are never in infinite supply. The aggregate problem then becomes one of generating as much output (gross domestic product) as possible while using the most efficient combination of inputs. This has always been society's economic problem. In the immediate chapters to follow, we shall consider the salient factors that contribute to enhanced aggregate production and, consequently, higher standards of living.

Appendix: The Calculus of Production

For those of technical inclination, we might return to equation (1.4), $Q = f(R, L, K)$. Given the typical shape of the production function in Figure 1.5, we can vary all three independent variables, and reduce the equation to $Q = f(I)$, where I is any one combination of the variable inputs R, L, or K. In this instance, we could determine the following:

Table 1.7. Various Production Cases.

Case	Characteristics
Increasing Returns	$\frac{dQ}{dI} > 0$ $\frac{d^2Q}{dI^2} > 0$
Constant Returns	$\frac{dQ}{dI} > 0$ $\frac{d^2Q}{dI^2} = 0$
Decreasing Returns	$\frac{dQ}{dI} > 0$ $\frac{d^2Q}{dI^2} < 0$
Zero Returns	$\frac{dQ}{dI} = 0$
Absolutely Decreasing Returns	$\frac{dQ}{dI} < 0$

References

[1] Baumol, W.J., "America's Productivity 'Crisis': A Modest Decline Isn't All That Bad," *The New York Times*, February 15, 1987.

[2] Baumol, W.J., Blackman, S.A.B., and Wolff, E. *Productivity and American Leadership*, Cambridge: The MIT Press, 1989.

[3] Chew, W.B., "No-Nonsense Guide to Measuring Productivity," *Harvard Business Review*, January-February, 1988, pp. 110-118.

[4] Council of Economic Advisers,*Economic Report of the President*, Washington D.C., G.P.O.: 1994, 1996.

[5] Dertouzos, M.L., Lester, R.K., Solow, R.M., and the MIT Commission on Industrial Productivity, *Made in America: Regaining the Productive Edge*, Cambridge, The MIT Press.

[6] Liebhafsky, H.H., *The Nature of Price Theory*, revised edition, Homewood: The Dorsey Press, 1968.

[7] Rosegger, G., *The Economics of Production and Innovation*, second edition, Oxford: Pergammon Press, 1986.

[8] Solow, R.M., "Technical Change and the Aggregate Production Function," *Review of Economics and Statistics*, August, 1957, pp. 312-320.

[9] Williams, E.E., "The Emergence of Entrepreneurship In China," in Campbell, et. al. *Advances in Chinese Industrial Studies*, JAI Press, 1990, Vol. I, Part A, pp. 247-265.

[10] Williams, E.E., "The 'New Economics' of the People's Republic of China," *American Journal of Economics and Sociology*, July, 1990, pp. 351-373 (included in Sociological Abstracts, 1990).

[11] Williams, E.E., "Economic Transformation in Eastern Europe: Some Lessons from China," *The Sarmatian Review*, January, 1990, pp. 4-6.

[12] Williams, E.E. and Thompson, J.R., *The Economics of Production and Productivity: A Modeling Approach*, Austin: Capital Book Company, 1996.

Problems

Problem 1.1 Assume a production function of the form:

$$Q = \sqrt{2\alpha_1 KL - \alpha_2 K^2 - \alpha_3 L^2}$$

where $\alpha_1 > 0$, $\alpha_2 > 0$, $\alpha_3 > 0$, and $\alpha_1^2 > \alpha_2\alpha_3$. Let $\alpha_1 = 40$, $\alpha_2 = 40$, and $\alpha_3 = 6$. Determine Q if $K = 1$ and $L = 10$.

Problem 1.2 Assume the production function of problem 1.1. Calculate $\partial Q/\partial K$ and $\partial Q/\partial L$.

Problem 1.3 Assume the production function of problem 1.1. Let $L = 10$. Determine values for Q where $K = 0.78$; 1.00; and 1.50.

Problem 1.4 Assume the production function of problem 1.1. Let $L = 10$. Determine values for Q where K=2,3,4,5,6,7,8,9,10,11 and 12.

Problem 1.5 Assume the production function of problem 1.1. Let $K = 1$. Determine values for Q where $L = 12.80$; 10.00; 6.67; 5.00; 3.34; 2.50; 2.00; 1.67; 1.43; 1.25; 1.11; 1.00; 0.91; and 0.83.

Problem 1.6 Prepare a table for the results you obtained in problems 1.3 through 1.5 above. Determine Q/L and Q/K for each value. Calculate $\partial Q/\partial L$ and $\partial Q/\partial K$ for each value.

Problem 1.7 Label the return economies provided in the table you prepared in problem 1.6.

Problem 1.8 Assume the production function of problem 1.1. Determine Q if $K = 2$ and $L = 20$ (i.e., double all inputs). How would you describe this long-run production function?

Chapter 2

The Economics of Aggregate Production

2.1 Introduction

In the previous chapter, we discussed the nature of productivity and the elements that enter into production decisions. We shall now consider some macroeconomic aspects of productivity and production in a more concrete fashion. At the outset we should state that we believe market economies are the most efficient forms of economic organization in converting inputs to outputs. Socialist, communist, and other forms of statist economies have been proven to be the least able to satisfy the needs of the participants in an economy through efficiently producing goods and services. Mixed economies, partly market and partly statist, are moderately efficient; but the closer a mixed economy comes to being a statist economy, the less likely it is to be productive.

Unfortunately, market economies may be unstable in the short-run. There are times when market economies utilize all inputs (labor, capital, resources) to the maximum and get the greatest possible output for a given level of input. During the 1980s, for example, the United States, which is a mixed economy tending toward being more market than statist, operated with only a small amount of unemployment of resources. Labor unemployment averaged just over 7% (with 5-6% being considered essentially "full employment" by most economists for the U.S. economy), and plants operated at nearly 81% of capacity. This might be deemed a fairly efficient use of resources, since substantial diminishing returns (see discussion in Chapter 1) usually do not set in until the labor unemployment rate falls to 6% or so and plant utilization increases to 86% or so.

During war time, the U.S. economy has operated at near capacity levels; but due to the laws of diminishing returns, market oriented economies tend to be less efficient during those intervals than during a peace time prosperity. This is true even without considering the different nature of outputs produced during war and peace. In war time, bombs, guns, military equipment, etc. are produced in abundance. These goods may be ultimately of great benefit (e.g., their production kept the Nazis during World War II and the Soviets during the post WW II period from conquering the world); but ordinary consumer goods such as automobiles, housing, appliances, etc. are typically in short supply during wars. Indeed, it is not unusual even for market economies to ration consumer goods and control prices during periods of war. Thus, although wars can make for great utilization of inputs, peace time prosperity usually results in greater and more efficient production of consumer goods and services.

There are times when market economies utilize all inputs to the maximum and get the greatest possible output for a given level of input, but there are other times when market economies operate for extended periods of time with under- or unutilized inputs. During the Great Depression, for example, the labor unemployment rate in the United States approached 25%, and plants operated at levels as low as 50% of capacity levels. Questions may be raised as to why there are periods when peace time prosperity prevails and production takes place efficiently and why there are other periods when there is substantial underutilization of inputs and inefficient production. One of the goals of this book is to address these questions, and we shall develop a model of aggregate output to help us in this regard.

2.2 Aggregate Economic Activity

Aggregate output may be measured three ways. First, we may measure spending on goods and services by the major spending groups within an economy (consumers, business, government and foreigners). Second, we can measure the output of all industries within an economy (being careful not to double count by considering only the value added at each stage of production); and, third, we can measure the income of each group producing aggregate output. Each method will yield the same result if we make our calculations carefully. For our purposes in this book, we shall focus on the first method, frequently called the "spending" method. The model postulates that the level of aggregate economic production (Y) is the sum of all personal consumer spending (C), business investment (I), government purchases (G), and net exports (X) that take place in any single economic period (say, a year). Symbolically, we may write:

$$Y = C + I + G + X \ . \tag{2.1}$$

Thus, for 1995 in the United States, personal consumption was $4,925 billion, gross private domestic investment (business investment) was $1,065 billion, government purchases (at all levels, federal, state, and local) was $1,358 billion, and net exports were -$95 billion. Y, the sum of these, was $7,253 billion. Y may also be conceived as the aggregate output or production for an economy. In recent years, we have used the concept of *gross domestic product* or GDP as the measured value of Y.

We may also use the input/output notions presented in Chapter 1 to consider Y. That is, an aggregate economy will use inputs to produce its output. Production functions similar to those diagrammed in Figure 1.5 may be determined. These are called *aggregate production functions.* The shape of these functions depends upon whether an economy is evidencing increasing returns, constant returns, or decreasing returns over the relevant range of output. A mathematically convenient function which has been used with surprising effectiveness in economic research and which appears to have empirical support for its validity over the relevant range of aggregate economic activity is one of the form:

$$Q = \alpha K^n L^{1-n} \ . \tag{2.2}$$

In this function, resources are ignored (or, are assumed to be part of capital), α is an empirically determined scale factor which changes with technology, and n is an empirically determined positive fraction of value $0 < n < 1$. We shall examine this production function in greater detail later in this book when we consider the role of technology and innovation in economic growth, but an empirically determined function has been found to be [1]:

$$Q = 1.01K^{.25}L^{.75} .$$

In this equation, K is measured by an index number based on money additions to capital goods in a given period (year) and L is measured by an index number of workers employed during that period. Q is measured by an index of physical production in which physical quantities of a variety of products are reduced to index numbers and weighted by relative values added during the period. Q may be expressed in terms of Y by a transformation of the index to physical output and multiplication by price indices. Expressing output using equation (2.2) is considerably more difficult than using (2.1), and for this reason we shall use (2.1) in the immediate work to follow.

It should be clear that the entrepreneur plays the pivotal role in a market economy in determining the values of all of the variables in equations (2.1) and (2.2) except arguably G, which is essentially politically determined, and n. We shall define the entrepreneur as "a high achievement oriented individual who sets out to accomplish certain goals and does so successfully" typically in the creation of an institution that engages in commerce, e.g. a business entity [15, p. 254]. As entrepreneurs become successful, they create increasingly complex commercial entities which also make decisions in increasingly complex fashions. Nevertheless, both individual entrepreneurs and the organizations which they may ultimately build must make judgments about the same basic phenomena: namely, what is to be produced, how it is to be produced and in what quantities, what quantity and mix of inputs will be used, and what will be charged for what is produced. Of course, all of these decisions are based on feedback from the ultimate "king" of the market place, the consumer. There may be disagreement about whether small entrepreneurs do a better job of this than do large organizations (which may, in fact, have lost their entrepreneurial flair), and this is an issue to which we shall return in later chapters; but for now, both will be considered as identical in their role in the decision making framework.

In equation (2.1), consumers decide at what level and on what products and services they wish to spend. These decisions are then transmitted to the market place via purchasing or indications of a desire to purchase. C itself represents the sum of all consumer spending that actually takes place during a given period (say, for a year).

Entrepreneurs examine present levels of C and anticipate future levels and then make decisions about what they are presently producing and what they should produce in the future. In order to produce, they will commit for the purchase of inputs. Expenditures on labor will result in salaries and wages being paid that ultimately become C (that is, people consume out of their incomes). Expenditures for plant, equipment and inventory (called business investment, or I) are made based upon entrepreneurial expectations about future consumer behavior. Finally, expenditures on resources (land, raw materials, etc.) do not change aggregate output. Resources merely change ownership when they are considered as an input. They only result in a change in aggregate economic activity when they are combined with labor and capital to produce output.

In equation (2.1), G represents all levels of government spending. Government spending may take on certain characteristics of consumer spending (say, when the government buys consumer goods such as television sets, automobiles, etc.) or it may take on characteristics of business investment (say, when the government builds a highway or constructs a power plant). Because government spending is not subject to the rules applicable to the entrepreneur operating in the market place, however, its determination will be different from either C or I. Hence, it will be considered separately. Also in equation (2.1), X represents the net sales of one country to another. If we were considering the aggregate economic activity of the United States, X would be the exports (sales) of Americans to foreigners less the imports (purchases) of Americans from foreigners. Of course, this may be a negative number if Americans were selling less abroad than they were buying (which has been frequently the case in recent history).

2.3 Modeling Economic Activity

As we move into a more detailed consideration of the variables outlined above, it should be remembered that our model is simply an approximate representation of what is going on in an economy. As such, it may be used for analytical purposes (i.e., what are the relationships among the variables) or it may be used for forecasting purposes (i.e., what will happen to one variable if another one changes). We shall discuss forecasting in some detail in a later chapter so nothing more will be said at this point. In terms of our analytical model, however, certain basic points need to be understood. First, the model will be specified with some variables being *dependent* and others being *independent*. If $Y = f(i)$, Y is said to be a dependent variable and i is said to be an independent variable. If i changes, there will be a corresponding change in Y dictated by the functional relationship f. Unfortunately, it is not always easy to determine which variables are causes and which are effects. Under some circumstances, a variable may be deemed to be a cause. Other times, it may be an effect. It will be important, therefore, to consider carefully the nature of the analysis each time a set of variables is employed.

Second, some variables will be deemed to be *exogenous* and other *endogenous*. An exogenous variable is one which the model does not attempt to explain. It is merely taken as a given. Endogenous variables, on the other hand, are those which the model is trying to explain. "Effect" variables are always endogenous, but a variable may be a "cause" in a single relationship (equation) and become an "effect" in another one. The typical method of model construction is to start off with a number of relationships and try to make as many variables endogenous as possible. Those variables which remain as exogenous will be independent in every relationship in which they appear.

Third, the model will be specified with equations (and/or diagrams which presume or assume equations). Sometimes it is thought that the use of equations implies an equilibrium condition. That is, if $Y = f(i)$, and $Y = 5i$, it is assumed that each time i changes by any amount, Y will change by five times that amount. This is a truism of the equation, but what is not said is *how long* it may take for any change in i to result in a change in Y. Economists often use the term *equilibrium* to mean that a system is always at the point where all equations are satisfied. Technically, this may never be true. Since, in the real world, it takes time for economic changes to take place, a system may never be in true equilibrium. It may only be moving in that direction or there may be no equilibrium at all. Equilibrium may only be a figment of the economist's imagination.

2.4 Consumption

Consumer spending is the total amount spent by consumers for such things as food, clothing, appliances, services etc. Tastes influence consumer spending, and demographic factors are important too. Very young and very old people, for example, tend to spend more of their income than do middle-aged people. The most important determinant of consumption, however, is the overall level of gross domestic product or income. In general, as income (Y) rises, so does consumption. The relationship,

$$C = f(Y) \tag{2.3}$$

is called a consumption function. The shape of equation (2.3) depends upon whether we are examining the consumption of an individual (family) or of an aggregate economy. Suppose we were examining an individual's consumption and we found the consumption function described in Table 2.1.

Note that at very low levels of income, the individual consumes more than he or she earns. This difference between consumption and income, where $C > Y$, might come from dissaving (spending previously saved income), gifts from relatives, welfare, etc. Note also that, as income rises, consumption increases but *at a decreasing rate.* For example, as income rises from \$16 to \$25 (a \$9 increase) consumption only increases by \$1. From $Y = \$25$ to $Y = \$36$ (an \$11 increase), ΔC also is \$1. Finally, from Y = \$36 to Y = \$49 (a \$13 increase), $\Delta C = \$1$. This illustrates the principal of *diminishing marginal consumption*, which says that for most people consumption increases with income but at a decreasing rate. In marginal terms we would find:

$$b = \frac{\Delta C}{\Delta Y} \tag{2.4}$$

That is, as income changes (ΔY) so will consumption (ΔC). The factor "b" is called the *marginal propensity to consume.* For our individual, we could determine that his/her diminishing marginal utility consumption function is: $C = 10 + \sqrt{Y}$. At any point, ΔC could be determined discretely by examining ΔY, and b would decrease as Y increased. If our individual's consumption function were continuous, we could determine $b = dC/dY$, or $b = 1/(2\sqrt{Y})$.

Table 2.1. An Individual Consumption Function.

Consumption (C)	Income(Y)
$10	$0
11	1
12	4
13	9
14	16
15	25
16	36
17	49

For an aggregate economy, the consumption function is generally assumed to be linear. Consider the U.S. economy, for example, over the past thirty years:

Table 2.2. Aggregate Consumption Function of the U.S. 1960-1995 in Billions of Dollars.

Year	Personal Consumer Spending (C)	GDP (Y)	C/Y
1960	332	527	.63
1965	444	719	.62
1970	648	1,036	.63
1975	1,029	1,631	.63
1980	1,760	2,784	.63
1985	2,705	4,181	.65
1990	3,839	5,744	.67
1995	4,925	7,253	.68

Source: *Economic Report of the President*, 1996.

Consumption appears to average about 64% of GDP. As GDP rises, aggregate consumption increases by about 64% of the increase. It would be reasonable to say for the U.S. economy that $b \approx .64$.

2.5 National Income, Personal Income, and Consumption

Although it is common to see consumer spending related to GDP (as in Table 2.2), it is actually more correct to compare consumer spending with personal income. Aggregate (national) income accounting is beyond the scope of this book, but it is useful to keep the following definitions in mind:

$$Y + F_r - F_p = GNP \qquad (2.5)$$
$$GNP - D = NNP \qquad (2.6)$$
$$NNP - T_b + G_s = NI \qquad (2.7)$$
$$NI - \Pi_c + p_i = PI \qquad (2.8)$$
$$PI - T_p = PDI \qquad (2.9)$$

where:

Y = Gross Domestic Product.
F_r = Receipts by domestic (U.S.) residents of interest, dividends and reinvested profits of foreign affiliates of domestic (U.S.) corporations.
F_p = Payments to foreign residents of interest, dividends and reinvested profits of domestic (U.S.) affiliates of foreign corporations.
GNP = Gross national product.
D = Consumption of fixed capital (depreciation).
NNP = Net national product.
T_b = Indirect business taxes and transfers.
G_s = Net subsidies to government enterprises.
NI = National income.
Π_c = Adjusted corporate profits, interest and social insurance payments.
p_i = Personal interest and dividends plus government and business transfer payments to persons.
PI = Personal income.
T_p = Personal income taxes.
PDI = Personal disposable income.

Equation (2.5) merely adjusts GDP by certain financial receipts received by U.S. residents and payments made to foreign residents.

This adjusted number is called *gross national product* or GNP. Historically, GNP was the most common measure of U.S. output. It actually measures the volume of goods and services purchased by people *living in* an economy (say, the United States) rather than the volume of goods and services purchased in the economy. Table 2.3 provides us with GNP data over the past thirty-five years:

Table 2.3 U.S. Gross National Product, 1960-1995, Billions of Dollars.

Year	GDP	$F_r(+)$	$F_p(-)$	GNP
1960	527	5	2	530
1965	719	8	3	724
1970	1,036	13	7	1,042
1975	1,631	28	15	1,644
1980	2,784	81	47	2,820
1985	4,181	108	88	4,201
1990	5,744	178	156	5,766
1995	7,253	208	215	7,246

Source: *Economic Report of the President*, 1996.

Equation (2.6) subtracts depreciation (called consumption of fixed capital, or plant and equipment in the national income accounts) from GNP to get *net national product* or NNP as in Table 2.4.

Table 2.4 U.S. Net National Product, 1960-1995, Billions of Dollars.

Year	GNP	$D(-)$	NNP
1960	530	61	469
1965	724	75	649
1970	1,042	112	930
1975	1,644	209	1,444
1980	2,820	368	2,452
1985	4,201	520	3,681
1990	5,766	693	5,073
1995	7,246	826	6,420

Source: *Economic Report of the President*, 1996

Next, equation (2.7) subtracts indirect business taxes (sales and excise taxes) and business transfers (such as gifts) and adds government subsidies to the businesses run by government to get *national income.* Some authorities [e.g., 5] argue that this is the most comprehensive income measure. National income is measured in terms of the prices businesses receive for what they sell rather than the prices paid by consumers, which is the way GDP and GNP are measured. Sales and excise taxes account for the difference between those prices. Table 2.5 provides national income data over the past thirty years.

Table 2.5 U.S. National Income, 1960-1995, Billions of Dollars.

Year	NNP	$T_b(-)$	$G_s(+)$	NI
1960	469	47	4	426
1965	649	65	3	587
1970	930	98	4	836
1975	1,444	145	-3	1,296
1980	2,452	223	-13	2,216
1985	3,681	351	22	3,352
1990	5,073	469	8	4,612
1995	6,420	626	20	5,814

(G_s includes statistical discrepancy) Source: *Economic Report of the President*, 1996

Finally, equation (2.8) subtracts out corporate profits, interest earned, and contributions made by corporations to social insurance programs (e.g., social security taxes) and adds personal interest and dividends plus transfers to persons from government (e.g., social security payments) and businesses (e.g., private retirement plans) to get *personal income.* From this, equation (2.9) subtracts out personal taxes to get *personal disposable income.* This is the actual income amount received by individuals available for consumption or saving. Table 2.6 provides personal disposable income figures for the past thirty-five years.

Table 2.6 U.S. Personal Disposable Income, 1960-1995, Billions of Dollars.						
Year	NI	$\Pi_c(-)$	$p_i(+)$	PI	$T_p(-)$	PDI
1960	426	82	67	411	48	363
1965	587	134	106	559	65	494
1970	836	178	178	836	109	727
1975	1,296	322	342	1,316	157	1,159
1980	2,216	584	654	2,286	313	1,973
1985	3,352	995	1,083	3,440	438	3,002
1990	4,612	1,355	1,535	4,792	625	4,167
1995	5,814	1,653	1,954	6,115	794	5,321

Source: *Economic Report of the President*, 1996

Since consumers actually spend out of personal disposable income, we might revise the consumption function derived in Table 2.2 (above). Where personal consumption was determined to be about 64 percent of GDP, we may now determine personal consumption to be about 90 percent of PDI (Table 2.7). Thus, the average American family consumes about nine-tenths of its income.

The information in Tables 2.1 through 2.6 may be generalized in equation form by noting that consumers consume out of income as per equation (2.3). However, they consume out of their *disposable* income, which means personal taxes must be subtracted from income and transfer payments (principally from government) must be added.

Table 2.7. U.S. Income and Consumption, 1960-1995 in Billions of Dollars.			
Year	Personal Consumer Spending (C)	PDI	$\frac{C}{PDI}$
1960	332	363	.91
1965	444	494	.90
1970	648	727	.89
1975	1,029	1,159	.89
1980	1,760	1,973	.89
1985	2,705	3,002	.90
1990	3,839	4,167	.92
1995	4,925	5,321	.93

Source: *Economic Report of the President*, 1996

A modified consumption function would thus become:

$$C = A + \bar{b}(GDP + F_r - F_p - D - T_b + G_s - \Pi_c + p_i - T_p) \quad (2.10)$$

where A is a given minimum amount of consumption that takes place independent of income, $\bar{b}$ is the *average propensity to consume*, and the other variables are defined as above. Now, in order to simplify, we shall ignore most of the variables that reduce GDP to personal disposable income (i.e., F_r,F_p, D, T_b, G_s. and Π_c). Two variables, p_i and T_p, are so important that they cannot be ignored, however. The variable p_i has several component parts, but we shall focus our attention only on that part of p_i which contains transfer payments from government to consumers, which we shall designate as T_r. Thus, our revised consumption function will become:

$$C = A + \bar{b}(Y - T_p + T_r) \quad (2.11)$$

where Y will be the relevant income number (henceforth, GDP), T_p will be the level of personal taxes paid by consumers, and T_r will be what consumers receive from government in the form of transfer payments (for example, social security payments, unemployment compensation, etc.). Given (2.11), we may compute the average propensity to consume for the economy as:

$$\bar{b} = \frac{C - A}{Y - T_p + T_r} \quad (2.12)$$

Changes in consumption would be given by:

$$\Delta C = b(\Delta Y - \Delta T_p + \Delta T_r) \quad (2.13)$$

where b was analogously defined in equation (2.4). Generally, $\bar{b}$ and b will be approximately the same for an aggregate economy (A is very small) but not for an individual consumer. Also, $\bar{b}$ and b will be essentially constant for an aggregate economy (see Tables 2.2 and 2.7) but not for an individual. We may solve for b as follows:

$$b = \frac{\Delta C}{\Delta Y - \Delta T_p + \Delta T_r} \quad (2.14)$$

For the United States, recall that b is approximately .64 if C is related to GDP (Table 2.2) and approximately .90 if C is related to PDI. In equation (2.14), we adopt an income measure that adjusts GDP for personal taxes and transfer payments only. In this instance, b is approximately .64 as we can see in Table 2.8.

Table 2.8. Adjusted *GDP* and Consumption 1960-1995 in Billions of Dollars.

Year	Personal Consumer Spending (C)	$Y - T_p - T_r$	$\frac{C}{Y-T_p+T_r}$
1960	332	$527 - 48 + 28$	.65
1965	444	$719 - 65 + 39$	.64
1970	648	$1,036 - 109 + 82$	.64
1975	1,029	$1,631 - 157 + 186$	.62
1980	1,760	$2,784 - 313 + 313$	.63
1985	2,705	$4,181 - 438 + 468$	.64
1990	3,839	$5,744 - 625 + 666$	.66
1995	4,925	7,253 - 794+1,000	.66

Source: *Economic Report of the President*, 1996

2.6 Business Investment

In a very simple system, what consumers do not consume, they save; and this savings becomes available for business investment. As we shall soon see, however, there is no immediately direct link between the decision of the consumer to save (not consume) and the decision of businesses to spend. It is quite possible that saving may actually discourage business spending if the decision to save means consumers consume less and, hence, businesses need less plant and equipment to produce what consumers want. In any case, what businesses ultimately spend on purchasing inventories, plant and equipment becomes part of aggregate economic output.

Business investment (I) is formally defined as the sum of spending by firms on plant, equipment, and inventories and by households on housing. Plant, equipment and housing are further categorized as being "fixed" or long-term in nature and can be divided into non-residential (automobile plants, office building, commercial vehicles, computer equipment, etc.) and residential (new houses and apartment building) components. Inventory investment consists of the net change in inventories of businesses over the period. Table 2.9 portrays I over the past thirty-five years.

Table 2.9. Business Investment 1960-1995 in Billions of Dollars.				
Year	Nonresidential Fixed	Residential Fixed	Change in Inventories	Total
1960	49	27	3	79
1965	74	34	10	118
1970	107	41	2	150
1975	169	63	– 6	226
1980	354	123	– 10	467
1985	504	186	25	715
1990	576	216	8	800
1995	739	289	37	1,065

Source: *Economic Report of the President*, 1996

2.7 Government Purchases

Government purchases (G) consist of the total purchases by federal, state and local governments of goods and services. Expenditures for schools, highways, hospitals, and the military are examples of government spending. It should be pointed out that government spending and the budgeted spending of governments are different. Welfare payments and interest on the public debt, for example, are part of government outlays but these are not part of total output and are not included within G in the GDP calculation. Table 2.10 portrays G over the past thirty-five years.

Table 2.10. Government Purchases, 1960-1995 in Billions of Dollars.			
Year	Federal	State and Local	Total
1960	66	47	113
1965	82	71	153
1970	116	120	236
1975	155	208	363
1980	248	325	573
1985	410	465	875
1990	504	672	1,176
1995	517	841	1,358

Source: Economic Report of the President, 1996

It is important to remember that where an item is classified in the national income accounts generally depends on the purchaser. An automobile bought by Mr. Brown for his personal use is part of C. The same automobile bought by a company for the use of a salesman would be part of I; and, if it were bought by the federal government for use by a bureaucrat in the Department of Labor, it would be part of G. The only exception to this is residential investment, which includes all housing purchases regardless of type of purchaser, and is always part of I.

2.8 The Simple Multiplier

We have now considered three of the four major variables making up *GDP* (C, I, and G). We shall consider the fourth (X) shortly, but there are some important exercises we can complete before we do so. Recall equation (2.1). Now let Y change such that:

$$\Delta Y = \Delta C + \Delta I + \Delta G + \Delta X \ . \tag{2.15}$$

Substituting equation (2.13) into (2.15) we find:

$$\Delta Y = b(\Delta Y - \Delta T_p + \Delta T_r) + \Delta I + \Delta G + \Delta X \ . \tag{2.16}$$

Now, for sake of simplicity, assume that:

$$\Delta T_p = \Delta T_r = \Delta G = \Delta X = 0 \ . \tag{2.17}$$

Then equation (2.16) reduces to:

$$\Delta Y = b\Delta Y + \Delta I \ . \tag{2.18}$$

Rearranging and factoring, we find:

$$\Delta Y(1 - b) = \Delta I \tag{2.19}$$

or

$$\Delta Y = \frac{1}{1-b}\Delta I \tag{2.20}$$

The quantity $[1/(1-b)]$ is called the *simple investment multiplier.* It indicates the amount by which the total level of income would rise (fall) if there were an exogenous increase (decrease) in business investment for plant and equipment. Thus, if we considered a simplified economy without taxes, transfer payments, government spending, or foreign trade and in which consumers had a marginal propensity to consume (b) of 0.8, autonomous investment would increase Y not just by ΔI but rather by $[1/(1-b)]\Delta I$, or $[1/(1-.8)]\Delta I = 5\Delta I$. A \$10 billion increase in business investment would add this amount to total aggregate income. But because such spending would induce further spending in the consumer sector, the total increase to income would be:

$$\Delta Y = \frac{1}{1-b}\Delta I = (5)(\$10) \text{ billion} = \$50 \text{ billion}$$

This may be seen by considering an example. Suppose business concerns become more optimistic about the future. They believe sales are going to increase, and extra plant and equipment will be needed to produce the goods to satisfy demand. Let $\Delta I = \$10$ billion. This would increase income since $\Delta Y = \Delta C + \Delta I$, but it would also cause an induced increase in consumption (and, hence, income) because $\Delta C = f(\Delta Y)$. If ΔI results in a \$10 billion increase in income, ΔC will equal \$8 billion since $\Delta C = b\Delta Y$ [i.e., $\Delta C =(.8)(\$10 \text{ billion}) = \$8 \text{ billion}$]. The increase in consumption due to more income will further produce an additional increase in income since consumption is a part of income, and more income will lead to yet more consumption. $\Delta C = b\Delta Y$, so $\Delta C = (.8)(\$8 \text{ billion}) = \$\ 6.4$ billion. In general, more consumption will lead to more income, which, in turn, will lead to more consumption until the following limit is reached:

$$\begin{aligned} \Delta Y &= \Delta C + \Delta I \\ \Sigma\Delta Y &= \Sigma\Delta C + \Sigma\Delta I \end{aligned} \tag{2.21}$$

or, \$10 billion + $(.8)^1$ (\$10 billion) + $(.8)^2$ (\$10 billion) + ... + $(.8)^n$ (\$10 billion). In the limit, where $n \to \infty$, the final term approaches zero. Arithmetically, we have: \$10 billion + \$8 billion + \$6.4 billion + \$5.12 billion + \$4.10 billion + ... + 0 = \$50 billion. It should be noted that an exogenous increase in government spending (or consumption for that matter) would produce the same result. If $\Delta I = 0$, but $\Delta G = \$10$ billion, the same \$50 billion increase in aggregate income would be effected.

2.9 Accelerated Investment

Admittedly, the economy postulated above is greatly simplified. In the first place, it is very likely that higher levels of income may not only stimulate consumers to spend more but may also encourage businesses to invest extra amounts. Hence, we may conceive of a *marginal propensity to invest*:

$$Z = \frac{\Delta I}{\Delta Y} \tag{2.22}$$

or:

$$\Delta I = Z\Delta Y \ . \tag{2.23}$$

The presence of this factor may add an "accelerator" effect to economic activity. Once again, consider equation (2.15):

$$\Delta Y = \Delta C + \Delta I + \Delta G + \Delta X \ .$$

Substituting (2.13) and (2.23) into (2.15), we find:

$$\Delta Y = b(\Delta Y - \Delta T_p + \Delta T_r) + Z\Delta Y + \Delta G + \Delta X \tag{2.24}$$

Now, let:

$$\Delta T_p = \Delta T_r = \Delta X = 0 \ . \tag{2.25}$$

Then equation (2.24) reduces to:

$$\Delta Y = b\Delta Y + Z\Delta Y + \Delta G \tag{2.26}$$

or:

$$\Delta Y(1 - b - Z) = \Delta G \ . \tag{2.27}$$

Solving for ΔY, we find:

$$\Delta Y = \frac{1}{1 - b - Z}\Delta G \ . \tag{2.28}$$

Suppose in the previous example $Z = 0.1$. The change in national income, given an exogenous increase in government spending (or investment) of \$10 billion, would be:

$$\Delta Y = \frac{1}{1 - .8 - .1}(\$10 \text{ billion}) = \$100 \text{ billion.}$$

2.10 Taxes

In the real world, $\Delta T_p \neq 0$. That is, we generally find economies where governments collect taxes such that $T > 0$. In a world of proportional taxes, total taxes (T) collected by government could be expressed as (tY), where t is the rate of taxation. This was not a bad assumption for the federal income tax structure of the United States between 1986 and 1990 due to the passage of the Tax Reform Act of 1986. This Act implemented an essentially flat tax of 28% on personal income and eliminated the steeply "progressive" tax rates that had been in place since World War II. These rates increased as income rose such that those with "high" incomes might pay a tax rate several times larger than those who earned "low" incomes. The Omnibus Budget Reconciliation Act of 1990 and the Omnibus Budget Reconciliation Act of 1993 have made our federal structure more "progressive," but the long run trend in federal, state, and local tax policy is toward proportional taxation.

The terms "progressive" and "regressive" may be somewhat biased. As used here, we simply mean that the percentage of income collected in taxes increases with income if the system is progressive and the percentage decreases if it is regressive. A system where the percentage stayed constant would be termed "proportional." State and local taxes are typically regressive since these entities depend mainly on sales and property taxes for their revenues. Under sales and property taxes, high income tax payers will typically pay more taxes than low income earners (since they will typically consume more and own more valuable property); but as their incomes rise, the percentage of total income paid in taxes generally declines. We shall return to the issue of taxation and production several times in this book, but for the time being we shall assume that total taxes (federal, state and local) are collected roughly proportionally. Tax payments would thus be given by:

$$\begin{aligned} \Delta T &= t\Delta Y \\ &\text{and} \\ T &= tY . \end{aligned} \tag{2.29}$$

2.11 Transfer Payments

Transfer payments result from government providing outright cash payments or payments in kind to certain elements of society. These elements generally include poor people, but they also include individuals who are not poor at all. For the United States, welfare payments, unemployment benefits, federal aid to dependent children programs, food stamps, Medicare and Medicaid, and social security payments are all examples of transfer payments. Often, these payments are made without regard to any *quid pro quo* from the recipients and resemble gifts. Some might object and argue that certain of these payments, in particular social security benefits, are not "gifts." It very likely will be the case for many people now in their 20s, 30s, 40s, and even 50s, that they will have paid substantially more into social security than they ever will receive from it. Present beneficiaries, however, generally receive many times more out of social security than they ever put in (even if interest on their contributions is included), and these receipts are really gifts from the government.

For purposes of analysis, we shall separate out the tax elements of transfer payments from the payments themselves. The reason for so doing is that there is no necessary reason for taxes actually to be collected in order for the payments to be made. Indeed, for many years now a substantial percentage of such payments have basically been made from deficit spending rather than tax collections. Thus, any taxes collected regardless of what such taxes are called will be deemed "taxes" for our purposes. Even so-called social security "contributions" are not contributions at all since one can go to jail for refusing to pay them just the same as one can go to jail for not paying income taxes. Of course, there are those who cheat and do not pay (or underpay) such taxes, but there are also people who do the same regarding income taxes.

Historically, transfer payments within an economy have been negatively correlated with national income given an initial base level. That is, as national income rises, transfer payments have gone down; and, as national income has fallen, transfer payments have increased. It is still true that certain of these payments are inversely related to national income. During periods of recession, for example, there are more people collecting unemployment benefits and more who go on welfare. Unfortunately, as many of these transfer payments have become entitlements, the negative correlation is not very strong and may, in fact, have become independent of national income. For our purposes, we shall continue to show this relationship as being inverse, although the coefficient will be quite small. Thus, if we assume transfer payments are inversely proportional to income, changes in total payments (ΔT_r) may be expressed as

$$\Delta T_r = -t_r \Delta Y \qquad (2.30)$$

and

$$T_r = -t_r Y. \qquad (2.31)$$

The symbol t_r will stand for the *income elasticity or marginal rate of transfer payments*, or what happens to transfer payments as income changes.

2.12 A More Complex Multiplier

Given the above discussion, a more complex multiplier may be obtained. Ignoring the accelerator effect ($Z = 0$) and net exports ($\Delta X = 0$), we can assume an exogenous change in either investment ($\Delta I \neq 0$) or government spending $\Delta G \neq 0$). Actually, both could change and the combined effect could be added together. Reiterating equation (2.15):

$$\Delta Y = \Delta C + \Delta I + \Delta G + \Delta X \ .$$

Substituting in equation (2.13) where $Z = \Delta X = 0$, and letting the change in total taxes collected be ΔT, rather than ΔT_p (i.e., we shall assume that all taxes are personal taxes), we find:

$$\Delta Y = b(\Delta Y - \Delta T + \Delta T_r) + \Delta I + \Delta G + 0 \ . \qquad (2.32)$$

Substituting in equations (2.29) and (2.30), we find:

$$\Delta Y = b[(\Delta Y) - (t\Delta Y) + (-t_r \Delta Y)] + \Delta I + \Delta G \ . \qquad (2.33)$$

Rearranging produces:

$$\Delta Y = b\Delta Y - bt\Delta Y - bt_r \Delta Y + \Delta I + \Delta G \ . \qquad (2.34)$$

Or,

$$\Delta Y(1 - b + bt + bt_r) = \Delta I + \Delta G \ . \tag{2.35}$$

Solving for ΔY:

$$\Delta Y = \frac{1}{1 - b(1 - t - t_r)}[\Delta I + \Delta G] \ . \tag{2.36}$$

If $\Delta I = 0$, $\Delta G \neq 0$, then:

$$\Delta Y = \frac{1}{1 - b(t - t - t_r)}\Delta G \ . \tag{2.37}$$

If $\Delta I \neq 0$, $\Delta G = 0$, then:

$$\Delta Y = \frac{1}{1 - b(1 - t - t_r)}\Delta I \ .$$

For the society discussed above, let the marginal propensity to consume (b) be .8, the rate of taxation (t) be thirty percent and the marginal rate of transfer payments (t_r) be 0.10. If ΔI =\$10 billion, and ΔG = \$0 billion,

$$\Delta Y = \frac{1}{1 - b(1 - t - t_r)}\Delta I \ .$$

$$\Delta Y = \frac{1}{1 - .8(1 - .3 - .1)}(\$10 \text{ billion}) \ .$$

$$\Delta Y = \frac{1}{1 - .48}(\$10 \text{ billion}) = \$19.2 \text{ billion.}$$

Notice that the multiplier effect is greatly reduced because added taxes and the existence of transfer payments tend to dampen the stimulating aspects of the increase in business investment.

2.13 Net Exports

We may complete the basic model by adding in imports and exports. Imports (goods and services purchased from abroad) and exports (goods and services sold abroad) will be influenced by a host of factors which are beyond the scope of this book, but for our purposes here we shall only consider the relationship between income (Y) and imports and exports.

We have defined net exports as X above. This merely subtracts the level of imports from the level of exports in any period (year). If exports > imports, $X > 0$. Vice versa, if imports > exports, $X < 0$. Now, we know from experience that imports are a function of income levels. That is, as an economy grows it will, in general, import more. Exports, however, do not typically depend *directly* on income levels of the exporting country. Rather, it is the income of other countries that would determine the exporting country's level of exports. This means that *net exports* (X) will vary inversely with a nations national income, such that:

$$m = -\frac{\Delta X}{\Delta Y} \tag{2.38}$$

or:

$$\Delta X = -m\Delta Y \; . \tag{2.39}$$

We may designate m as the *marginal propensity to net export.* Let's say country A had national income of \$100 billion and that any increase in income (say $\Delta Y = \$10$ billion) would result in an increase of imports of \$1 billion. Since exports do not directly depend on Y, if $\Delta Y = \$10$ billion, $\Delta X = -\$1$ billion. The marginal propensity to net export would be:

$$m = -\frac{\$1 \text{ billion}}{\$10 \text{ billion}} = -.1 \; . \tag{2.40}$$

2.14 A Complete Basic Model

We may complete the basic model algebraically. Reiterating equation (2.15):

$$\Delta Y = \Delta C + \Delta I + \Delta G + \Delta X \; .$$

Substituting equations (2.13), (2.23), and (2.39) into (2.15), and letting total taxes collected be T rather than T_p (i.e., we are taking all taxes into account and not just personal taxes), we find:

$$\Delta Y = b\Delta(Y - T + T_r) + Z\Delta Y + \Delta G - m\Delta Y \; . \tag{2.41}$$

Expanding, we find:

$$\Delta Y = b\Delta Y - b\Delta T + b\Delta T_r + Z\Delta Y + \Delta G - m\Delta Y \; . \tag{2.42}$$

And substituting (2.29) and (2.30) into (2.42), we find:

$$\Delta Y = b\Delta Y - bt\Delta Y - bt_r\Delta Y + Z\Delta Y + \Delta G - m\Delta Y \ . \qquad (2.43)$$

What we do with this depends on what happens to any one of the variables exogenously. Any factor (besides income change in and of itself, which would be an endogenous change) may be affected by exogenous factors which may then affect all of the endogenous variables. Let us consider an example. Assume the following:

$$\begin{aligned} b &= .8 \\ Z &= .1 \\ t &= .3 \\ t_r &= .01 \\ m &= .02 \end{aligned}$$

Now suppose government spending increases, *cet. par.* This represents an exogenous element since government spending is not a function of income. [Note that tax collections (T) depend on (Y), but (G) does not.] Let $\Delta G = \$10$ billion. Using equation (2.42), we may introduce the assumed coefficients and solve for ΔY:

$$\begin{aligned} \Delta Y &= (.8)\Delta Y - (.8)(.3)\Delta Y - (.8)(.01)\Delta Y + (.1)\Delta Y + 10 \\ &\quad -(.02)\Delta Y \\ \Delta Y &= (.632)\Delta Y + 10 \\ .368\Delta Y &= 10 \\ \Delta Y &= \$27.17 \text{ billion} \end{aligned}$$

This could be determined directly from (2.43) by solving for ΔG:

$$\Delta Y - b\Delta Y + bt\Delta Y + bt_r\Delta Y - Z\Delta Y + m\Delta Y = \Delta G \ . \qquad (2.44)$$

Factoring, we find:

$$\Delta Y(1 - b + bt + bt_r - Z + m) = \Delta G \ . \qquad (2.45)$$

And, dividing by the factor, we determine:

$$\Delta Y = \Delta G \frac{1}{1 - b - Z + bt + bt_r + m} \qquad (2.46)$$

Equation (2.46) contains the *complex multiplier* which is given by the term:

$$\frac{1}{1 - b - Z + bt + bt_r + m}\,. \tag{2.47}$$

For the example above, the multiplier would be:

$$\frac{1}{1 - .8 - .1 + (.8)(.3) + (.8)(.01) + .02}$$

which equals:

$$\frac{1}{.368} = 2.72$$

Given the assumptions of the model, an exogenous change in any of the variables (C,I,G, or X) will cause Y to advance by 2.72 times the exogenous change in the variable. Thus, if C or I or X changed for reasons other than changes in income, that would cause a multiplier effect on income. Of course, since C, I, and X (but not G) can also change because of a change in Y, it is important to ascertain carefully that the change was independent of a change in Y. For the U.S. economy in recent years, the complex multiplier has been about 2.0.

References

[1] Cobb, C.W. and Douglas, P.H., "A Theory of Production," *American Economic Review*, March, 1928, pp. 135-69.

[2] Council of Economic Advisors, *Economic Report of the President*, Washington, D.C., G.P.O., 1996.

[3] Davidson, P. and Smolensky, E., *Aggregate Supply and Demand Analysis*, New York: Harper & Row, 1964.

[4] Figgie, H.E. with Swanson, G.J., *Bankruptcy 1995*, Boston: Little, Brown and Company, 1992.

[5] Hall, R.E. and Taylor, J.B., *Macroeconomics*, fourth edition, New York: W. W. Norton & Company, Inc., 1993.

[6] Hall, P.A., *The Political Power of Economic Ideas*, Princeton: Princeton University Press, 1989.

[7] Hicks, J.R., "Some Questions of Time in Economics," in *Evolution, Welfare and Time in Economics*, A.M. Tang, F.M. Westerfield and J.S. Worley, eds., Lexington: Lexington Books, 1976.

[8] Keynes, J.M., *The General Theory of Employment, Interest, and Money*, New York: Harcourt Brace Jovanovich, 1936.

[9] Kirzner, I.M., *Competition and Entrepreneurship*, Chicago: University of Chicago Press, 1973.

[10] Patinkin, D., "Keynes, Lost and Found," *The Economist*, January 23, 1993, p. 65.

[11] Schumpeter, J.A., *The Theory of Economic Development*, Cambridge: Harvard University Press, 1934.

[12] Thompson, J.R., *Empirical Model Building*, New York: John Wiley & Sons, 1987, pp. 42-50.

[13] Williams, E. E., "Entrepreneurship, Innovation, and Economic Growth," *Technovation*, February, 1983, pp. 3-15.

[14] Williams, E. E., "Innovation, Entrepreneurship, and Brain Functioning," in *Frontiers of Entrepreneurship Research*, Babson Park: Babson Center for Entrepreneurship Studies, 1981, pp. 516-536.

[15] Williams, E. E., "The Emergence of Entrepreneurship in China," in *Advances in Chinese Industrial Studies*, Vol. 1, Part A, J.A.I. Press, 1990, pp. 247-265.

[16] Williams, E.E. and Thompson, J.R., *The Economics of Production and Productivity: A Modeling Approach*, Austin: Capital Book Company, 1996.

Problems

Problem 2.1 Ignoring taxes, transfers, net exports, government spending and the accelerator effect (Z), if b = .9 and ΔI = \$5 billion, what is ΔY?

Problem 2.2 If $t = t_r = m = 0$, and $b = .7$, $Z = .1$, and ΔG = \$1 billion, what is ΔY?

Problem 2.3 If $b = .7$, $t = .2$, $t_r = 0$, $m = 0$, $Z = 0$, and ΔG = \$5 billion, what is ΔY?

Problem 2.4 Answer problem 2.3 above assuming $t_r = .1$.

Problem 2.5 Define the term "progressive income tax."

Problem 2.6 Explain how the "Law of Diminishing Marginal Utility" might be used as a rationalization for the progressive income tax.

Problem 2.7 Critique your rationalization in problem 2.6 above.

Problem 2.8 Is the total American tax structure (federal, state, and local) progressive? Explain.

Chapter 3

Economic Growth and Enhanced Production

3.1 Introduction

In the last chapter, we developed what economists call a short-run equilibrium model. Our concern was centered on determining the level of aggregate economic activity (Y) that takes place during an economic period (say, a year). Now we shall consider how an economy achieves long-run economic growth and enhanced production (productivity). Some of the ideas we shall describe have micro analogies which we will develop in the remaining chapters of the book.

Let us return to the production function initially posited in equation (2.2)

$$Q = \alpha K^n L^{1-n} .$$

In this equation, K is measured by an index number based on money additions to capital goods in a given period and L is measured by an index number of workers employed during the period. Q is measured by an index of physical production in which physical quantities of a variety of products are reduced to index numbers and weighted by relative values added during the period. Q is expressed in terms of Y by a transformation of the index to physical output and multiplication by price indices. The coefficient α is an empirically determined scale factor which changes with technology and the exponent n is an empirically determined positive fraction of value $0 < n < 1$.

It is clear from equation (2.2) that output (Q) will increase if either capital or labor inputs increase. It is also clear that the degree of increase will depend on the empirically estimated values for α and n. Growth in the capital stock will depend on how much net investment takes place each period. In turn, the amount of net investment will depend on such variables as the rate of interest and the economy's marginal efficiency of capital schedule. Net investment may also depend on the domestic saving rate and the amount foreigners are willing to invest in the domestic economy. Growth in the labor force will be determined by population trends (birth rates, death rates, etc.) and the degree of net migration into the economy. Various economists have estimated α and n and the results indicate that both variables are highly stable over time. Indeed, empirical estimates for α suggest the existence of values close to unity over a long period of time and values for n have been estimated between .25 and .30, also over a long period of time.

We might consider an example using assumed indices for an aggregate production function but with empirically determined values for n and α. Let our index of capital inputs be 100. Similarly, let the index for labor inputs be 100. If α is empirically determined to be unity and n is empirically determined to be .25, we could compute the index value of Q as follows:

$$\begin{aligned} Q &= (100^{.25})(100^{.75}) \\ &= (3.1623)(31.6228) = 100 \end{aligned}$$

Now, if we increase capital and labor inputs, say, by ten percent, we would find the following:

$$\begin{aligned} Q &= (110^{.25})(110^{.75}) \\ &= (3.2385)(33.9660) = 110. \end{aligned}$$

Thus, we would find that an increase of all inputs of ten percent would increase output by ten percent. A production function of this kind, i.e., where a change in inputs by a constant percentage results in a change in output by the same constant, is called a *linearly homogeneous production function* or a *production function homogeneous of degree one.* Linearly homogeneous production functions evidence constant returns to scale (see discussion in Chapter 1) and are generally believed to exist for the aggregate U. S. economy over time.

3.2 Long-Run Production Growth

In order to study long-run production growth, we might begin with a famous study done by Robert Solow of the Massachusetts Institute of Technology [14]. Winner of the Nobel Prize in Economics in 1987, Solow's work carried forward the previous efforts of pioneers in production and growth theory such as C. W. Cobb and Paul Douglas [2], Roy Harrod [8] and Evsey Domar [4] among many others. Solow's model assumes that an economy travels along a balanced path. He also assumes initially, for the sake of simplicity, that the economy is closed (no international trade) and that there is no technological change. These assumptions may be relaxed eventually.

Assumptions about growth in inputs are required for the Solow model to provide results for growth in production. Fortunately, growth in the labor force is predicted by the Bureau of Labor Statistics for the U. S. economy to the year 2010. These predictions are quite accurate because most of the people who are or will be in the labor force over this period (those of age 16 and above) have already been born. Growth in capital inputs is much more difficult to predict, but this difficulty is avoided if the growth of the economy is balanced. By *balanced growth*, we mean that growth takes place steadily over time with all factor inputs growing at the same rate. Although there is no a priori reason for an economy to grow in a balanced fashion, Solow showed that there are natural forces in an economy that work to assure balanced growth.

The model begins with an assumed (or empirically determined) growth rate for labor inputs. Let h be that growth rate. Now under balanced growth, if labor inputs are growing at rate h, so will capital inputs. Thus, if the capital stock (capital inputs) at a point in time is K, the growth rate in the capital stock would be hK. This would also be the amount of net investment that would take place over each period. Saving may be defined as:

$$S = sY \tag{3.1}$$

where S is aggregate saving for an economy, s is the aggregate rate of saving taking place in an economy, and Y is total output or GDP. Since saving equals net investment, we can write:

$$sY = hK \tag{3.2}$$

which is Solow's condition for balanced growth.

Equation (3.2) may be rewritten as:

$$K/Y = s/h \tag{3.3}$$

In this rewritten version, the left-hand side of the equation becomes the *capital output ratio*, which the value of the capital stock of the economy divided by output. If an economy had a capital stock of \$16 trillion and total output of \$8 trillion, it would have a capital output ratio of two. This ratio is approximately the one that exists for the United States economy.

Equation (3.3) tells us that, for a balanced economy, the capital output ratio equals the ratio of the saving rate to the growth rate of factor inputs. In the United States, the net saving rate (the ratio of net saving to GDP) has been about two percent in recent years. If the growth in factor inputs has been approximately one percent (which is also empirically true), then s/h is about two. We saw above that this is approximately the capital output ratio for the United States. Thus, it appears that the U. S. economy is following a balanced growth pattern.

3.3 Saving and Growth without Technological Change

A key implication of the Solow model is that the balanced growth path is stable. Prior to Solow's work many growth economists believed that imbalances between K/Y and s/h could lead to economic instability, resulting in an increasing amplitude for the business cycle. Fortunately, Solow's efforts suggested these fears were unfounded. A proof of Solow's results may be provided. Let:

$$sY > hK \tag{3.4}$$

or,

$$K/Y < s/h \tag{3.5}$$

Here net investment would exceed balanced growth investment. With capital inputs growing more rapidly than labor inputs, the diminishing marginal product of capital (see Chapter 1) should cause the capital output ratio to rise until it equals s/h. In the reverse case, if $sY < hK$ or $K/Y > s/h$, capital inputs would be growing more slowly than labor inputs, and the marginal productivity of capital would be increasing. This would result in the capital output ratio falling until it equaled s/h. In either case, the economy would return to a balanced growth pattern.

Another implication of the Solow model as it has been presented thus far is that along the balanced growth path, *growth in Y is not a function of the saving rate.* This rather surprising result may be explained. Let:

$$s/h > K/Y \tag{3.6}$$

Under this circumstance, capital inputs would grow more rapidly than labor inputs and the capital output ratio would increase until the economy returned to balanced growth. Thus, if the saving rate increased, the capital output ratio would simply rise to the point where $s/h = K/Y$. There would be a short-run increase in the growth rate beyond that suggested by the balanced growth path (as K/Y was rising), but there would be no long-term effect. It should be remembered, however, that the model developed thus far ignores the role of technological change. Once this factor is included, we will see that the saving rate is quite important as a determinant of the long-run economic growth rate.

3.4 Saving and Growth with Technological Change

Although the simple Solow model presented above is powerful, it is not in complete agreement with what we know about economies over time. In particular, we know that economies do experience different growth rates over varying periods. What this implies is that economies are rarely on a balanced growth path for extended periods. Instead, it may be the case that movement from one growth path to another is the more likely scenario. Also, some economies grow faster than others. Why?

One possible explanation for differing rates of economic growth across economies comes from the observation that many countries with low levels of GDP per capita of those employed ("low GDP countries") have higher rates of growth than do countries with high levels of GDP per capita of those employed ("high GDP countries").

Eventually, however, the higher rates of GDP growth enjoyed by low GDP countries will increase GDP to the point where the level of GDP per capita of those employed will be the same as for high GDP countries. When this happens, we would expect that the growth rate for the formerly low GDP country would converge (i.e., decline) to that of high GDP countries.

To some extent, this "convergence" hypothesis has been observed in the world. However, there are situations where it may not apply. Also, we do find situations where some high GDP countries grow even faster than other "high GDP countries" (and soon become "super-high GDP countries") without immediate signs of convergence. Thus, there must be other explanations as well.

Fortunately, the assumptions of Professor Solow's model may be relaxed to help us in this regard. First, if we allow open economies, capital will be allowed to flow across borders. This will serve to abed convergence since low GDP countries may offer higher investment returns than high GDP countries. Second, if we permit technological improvement, we can see a reason for differing growth rates across countries. Improved technology will increase capital requirements in the same way a larger labor force will. If labor inputs are growing at one percent, it may make sense for capital inputs also to have to grow at one percent. With technological improvement, however, increased labor efficiency is possible, and capital requirements will be higher. More formally, if we let the growth rate in technology (admittedly, a difficult to measure variable) be j, and if the growth in labor inputs remains as h, balanced growth investment requires growth of $h + j$. If we equate net saving with net investment as before, we find:

$$K/Y = s/(h + j) \tag{3.7}$$

Thus, the same capital output ratio will require a higher rate of saving. If the United States, for example, had a capital output ratio of two, a growth rate in labor inputs of one percent, and a saving rate of two percent, the implied growth rate of technology would be zero, i.e., (2.00) = (.02)/(.01 + .00). Alternatively, if technological improvement was possible to the extent of even a one percentage point increment, with the capital output ratio remaining at two and the growth rate in labor inputs remaining at one percent, the implied saving rate would be: (2.00) = (.04)/(.01 + .01) = .04, or four percent. A saving rate of less than four percent would mean that insufficient capital investment would be made, and the production growth rate would be lower than its potential. *It is because of technological advances that saving is important.* Quite possibly, the growth rate of GDP in the United States has been stunted for a number of years because of excess consumption and insufficient saving.

3.5 The Importance of Stimulating Saving and Production Growth

During the 1960s and 1970s, gross saving (personal, business, and governmental, but before taking depreciation into account) in the United States averaged about 17 percent of GDP. By the 1980s, gross saving declined slightly to about 15 1/2 percent of GDP. During 1990-1993, however, the rate fell precipitously to only about 12 1/2 percent of GDP. This decline reflected the deteriorating fiscal position of government, at all levels federal, state, and local since the 1960s [3 p. 117]. Measured on a national income accounts basis, the deficit of the government sector was only 0.2 percent of GDP during the 1960s. The deficit rose to about one percent of GDP during the 1970s, and grew to 2.5 percent of GDP in the 1980s. The average has been even worse since 1990, although political pressures to reduce deficits have mounted in recent years.

Gross personal saving (excluding business and government) has also declined from about 4.5 percent of GDP during the 1960s and 5.5 percent during the 1970s to only 3.5 percent during the early 1990s. Over this period business saving has been almost flat, while government deficits have siphoned off much of the saving that has taken place. Gross saving is a good measure of an economy's saving effort, but saving net of depreciation is the best measure of the domestic resources available for increasing the capital stock. Sadly, the trend in net saving has been even worse than that of gross saving. Net saving has declined from about eight percent of GDP in the 1960s *to average only two percent of GDP since 1990.*

Even liberal economists have come to accept the importance of increasing the saving rate in order to promote economic growth. Of course, as we saw in the last chapter, the potential for periodic economic slowdowns is enhanced if consumption is inadequate. Nevertheless, it is becoming increasingly apparent that governmental policies designed to dampen the amplitude of the business cycle (Keynesian contra-cyclical monetary and fiscal policies) may have had the side-effect of reducing long-term economic growth. The Clinton Administration's Council of Economic Advisers has indicated its concern about insufficient saving in the United States as follows [2, pp. 116-7]:

> Without a doubt, the future rate of increase in the economy's productive capacity will be largely determined by the decisions of the millions of individual businesses and households in the private economy. The role of government is, and will continue to be, a limited one: to foster an open and competitive market environment, and to help the market work better when it would otherwise generate an inefficient result.
>
> Government policies to advance these objectives generally fall into two broad categories. First, government must address the question of national saving. Historically nations that have saved the most have also invested the most, and investment has been strongly correlated with productivity. Therefore, it is a matter of considerable concern that the national saving rate in the United States is low by international standards and has declined in the last 20 years.

What can be done to increase the saving rate in the United States? As a first step, there should be increased public (governmental) saving, or at least less public dis-saving. This means governmental deficits must be brought under control. Unless this happens, one cannot be too sanguine about the long-run growth potential for the United States. Second, there must be more private saving. Unfortunately, the political system in the United States does not encourage private saving. In addition, the tax structure in the United States does not reward saving. For long periods of time, people can actually suffer negative real after-tax returns on their savings. For example, during 1997, the average passbook rate on saving accounts was about three percent. For an individual in the highest federal and state tax brackets, this resulted in an after-tax return of only about 1.5 percent, which was substantially below the rate of inflation that has been experienced in recent years. Even with higher interest rates, those in the top brackets (who, in fact, do most of the saving) must earn nearly double the inflation rate in order to break even on an after-tax basis. The only way one can do this is by taking substantial risk, but even here the tax structure is punishing. If a high income person invests in the stock market and secures a capital gain, he/she is taxed at a combined federal and state capital gains tax rate of about 35 percent (as this is written). If that person, for example, enjoys a gain of $100,000, he/she would get to keep (say, for re-investment purposes) only $65,000. If that person lost $100,000 in the stock market, on the other hand, current federal (and most state) rules allow only a write-off of $3,000 per year. At a 15 percent interest rate, the discounted present value of that write-off would be less than $10,000!

Why do such ridiculous tax laws exist? Unfortunately, there seems to be an opinion widely-held in certain quarters that successful people should be taxed as heavily as possible. It is felt somehow that all high income persons do not deserve their salaries and other income, but there is no evidence that high income individuals are in that position because they are dishonest or somehow get their incomes at the expense of the poor. Even if they were both, however, for our purposes (i.e., attaining higher levels of aggregate saving), these are the very people who we should expect to save the most if they are given a chance. Remember from Chapter 2 that those with high marginal and average propensities to save are those with the high incomes.

From the perspective of generating more saving, one could make a very good case for real tax reform in the United States. By real reform, we do not mean the sorts of tinkering that has taken place consistently over the past forty years. In this world, the winners are the loop-hole lobbyists and the Congressmen and Congresswomen who get their campaign funds from writing the loop-holes. With real reform, we might even see the income tax abolished in favor of consumption taxes. This would quite likely encourage saving in the United States. Interestingly, the Ways and Means Committee of the U. S. House of Representatives is seriously considering this idea. Past history does not make one optimistic in this regard, however.

Even if the income tax remains, however, there are several reforms that would greatly reduce the dis-incentives to save. First, the capital gain tax could be abolished. Not only is this an unfair tax (since the income earned in order to produce capital gains has already been taxed) but it can result in silly situations such as that described above. Also, this tax does not take inflation into account, and a tax payer can wind-up with a large tax bill on phantom income. Second, the tax on dividends and interest could be eliminated. Dividend income is taxed twice in the United States, initially by the corporation that earned a profit and then by the stockholder who gets the dividend. For high income stockholders in large, profitable corporations, the effective tax on dividend income can be well over 60 percent. Interest income is taxed at the highest individual rates, with the absurd result that those who invest in relatively secure instruments such as treasury bills or bank deposits frequently do not earn an after-tax return that even equals the rate of inflation. Third, depreciation deductions for investment in real plant and equipment could be made larger. In some countries, business investment of this type is fully deductible in the year the investment is made. This encourages both higher saving rates and higher levels of business investment.

Finally, if all else fails, the income tax could at least be a flat tax with no deductions. Those who argue for fairness in taxation do not seem to understand that with a flat tax a person making ten times more than another person still pays ten times more tax. By what fairness standard should that person pay twenty or even fifty times more? Certainly if one wants to encourage saving (rather than government spending), taxing all people at the same rate should be an objective. Moreover, without deductions (loop-holes) we can get the government out of the business of determining that some investments (say, private housing which is encouraged by allowing homeowners to deduct interest costs) are better than others. As a bonus, we can also reduce the degree of political corruption that takes place when politicians who write the tax laws get funded by special interests who can benefit from those laws.

3.6 An Aggregate Growth Formula

Given the demonstrated fact that saving is a critical ingredient in enhancing production growth, we can return to a reformulation of the

Solow model which may be used whether or not an economy is enjoying balanced growth. The formula is derived from the production function identified in equation (2.2) and appears as follows:

$$\Delta Y/Y = \Delta H/H + .75\Delta L/L + .25\Delta K/K \tag{3.8}$$

where $\Delta Y/Y$ is the growth rate of aggregate production (GDP), $\Delta H/H$ is the growth rate of technology,$\Delta L/L$ is the growth rate of labor inputs, and $\Delta K/K$ is the growth rate of capital inputs. The coefficients are, once again, empirically determined from the aggregate production function and some authorities use .7 as the labor input growth coefficient and .3 as the capital input growth coefficient [7]. Also, these coefficients are for the economy of the United States. Other countries may have different coefficient.

Equation (3.8) provides a formula to determine production growth given growth in technology, labor inputs, and capital inputs. Suppose all three variables are growing at a one percent rate. The rate of production growth would be: $\Delta Y/Y = .01 + .75(.01) + .25(.01) = .02$, or two percent per period. If technology was growing at a rate of two percent, the production growth rate would become .03, or three percent, etc. Notice that, given the coefficients, technology is the most important element in the growth formula. There is a one-to-one correspondence between the technological growth rate and the production growth rate. Labor input growth is second in importance. For every one percentage point increase in labor inputs, the production growth rate increases by about three-quarters of a percentage point. Finally, growth of one percentage point in capital inputs will increase the production growth by about one-quarter of one percentage point.

From equation (3.8), we can see a reason for the slow down in the growth rate of the U. S. economy. That rate reached a peak around 1970, and has been declining since then [7, p. 105]. The major explanation for the decline is that the rate of technological improvement has fallen precipitously. The rate of increase of labor inputs actually increased somewhat due to the entrance of the baby boomers into the work force over this period, and the rate of increase of capital inputs has been steady.

The decline in the technological growth rate may be due to several factors. As we saw above, the saving rate has also fallen dramatically since the 1960s, and it is entirely possible that lack of saving has made it impossible for entrepreneurs to get adequate financing for improving technology. There may be other factors at work as well. Increased governmental regulation and red-tape has almost certainly made business less efficient and been a contributor to lower rates of productivity growth. Incentives for Americans to engage in entrepreneurial activities may also have declined. As we saw above, the tax structure may have contributed to this. It is also possible that individuals are less inclined to be entrepreneurs if they are going to be socially ostracized for their actions. There seemed to be an increase in entrepreneurial activity in the 1980s, perhaps due to a more favorable tax structure and a more optimistic political spirit, but that climate began to dissipate in the 1990s. Indeed, it has been popular in some quarters to refer to the 1980s as a "decade of greed" and to disparage entrepreneurs who were successful during that time. There is nothing like social condemnation (and higher taxes) to reduce the incentives for people to go out and start their own businesses or grow existing ones.

The decreasing growth rate of production in the United States has serious implications. If it continues, the standard of living for Americans will suffer. That trend may already have begun for some people. Unfortunately, when a decline in living standards sets in, one likely consequence is that people begin fighting over who gets how much of the economic pie rather than concentrating on how to make the pie bigger. We are seeing evidence of this behavior as this book is written.

3.7 Enhancing Labor Inputs for Greater Production

Although the analysis presented above is not encouraging, there are steps that can be taken to arrest the declining growth rate of production in the United States. Growth of all three variables, labor, capital, and technology can be stimulated in the long-run.

For example, even though population demographics are pretty much set for the next couple of decades, it may be possible to induce more labor into the work force. Reducing incentives for people not to work (welfare, etc.) may be helpful in this regard. Also, education may play a role in retraining willing workers whose skills are rusty or obsolete. Even the tax structure may be a factor.

We know from microeconomics that the supply of labor is a function of wage rates. If after-tax wages are higher, then more people will be willing to work more hours. There is a contra-indication to this rule, however. As people make more money, they tend to want to substitute leisure time for work time. Indeed, it is possible that higher wages may even have the perverse effect of reducing the supply of labor rather than increasing it if this substitution effect is large enough. One way around this dilemma is to reform the tax structure so that the *level* of taxation is the same but the *rates* are lower, and this was an objective of tax policy during the 1980s.

Now it may not be obvious how tax rates can be lowered even though the level of taxation is the same. Actually, how to accomplish this is rather simple: Reduce rates and eliminate deductions at the same time. If one's marginal rate of tax declines, say, from 40 percent to 20 percent, for every extra dollar of income that person earns, he/she gets to keep $.80 rather than $.60. There is a clear incentive to work more as a consequence. However, if certain tax deductions (say, mortgage interest payments) are eliminated, the overall dollar burden of tax may stay the same. Thus, there would be no incentive to substitute leisure time for work. Here we have the best of all possible worlds: People are encouraged (through lower tax rates but constant tax payments overall) to work, and they are allowed to spend their money as they see fit without governmentally imposed distortions via the tax code. Indeed, this is all so simple it is amazing we have not adopted this system of taxation.

3.8 Enhancing Capital Inputs for Greater Production

There are ways to stimulate the rate of growth of capital inputs as well as for labor inputs. As we have seen above, growth of the capital stock requires continuous high levels of business investment.

Once again, however, tax rules seem to get in the ways of more adequate levels of investment. Under the present structure, more rapid depreciation allowances and investment tax credits (ITCs) might be made available. Both have been shown to encourage business investment by increasing the rate of return on investment (as we shall see in greater detail in the next chapter). Larger depreciation allowances reduce the present value of tax payments, and hence reduce the real amount of business taxes paid. ITCs actually reduce the cost of investment by allowing a percentage of the amount spent to be *credited* to a companys tax bill. For example, if we had a 10% ITC in effect and a firm bought a piece of machinery for $100,000, it could subtract from its total tax bill in the year the machinery was purchased an amount equal to: (.10)($100,000) = $10,000. If total taxes due were $10,000, the firm would pay no tax. Although one must be careful with the incentive aspect of ITCs (since demand elasticities may allow some of the value of an ITC to be captured by businesses that produce capital goods, who themselves might then see higher returns on investment and hence invest more), they have worked in past years to accomplish higher levels of business investment. One authority has calculated that the investment tax credit feature added to the tax code by the Kennedy Administration in 1962, actually increased business investment by about 30 percent [7, p. 108].

It is unfortunate that we must spend so much time discussing tax rules when we are analyzing production growth. It is sad but true, however, that high levels of taxation distort *all* economic decisions, and at high enough levels one's investment in accountants and lawyers becomes more important than one's investment in improving real production. It is probably the case that our very complicated (and ever changing) income tax laws have been a major burden on production and productivity growth. The complication factor is clearly important, and it has been estimated that the cost of compliance alone with federal, state, and local tax rules runs many billions of dollars a year. When added to the cost to the government of having to operate the Internal Revenue Service (plus state and local equivalents), the income tax is undoubtedly a major drain on production. After all, what does a tax lawyer really produce?

One should not overlook the ever changing element of the tax rules as a factor in reducing production as well. Billions of man-hours are spent every year just keeping up with the thousands of changes in the rules either produced by Congress (or state and local authorities) or by the IRS (and its state and local equivalents). Some of the change is due to a fickle public who does not understand economics. For example, although the Kennedy ITC worked well, it was eventually repealed. Why? The answer is that it worked too well. Many companies invested heavily in plant and equipment and cut their tax bills accordingly. Soon, politicians were screaming about "big corporations not paying their fair share" of taxes, and the rules were changed. Periodic rule changing may be a cost of democracy, but there is little doubt that businesses invest less in an uncertain environment. Changing the tax rules whimsically and regularly adds an unnecessary degree of risk to a naturally risky world, and is a luxury one can only afford if the objective of society is something other than maximizing production. [Note: Socialist economies, for example, do not make output maximization a goal. Rather, a "fair and equal" distribution of income is the major objective. The economy may not be very productive, but at least it should not evidence rich and greedy people lording over those in poverty. Everyone should starve equally in such an economy! In the real world, unfortunately, the experiment with socialism in eastern Europe and Asia during the twentieth century merely resulted in economies that were highly inefficient and unproductive. Vast income inequalities still existed, only it was greedy commissars rather than capitalists lording over everyone else.]

From the standpoint of increasing production, it seems clear that the best macro policy an economy could have would be not to have an income tax. Congressman Bill Archer of Texas, who as this is written is the Chairman of the Ways and Means Committee of the U. S. House of Representatives (which writes the U. S. tax laws) has stated that the income tax should be torn out by its roots. He advocates repeal of the amendment to the U. S. Constitution that allows income taxes just like the one providing for prohibition of the manufacture and sale of alcoholic beverages was repealed. It was pointed out in Section 3.5 above that abolishing the income tax would also encourage saving. Thus, we have two very good reasons for eliminating income taxes in favor of consumption taxes: higher saving rates and higher levels of production.

There is one other area that must be referred to when macro policy decisions are discussed and that is the ever changing element of monetary policy, which has become the focal point in fighting inflation since the U. S. federal budget is always in deficit. Thus, fiscal policy can not be counted on to contain inflation (to the contrary, it can be counted on to stimulate inflation). An unfortunate aspect of monetary policy, however, is that it contains inflation by reducing the aggregate demand for business investment. Thus, when monetary policy is employed to reduce inflationary pressures it is by definition reducing the growth rate of the capital stock, and hence the long-run economic growth rate. The United States is thus in the most unenviable position of having all of its macro policies directed to stimulate consumption at the expense of saving, and its monetary policy is directed to reduce both saving and investment. It is no wonder that many economists believe that no policy would be better than these policies. These economists advocate the following:

- The elimination of the income tax in favor of consumption taxes.
- Large reductions in spending at all levels of government.
- A monetary policy that does not attempt to guess which way the economy is going but rather increases the money supply by a fixed rate equal to the overall real growth rate of GDP.

3.9 Enhancing Technology for Greater Production

As it turns out, improvements in technology may have the greatest impact on production. Unfortunately, this is the area where the least is known. One thing that we do know, however, is that encouraging entrepreneurship is a critical element in enhancing the rate of technological improvement [18]. The next chapters in this book deal with production at the level of the entrepreneurial firm, and they outline some thoughts on how the level of entrepreneurial activity may be increased.

Research and development (R&D) is also at the core of enhancing technology. Larger firms as well as entrepreneurial endeavors depend on research and development to come up with new products, to improve on older ones, and to find ways to produce for lower costs. The final chapters in this book examine ways companies can produce more at lower costs through statistical process control procedures.

R&D investment can be encouraged under present tax laws in the same way capital investment can be encouraged. Immediate write-offs for R&D expenditures and/or R&D credits would provide financial incentives which would result in greater efforts by enterprises.

If the tax laws are reformed, as we have strongly advocated above, there would be a free market approach to research and development. Many economists believe this would be the best way to proceed.

The United States has historically been an innovative and pioneering nation when it comes to invention. The past two centuries witnessed one major development after another. From mechanical inventions in the Nineteenth Century to high-tech space and computer applications in the Twentieth Century, invention after invention has been discovered, produced, and marketed by American companies. Although there appears to be some slow-down in this regard, only the pessimistic believe there has been a fundamental change in the American character.

References

[1] Baumol, W.J., "America's Productivity 'Crisis': A Modest Decline Isn't All That Bad," *The New York Times*, February 15, 1987.

[2] Cobb, C.W. and Douglas, P.H., "A Theory of Production," *American Economic Review*, March, 1928, pp. 135-169.

[3] Council of Economic Advisers,*Economic Report of the President*, Washington D.C., G.P.O.: 1995.

[4] Domar, E., "Expansion and Employment," *American Economic Review*, March, 1947, pp. 34-55.

[5] Eubank, J.T., *Attitudes Towards Wealth*, Los Angeles: The American College of Probate Counsel, 1986.

[6] Gillis, M., Perkins, D.H., Roemer, M. and Snodgrass, D.R., *Economics of Development*, Third Edition, New York: W.W. Norton & Co., 1992.

[7] Hall, R.E. and Taylor, J.B., *Macroeconomics*, fourth edition, New York: W.W. Norton & Co. , 1993.

[8] Harrod, R.F., *Towards a Dynamic Economics*, London: Macmillan, 1948.

[9] Lindsey, L.B., *The Growth Experiment*, New York: Basic Books, Inc., 1990.

[10] Pilzer, P.Z., *Unlimited Wealth*, New York: Crown Publishers, 1990.

[11] Rosegger, G., *The Economics of Production and Innovation*, second edition, Oxford: Pergamon Press, 1986.

[12] Rosenberg, N. and Birdzell, L.E., *How the West Grew Rich*, New York: Basic Books, 1986.

[13] Rothbard, M., *Power and Market*, Second Edition, Kansas City: Sheed Andrews and McMeel, Inc., 1977.

[14] Solow, R.M., "Technical Change and the Aggregate Production Function," *Review of Economics and Statistics*, August, 1957, pp. 312-320.

[15] Solow, R.M., "Technical Progress, Capital Formation, and Economic Growth," *American Economic Review*, May, 1962, pp. 76-86.

[16] Wagner, R.E., *Inheritance and the State*, Washington, D.C.: American Enterprise Institute, 1977.

[17] Williams, E.E., "Innovation, Entrepreneurship and Brain Functioning," in K. Vesper, *Frontiers of Entrepreneurship Research*, Wellesley. Mass.: Center for Entrepreneurial Studies, 1981.

[18] Williams, E.E., "Entrepreneurship, Innovation, and Economic Growth," *Technovation*, February 1983, pp. 3-15.

[19]Williams, E.E. and Thompson, J.R., *The Economics of Production and Productivity: A Modeling Approach*, Austin: Capital Book Company, 1996.

Problems

Problem 3.1 Using Solow's balanced growth formula, assume the technology of the U.S. economy is growing by one percent, labor inputs are also growing by one percent, and the capital/output ratio of the economy is two. Ignoring technology, determine the growth rate of capital inputs.

Problem 3.2 Again ignoring technology, what is the overall growth rate for the economy described in problem 3.1 above?

Problem 3.3 Again ignoring technology, what is the equilibrium saving rate for the economy described in problems 3.1 and 3.2 above?

Problem 3.4 Determine the overall growth rate of the economy of problems 3.1-3.3 above assuming the existence of technological improvement.

Problem 3.5 Determine the equilibrium saving rate for the economy in problem 3.4 above.

Problem 3.6 What has been the growth rate record of the U.S. economy in recent years? Explain why the growth rate has diminished.

Problem 3.7 List six changes that might be effected to improve the growth rate of the U.S. economy.

Chapter 4

Production at the Enterprise Level: The Entrepreneurial Firm

4.1 Introduction

At this point, we turn our attention from aggregate to firm-specific production. Here we shall still be concerned with inputs and outputs just as we were when we looked at the production of economies. Now, however, we must focus our attention on decision making and decision makers.

Part of the problem in constructing theories of production and productivity at the microeconomic level is that there are really two very different types of enterprises to model. On the one hand, we find highly complex, institutionally driven, quasi-political entities which we call publicly-held corporations. On the other, we find more simple, non-institutional, generally apolitical entities that we shall call *entrepreneurial firms*. Historically, microeconomics has not clearly distinguished between the two, and the neoclassical theory of the firm which is usually taught in microeconomics is really a theory of proprietors operating in generally competitive markets. Although the theory of monopoly and monopolistic competition is considered, the focus remains on competitive markets. Unfortunately, most of the large, publicly-held corporations in the world by no means operate in generally competitive markets, at least as economists use the term "competitive." As a consequence, real world results often are hard to ferret out in microeconomic treatments. One must add insights from disciplines other than economics to get a firm grasp on reality. Of course, one should be careful not to throw out the baby with the bath water. As we have said several times before in this book, the market place is a powerful arena. Generally speaking, allowing the free market to operate will result in greater production and higher levels of productivity than will be the case when the market is fettered. Unfortunately, government is not the only influence which can fetter the free market. Big business can do so as well.

Any realistic theory of the entrepreneurial firm must take into account the important characteristics of these entities. By definition, for the entrepreneurial firm, there is no separation of ownership and control, which produces an important set of issues that can have a major impact on analysis. Also, decisions of the entrepreneurial firm are made under conditions of pure uncertainty. Although there are some occasions where, due to the existence of large data bases and the repetition of experiments, the long-existing entity (which is also typically large and publicly-held) may be able to use probabilistic approaches and Bayesian analysis, this is frequently not true for the entrepreneurial concern. New enterprises usually have the least data with which to work of all businesses, and other entrepreneurial endeavors usually do not have the resources to put together requisite data bases. Although these entities may prepare business plans with elaborate projections and forecasts, there is rarely a solid foundation for these numbers [see Chapters 5 through 7]. Thus, entrepreneurial firms are like their large, publicly-held corporate cousins in that they face a world of fundamental uncertainty. They are unlike the publicly-held institutions regarding ownership conflict issues which may obscure production plans from the beneficiaries of those plans.

4.2 Psychology and Entrepreneurs

Whereas certain socio-political issues influence the structure and decision making of the publicly-held entity, it is probably true that the psychological make-up of the entrepreneur may be more important to the entrepreneurial firm. Fortunately, this is one area where quite credible and applicable academic work has been done (practically all by psychologists and sociologists).

Much of the early scholarly research in entrepreneurship centered on the socio-psychological characteristics of entrepreneurs. From Collins and Moore [6] onward, professors have been probing into the psyche of those individuals who decide to start a business of their own. The early view that entrepreneurs were men who failed in the traditional and highly structured roles available to them in society [6, p. 243] has been displaced in the literature with the view that most founders of new enterprises experience a generally higher than average level of success as employees [22, p. 3] and, in fact, are quite capable of functioning in a structured environment.

It is also generally accepted that at both the individual and societal level needs are far more complex than those simple requirements typically envisioned by economic models. Work by Maslow [24], Boyatzis [4], Winter [44], McClelland [26, 27], and others have identified the need for achievement (n-achievement), the need for affiliation (n-affiliation), the need for autonomy (n-autonomy), and the need for power (n-power) as the driving forces behind human behavior.

A striking conclusion of much of the socio-psychological research is that monetary reward is only of secondary importance in motivating individuals. One observer has attempted to synthesize humankind's needs in a so-called "money motive," but this is a rather different phenomenon from the one generally contemplated in economic models [45]. Indeed, it turns out that people have ambivalent attitudes about money. Anal types continue to amass it for no other reason than for its collection value, but others are actually repelled even by the discussion of monetary matters – at least when applied to themselves.

In discussing the achievement motive, McClelland found that high achievers were not much influenced by monetary reward except as a score-keeping device. Lower achievers, on the other hand, might be motivated by money and might be encouraged to work harder for financial incentives. Perhaps most significant of all the conclusions, however, is the general indictment by psychologists of the rationality postulate generally assumed in economic models.

As McClelland has put it, "...(Freud) destroyed forever (except, perhaps in the minds of economic theorists) the notion that motives are rational or can be rationally inferred from action. By concentrating his attention on notable irrationalities in behavior – slips of the tongue, forgetting of well-known facts, dreams, accidents, neurotic symptoms – he demonstrated over and over again that motives 'are not what they seem.'

In fact they might be just the opposite. It could no longer be safely assumed that a man walks across the street just to get to the other side. He might, in fact, want just the opposite – to enter a tavern on this side, a desire revealed indirectly by his exaggerated avoidance behavior" [27, p. 38]. See also [36] and [37].

Thus, it appears that any model attempting to explain entrepreneurial behavior which postulates maximizing profit, wealth, or some such monetarily-oriented objective, will fail to capture all of the essential determinants. Many entrepreneurs appear to be irrational and even quixotic, and pecuniary maximization models do not always handle well this sort of behavior. To be sure, many of the great economists of the past have recognized that irrational (non-economic) motives might dominate the entrepreneurial decision-making process.

Schumpeter [29], for example, argued frequently that such motives as the desire to found a private dynasty, the will to conquer in competitive battle, or the sheer joy of creation, could rule the judgments of the entrepreneur. Lord Keynes [20] also believed that animal spirits might be far more important than perhaps any other factor in explaining the stock market or even real investment activity, and Williams [36] suggests that "whim and fancy" may be more important than quantifiable variables in economic analyses.

In the neoclassical competitive models, however, the entrepreneur often is a sterile eunuch, a puppet manipulated by the invisible hand. In the condition of competitive equilibrium envisaged by these models, the entrepreneur does nothing. He/she does not create. He/she does not innovate. He/she merely reacts. It is fortunate for human progress that the entrepreneur of the real world does not behave exclusively in the fashion envisaged so often by neoclassical economic theory.

4.3 Economics and Entrepreneurs

One might be pardoned for thinking that there exists an extensive literature on the role of the entrepreneur in economic theory. Unfortunately, there does not. As Professor William Baumol has observed, "The entrepreneur is at the same time one of the most intriguing and one of the most elusive characters in the cast that constitutes the subject of economic analysis. He has long been recognized as the apex of the hierarchy that determines the behavior of the firm and thereby bears a heavy responsibility for the vitality of the free enterprise society. In the writings of the classical economist his appearance was frequent, though he remained a shadowy entity without clearly defined form and function. Only Schumpeter and, to some degree, Professor Knight succeeded in infusing him with life and in assigning to him a specific area of activity to any extent commensurate with his acknowledged importance. In more recent years, while the facts have apparently underscored the significance of his role, he has at the same time virtually disappeared from theoretical literature. And, as we will see, while some recent theoretical writings seem at first glance to offer a convenient place for an analysis of his activities, closer inspection indicates that on this score matters have not really improved substantially" [2, p. 64].

Baumol goes on to discuss *why* economic theory has failed to develop an illuminating formal analysis of entrepreneurship, principally because economic models are essentially mechanistic and automatic and call for no display of entrepreneurial initiative [2, p. 68]; and he maintains that such analysis is not likely to be forthcoming in the foreseeable future. Nevertheless, he argues, "If we are interested in explaining the 'really big dissimilarities in economic life,' we must be prepared to concern ourselves with entrepreneurship" [2, p. 65]. Among those really big dissimilarities are those associated with economic development. Baumol tells us, "It has long been recognized that the entrepreneurial function is a vital component in the process of economic growth. Recent empirical evidence and the lessons of experience both seem to confirm this view. For example, some empirical studies on the nature of the production function have concluded that capital accumulation and expansion of the labor force leave unexplained a very substantial proportion of the historical growth of the nations output. Thus, in a well-known paper, Solow [30] has suggested on the basis of American data for the period 1909-49 that 'gross output per man-hour doubled over the interval, with 87.5% of the increase attributable to technical change and the remaining 12.5% to increase in the use of capital.' But any such innovation, whether it is purely technological or it consists in a modification in the way in which any industry is organized, will require entrepreneurial initiative in its introduction. Thus we are led to suspect that by ignoring the entrepreneur we are prevented from accounting fully for a very substantial proportion of our historic growth" [2, pp 65-66].

Baumol concludes, "In a growth-conscious world I remain convinced that encouragement of the entrepreneur is the key to the stimulation of growth. The view that this must await the slow and undependable process of change in social and psychological climate is a counsel of despair for which there is little justification. Such a conclusion is analogous to an argument that all we can do to reduce spending in an inflationary period is to hope for a revival of the Protestant ethic and the attendant acceptance by the general public of the virtues of thrift! Surely we have learned to do better than that, in effect by producing a movement along the relevant functional paths rather than undertaking the move heroic task involved in shifting the relationships. This is precisely why I have just advocated more careful study of the rewards of entrepreneurship. Without awaiting a change in the entrepreneurial drive exhibited in our society, we can try to learn how one can stimulate the volume and intensity of entrepreneurial activity, thus making the most of what is permitted by current mores and attitudes. If the theory succeeds in no more than showing us something about how that can be done, it will have accomplished very much indeed" [2, p. 71].

Although Professor Baumol's conclusions are grounded more in intuition than rigorous economic theory, it does not differ from the findings of the economic historians who have analyzed the role of the entrepreneur in the development of the United States. There is a more complete literature in this area [see 5, 16, 31], although business history has not yet created a satisfactory general hypothesis of the role of entrepreneurship [see 31, p. 90]. One economist who believes that an axiomatic-theoretic approach to entrepreneurship may be adopted is Professor Harvey Liebenstein, yet his views are quite compatible with Baumol's. Liebenstein maintains, "Although there is no universally accepted theory of development, we can point to two important elements in the process: (1) Per capita income growth requires shifts from less productive to more productive techniques per worker, the creation or adoption of new commodities, new materials, new markets, new organizational forms, the creation of new skills, and the accumulation of new knowledge. (2) Part of the process is the interaction between the creation of economic capacity and the related creation of demand so that some rough balance between capacity growth and demand growth takes place. The entrepreneur as a gap-filler and input-completer is probably the prime mover of the capacity creation part of these elements of the growth process."

Professor Liebenstein continues, "We now know that development is not simply a process of physical and human capital accumulation in the usual sense. If that were all that were involved, then development would simply be a function of the willingness to save. Experience has shown that this is not the case. The work of Solow and others have shown that growth cannot be explained by the contributions of the increase in standard inputs. The work of Chenery and Strout emphasizes that the degree of capital absorption can be a significant constraint to growth in developing countries. The existence of and need for gap-filling and input-completing capacities could explain why standard inputs do not account for all outputs and why capital absorption should be a problem. Economic planning experience in many countries reveals that there is frequently a considerable divergence between plan targets and results. This divergence may be partly explained by the fact that entrepreneurship is not a normal input whose contribution can be readily determined, predicted, planned for, or controlled" [21, pp. 77-78].

Thus, even though we may not have a good economic theory of entrepreneurship, few could argue with the proposition that entrepreneurship is an essential determinant of economic development. Moreover, it is very likely to be the case that entrepreneurship is even more important than other variables such as the rate of saving, the capital stock of society at a point in time, etc., which we have discussed in previous chapters in this book. This conclusion has some incredibly important implications because, unlike other economic factors, the supply of entrepreneurship can be limitless. Entrepreneurial activity involves creation and innovation, and the creative process may be fostered. It is altogether possible that creativity can even be taught. If this is, in fact, the case, then there can be no logical limits to economic growth. The usual bane of the economist, natural resources, becomes fundamentally unimportant because entrepreneurial talent should be able to find better and better techniques that require fewer and fewer resources. Given the natural conservation laws of physics, it might even be argued that resources are not an essential requirement for economic growth! Unfortunately, in the past, economists have spent most of their time worrying about the scarcity phenomenon (scarce capital, scarce savings, etc.) when they really should be concentrating on the abundance of entrepreneurial talent that exists in the world and figuring out ways to encourage the development of entrepreneurs.

4.4 An Entrepreneurial Model

Despite the fact that there really is no good or well developed economic theory of entrepreneurship, we shall construct a production model for the entrepreneurial firm. Although this model is rigorous and assumes maximizing behavior, there is still room for entrepreneurial whim and fancy to play a role if the entrepreneur so wishes. It should be recognized that whim and fancy may be "costly" to the extent that their presence in decision making may reduce the competitive position of the entrepreneaurial firm in the market place. However, if the entrepreneur elects to incur these costs, they can be subsumed into the cost functions of the firm. There are limits, of course, to the extent that unprofitable whim and fancy, if too often indulged, may result in the bankruptcy (and elimination) of the enterprise.

Antecedents to the model we shall develop were posed a number of years ago for the publicly-held entity [32, 43]. These models were refined allowing for a simultaneous solution, providing for a correct interpretation of the "marginal productivity (efficiency) of investment capital" and positing a firm producing a products with z inputs or factors of production, but they still focused on the large, publicly-held entity. In the work to follow, our attention will center on the entrepreneurial firm.

We begin with an entrepreneur who wishes to maximize the wealth position of his/her enterprise as follows:

$$W = \frac{1}{\rho(K_{vc}/E)}[p(Q)f(K,L) - \gamma_1 K - \gamma_2 L - r_{vc}(K_{vc},E)K_{vc}] - E \tag{4.1}$$

subject to the constraint:

$$K_{vc} + E = g(Q) + k_1K + k_2L \tag{4.2}$$

Thus, we have the Lagrangian solution:

$$\begin{aligned} W &= \frac{1}{\rho(K_{vc}/E)}[p(Q)f(K,L) - \gamma_1 K - \gamma_2 L - r_{vc}(K_{vc}, E)K_{vc}] \\ &\quad -E + \lambda[K_{vc} + E - g(Q) - k_1K - k_2L] \end{aligned} \tag{4.3}$$

where:

W = the owner's net value of the enterprise;

ρ = the owner's opportunity capitalization rate;

r_{vc} = the average rate of return expected by outside venture capital;

E = the amount of owner's equity capital invested in the firm (optimized where W is maximized);

K_{vc} = the amount of venture capital employed by the firm (optimized where W is maximized);

p = the unit selling price of the firm's product;

$Q = f(K, L)$= the quantity of output of the product produced (optimized where W is maximized);

K, L = input factors of production;

γ_1, γ_2 = the unit factor costs of inputs K and L respectively;

$g(Q)$ = a net working capital requirement;

k_1, k_2 = capital requirement coefficients to finance K and L respectively.

Although this framework looks fairly imposing, the ideas behind equations (4.1) - (4.3) are fairly simple. The variable ρ is merely a discount rate. It is that rate of return which the entrepreneur expects to earn on the capital (designated as E in the model) he/she has invested in the business, given the risk assumed by the entrepreneur. Thus, if entrepreneur Smith has embarked on a new venture with $100,000 of his savings, he must determine a proper return to justify the risk he has assumed on his capital.

In order to arrive at ρ , it will be necessary for Smith to see what he could earn on his money from alternative investments. One way for Smith to do this would be to use the *capital asset pricing model* (CAPM) which has become prevalent in the finance literature. In its most simple form, the CAPM merely suggests that as investments increase in risk, they should also have higher returns. Or, put another way, in order to get investors to invest, they must be accorded *expected* returns to justify the risk they have assumed.

A short-term note (called a "bill") issued by the U.S. government is deemed to be almost riskless. Unless the U.S. government defaults during the term of the bill (say 90 days), the holder of the bill will be paid his/her principal plus whatever interest the bill bears. (Typically, treasury bills are issued at a discount, so technically Smith would buy the bill at the discount and receive its face value upon maturity). Suppose Smith can earn 4% on a 90 day treasury bill. Is his investment in a new business riskier than buying the treasury bill? The answer is definitely yes, and he should therefore expect a higher rate of return on his investment than 4%.

Other investments Smith might make include longer term U.S. treasury bonds which have some risk attached to them due to the possibility of fluctuating interest rates (see discussion in Chapter 3 regarding the inverse relationship between bond prices and interest rates), long term corporate bonds, common stocks, and stock in small capitalized public companies. Table 4.1 provides historical yields on these investments. It should be clear that the new business Smith wishes to initiate is riskier than all of the investments in Table 4.1. What does this mean? Clearly, the implication is that Smith should expect to earn an even larger amount since his investment in a new enterprise is even riskier than all of theses alternatives.

Given the data in Table 4.1, suppose Smith decides that he should earn a 25% return on his investment in his new enterprise. This would become the discount rate ρ in equation (4.1). It should be noted that ρ is an expected rate and is not necessarily what Smith *will* earn. It is the risk that Smith may lose all of his investment (or make even more than 25%) that gives ρ it meaning. It is essentially the mean value of a probability distribution with a fairly large variance.

Table 4.1 Arithmetic Mean Returns on Various Investments in the United States, 1926-1992.	
U.S. Treasury Bills	3.9%
Intermediate Term U.S. Government Bonds	5.3%
Long Term Corporate Bonds	5.7%
Common Stocks	12.4%
Small Company Stocks	17.5%

Source: Ross, Westerfield, and Jaffe, *Corporate Finance*, Homewood: Irwin, 1996.

The variable r_{vc} is also a discount rate. It is the rate of return expected by other investors in Smith's business. These other investors are called *venture capitalists*, and they typically structure their investments to have a *prior return* to that of the entrepreneur. Sometimes this is done by having the venture capitalists have a senior form of common stock, sometimes it is done with preferred stock, and sometimes it is done with debt (loans to the firm). Sometimes the venture capitalist uses a combination of all of the above with even more exotic elements such as rights (called *warrants*) to buy more stock at a given price and conversion privileges which allow preferred stock and/or debt to be converted to common stock. The important factor here is that the venture capitalist has a more secure position than the entrepreneur. Hence, the expected return to the venture capitalist is lower. In the case of Mr. Smith, suppose he has secured \$500,000 (designated as K_{vc} in the model) from venture capitalists who have purchased convertible preferred stock and expect to earn 20% on their investment.

Within equation (4.1), it is assumed that ρ is functionally dependent on E and K_{vc} (the amounts of owner and venture capital employed by the firm) and that r_{vc} is a function of K_{vc}. The reason for this is that the existence of venture capital increases the riskiness to both the entrepreneur and to the venture capitalist. If Smith could finance his business entirely on his own without the use of more senior capital, his risk would be reduced. By securing convertible preferred stock from outsiders, Smith risks having to allow others a positive return on their capital before he gets any on his own. In addition, he has to take into account the wishes of his investors in certain of his decisions in running the business. If he had no outside investors, he could make all of the decisions and he would be entitled to all of the profits made without having to give others a preference. The venture capitalist is also less secure as the amount of capital he/she supplies increases. In the example with Mr. Smith, the venture capitalist is supplying \$500,000 out of the total of \$600,000 being raised. If Smith were putting up \$500,000 and the venture capitalist were only investing \$100,000, the risk assumed by the venture capitalist would be reduced (and so, therefore, would the expected return to the venture capitalist).

The variables p and Q in equation (4.1) indicate the price Smith will charge for his product (or service) and the amount he expects to sell. These variables are typically made by forecasts in a business plan, which will occupy our attention in Chapters 5 through 7. In equation (4.1), p is shown to be a function of Q ,which, in turn, is a function of K and L. This, of course, implies that the entrepreneur is not operating in a competitive product market, which is the usual assumption microeconomists make about new firms. In a competitive market, the entrepreneur would be unable to influence the price he/she charged. He/she would be deemed a *price taker* and would have to sell at the competitive market price. Instead, we are suggesting in equation (4.1) that the *purpose* of the entrepreneurial enterprise is to differentiate its product or service. When the entrepreneur effectively does this, he/she will face a negatively sloped demand curve, where p is a function of Q. That is, for the entrepreneur to sell more of his/her product or service, he/she will have to sell at a lower price. In Smith's case, suppose he has determined to sell his product at \$5 per unit and at this price he expects to sell 100,000 units. His expected revenue would be: $\$5 \times 100{,}000 = \$500{,}000$.

Now in Smith's business plan he has calculated that he will have to hire a given number of employees and utilize a plant of a given size with given raw material inputs to produce 100,000 units. Hiring employees and operating a plant give rise to costs. Although some of the costs may be fixed (i.e., they exist regardless of the amount produced), others are variable (i.e., the vary in direct proportion to the amount produced). In Smith's case, he has attempted to reduce the fixed element of his costs as much as possible, since the existence of fixed costs gives rise to risk. This is because even if he has no sales, he would incur costs (and, hence, losses) if he had fixed costs.

It may not be possible to eliminate all fixed costs, but the resourceful entrepreneur will often find ways to reduce or even eliminate most of them. Suppose Smith has been able to hire employees on a "piece work" basis. This means that they will be paid only for the output produced. Assume Smith has been able to accomplish this for $1 per unit. This would become the variable γ_2 in equation (4.1). Suppose further that Smith has worked out a lease arrangement for his plant and equipment which is also based on production and that his raw materials cost will varying in direct proportion with sales. He has agreed to pay $1 per unit for the use of plant and equipment and will incur another $1 per unit in raw materials costs, for a total cost of $2 per unit. This would become the variable γ_1 in equation (4.1).

Given the above, we may make the following calculation for equation (4.1) in the case of Mr. Smith:

$$\begin{aligned} W &= (1/.25)[(5 \times 100,000) - (2 \times 100,000) - (1 \times 100,000) \\ &\quad -.20(500,000)] - 100,000 \\ &= (4)(500,000 - 200,000 - 100,000 - 100,000) - 100,000 \\ &= (4)(100,000) - 100,000 \\ &= \$300,000 \end{aligned}$$

This amount is the net value of the enterprise to Mr. Smith, if all of the above assumptions about the variables turn out to be correct. Smith will sell $500,000 in product. He will incur capital costs (plant and equipment plus raw materials) of $200,000 and labor costs of $100,000. He will pay his venture capitalists a return of $100,000 on their investment, and he will have a profit of $100,000 left for himself. Assuming this profit will continue to be earned over a long period of time, it may be "capitalized" to a present value. This is done by dividing the expected profit by the appropriate owner's opportunity capitalization rate (ρ). Capitalizing the $100,000 at a rate of 25% gives the firm a gross value of $400,000, or a net value of $300,000 once Smith's investment is taken into account.

We might inquire as to the nature of the $300,000 net value to Mr. Smith. First, it should be observed that this is an amount above and beyond the $100,000 he invested in the business. He expected to earn a return on that $100,000 as a *capitalist* (i.e., one who has invested his capital in a business); but, if his expectations are met, he has a firm worth $300,000 more than his investment. This may be deemed the *returns to entrepreneurship*, which are due to the skills mustered by Smith as an entrepreneur. Professor Kirzner [19] has distinguished between the role of the capitalist (which Smith is assuming by investing $100,000 in his business) and that of the entrepreneur (which Smith is assuming by having built a business). Some entrepreneurs are able to build businesses without having to invest any of their own money. In these instances, the business values are entirely due to entrepreneurial skills and the gross value of the business is equal to the net value since $E = 0$.

Now the example of Mr. Smith is an altogether simple one. Indeed, we have really assumed some of the results which would have to be worked out by optimization in equation (4.1). Suppose Smith knows what the demand for his product is at varying prices and he knows his input costs. He does not know, however, how much he should produce (i.e., Q) to maximize the net value of his business, and he does not know how much money he will need to raise (K_{vc} and E) in order to maximize net value. An approach to maximizing while providing a completely simultaneous solution for all the variables can be worked out. The mathematics are a little complicated but the method is the usual Lagrangian process. First, a set of simultaneous equations are derived necessary to solve for the optimization values of K , L , K_{vc} , and E :

$$\frac{\partial W}{\partial K} = \frac{1}{\rho(K_{vc}/E)}[\{p + Q\frac{dp}{dQ}\}f_K - \gamma_1] - \lambda[g'(Q)f_K + k_1] = 0 \quad (4.4)$$

and,

$$\frac{\partial W}{\partial L} = \frac{1}{\rho(K_{vc}/E)}[\{p + Q\frac{dp}{dQ}\}f_L - \gamma_2] - \lambda[g'(Q)f_L + k_2] = 0 \quad (4.5)$$

Simplifying the notation by letting:

$$\Pi = p(Q)f(K, L) - \gamma_1 K - \gamma_2 L - r_{vc}(K_{vc})K_{vc} \quad (4.6)$$

we find:

$$\frac{\partial W}{\partial K_{vc}} = [-\frac{\Pi}{\rho^2(K_{vc}/E)}\frac{\partial \rho(K_{vc}/E)}{\partial (K_{vc}/E)}\frac{1}{E}] - [\frac{1}{\rho(K_{vc}/E)}(r_{vc} + K_{vc}\frac{\partial r_{vc}}{\partial K_{vc}})] + \lambda = 0 \quad (4.7)$$

and,

$$\frac{\partial W}{\partial E}=[\frac{\Pi}{[\rho(K_{vc}/E)]^2}\frac{\partial\rho(K_{vc}/E)}{\partial(K_{vc}/E)}\frac{K_{vc}}{E^2}]-[\frac{1}{\rho(K_{vc}/E)}K_{vc}\frac{\partial r_{vc}}{\partial E}]-1+\lambda=0 \tag{4.8}$$

Equations (4.4) and (4.5) simply say that we should employ a given quantity of K and a given quantity of L . It can be shown that the marginal revenue products for K and L (stated in terms of maximizing the net value of the enterprise) are equal. (For a refresher on these concepts, see Chapter 1):

$$\frac{f_K}{f_L}=\frac{\gamma_1/\rho(K_{vc}/E)+\lambda k_1}{\gamma_2/\rho(K_{vc}/E)+\lambda k_2} \tag{4.9}$$

Equations (4.6) and (4.7) provide us with optimal values for K_{vc} and E. In addition, we must bring in the constraint:

$$K_{vc}+E=g(Q)+k_1K+k_2L \tag{4.10}$$

This merely states that the sources of financing (K_{vc} and E) will equal what is required by the business to finance its investment in plant, equipment, raw materials inventory, and other working capital (such as receivables and operating cash balances). To illustrate, let us return to our example of Mr. Smith. Suppose after going through the analysis in equations (4.1) through (4.10), Smith determines that he should produce 100,000 units selling for \$1 per unit. He should also have raised \$500,000 from venture capitalists and \$100,000 from himself, and he should spend the \$600,000 he has raised as follows: (1) Required cash balances, \$150,000; (2) Accounts receivables requirement, \$200,000; (3) Inventory requirement \$100,000; (4) Advance lease payment on plant and equipment, \$100,000; and (5) Training programs for employees, \$50,000. The constraint envisaged in equation (4.10) merely says that K_{vc} and E will equal the required working capital (noted as $g(Q)$ and equaling the required cash, receivables, and inventory) plus the required investment in capital (k_1K) and labor (k_2L).

By bringing in the constraining equation, we may obtain an optimization solution for K , L , K_{vc} , E and λ which will maximize W when the second ordered conditions below are satisfied.

$$\begin{vmatrix} W_{KK} & W_{KL} & -k_1 \\ W_{LK} & W_{LL} & -k_2 \\ -k_1 & -k_2 & 0 \end{vmatrix} > 0 \tag{4.11}$$

$$\begin{vmatrix} W_{KK} & W_{KL} & W_{KK_{vc}} & -k_1 \\ W_{LK} & W_{LL} & W_{LK_{vc}} & -k_2 \\ W_{K_{vc}K} & W_{K_{vc}L} & W_{K_{vc}K_{vc}} & 1 \\ -k_1 & -k_2 & 1 & 0 \end{vmatrix} < 0 \tag{4.12}$$

$$\begin{vmatrix} W_{KK} & W_{KL} & W_{KK_{vc}} & W_{K_{vc}E} & -k_1 \\ W_{LK} & W_{LL} & W_{LK_{vc}} & W_{LE} & -k_2 \\ W_{K_{vc}K} & W_{K_{vc}L} & W_{K_{vc}K_{vc}} & W_{K_{vc}E} & 1 \\ W_{EK} & W_{EL} & W_{K_{vc}E} & W_{EE} & 1 \\ -k_1 & -k_2 & 1 & 1 & 0 \end{vmatrix} > 0 \tag{4.13}$$

It should be pointed out that the equations and analysis provided above yield a rigorous solution to the problems faced by Mr. Smith. In the real world, most new entrepreneurs do not have the analytical training or inclination to perform this analysis. Moreover, since the equations are never known with certainty, one may forgive the entrepreneur for using less sophisticated methods such as those presented in Chapters 5 through 7 below.

4.5 Business Taxes

The model described in equations (4.1) - (4.13) ignores taxes. This is not because taxes are unimportant in the real world. Rather, the means of handling the taxation issue would depend on the legal form of enterprise adopted by the entrepreneur. For example, were the entrepreneur to operate as a corporation and elect (or be required) to be taxed according to Subchapter C of the Internal Revenue Code, the business entity itself would be subject to tax before any distributions were made to the entrepreneur (or the venture capitalist unless the financing supplied by the venture capitalist were deemed to be debt). Were the entrepreneur to operate as a sole proprietorship or partnership, or be able to elect Subchapter S status (see discussion below), or be able to become a limited liability company, then the business entity itself would not be taxed. Instead, the owners of the business would be taxed directly and one layer of taxation would be avoided. The rules of taxation are arbitrarily decided by the U.S. Congress and the Internal Revenue Service. Such rules may have no economic rationale, although they definitely have an economic impact on business and production decisions. Since tax rules can influence the behavior of all economic actors, it might be wise for us to summarize very briefly the rudiments of business taxation (see [7] for a more extensive discussion).

For the purposes of taxation, an organization may qualify as a corporation even if it is not incorporated. The basic rule is whether the organization possesses the characteristics of a corporation, which include such things as long or unlimited life, limited liability, ease of ownership transfer, etc. If an organization so qualifies, then it is subject to income taxation as a corporate entity. Taxable income is generally equal to gross income less deductions allowed to corporations. The gross income of a corporation is generally derived from sources such as sales, dividends, interest, rent, royalties received, and net gains on the sale of capital assets. A contribution of capital is not income. Corporations taxed pursuant to Subchapter C of the Internal Revenue Code may usually exclude from their taxable income 70 percent of the dividends which they receive on common or preferred stock of other Subchapter C corporations. They may not exclude any of the interest received on debt that they hold. If the corporation sustains a net loss on capital asset transactions for the year, this may not be deducted from other income but may be carried forward for up to five years as a short-term capital loss and used to offset any capital gains that occur during that time. On the other hand, should the corporation end the year with net long-term capital gains (on assets held more than one year) that exceed net short-term capital losses, the net long-term capital gain in excess of net short-term losses is included in ordinary income. Finally, the corporation may also receive capital gains treatment on certain depreciable property and real property that is used in trade or business (Sec. 1231 property) if it is held over one year and recognized gains exceed recognized losses. Net losses for the year on Sec. 1231 property may be deducted as ordinary losses.

Corporations are allowed to deduct expenses from gross income to determine taxable income. There is no set list of these expenses, but the corporation is usually on strongest ground in claiming a deduction if the expense is an ordinary and necessary business expense and if it is reasonable in amount. Typical deductions claimed by corporations include costs of goods sold (such as wages, raw materials, rent, repairs, and depreciation), selling expenses (such as salaries, advertising, bad debts, and certain taxes), interest, amortization and depletion, contributions to pension and profit-sharing plans, the intercorporate dividend exclusion (described above), and net operating losses carried over from other years. Deductions for charitable contributions are only allowed up to 10 percent of the sum of taxable income plus contributions made. Any excess over this amount may be carried forward five years. Should a corporation sustain a net operating loss during the year, it may, if it meets certain conditions (e.g., that there has been no substantial change in the ownership or the nature of the business), carry this loss back three years and, if it is still not exhausted, forward five years. The resulting recomputation of taxable income in other years should result in either a recovery of taxes paid in earlier years or a lower tax burden in subsequent years.

After subtracting the deductions from gross income to determine taxable income, the tax rates may be applied to determine the federal corporate income tax due. (Most states also collect corporate income taxes, which are generally figured along the lines of the federal tax and are superimposed on that tax). All corporate taxable income is subject to a graduated rate structure which, at this writing, is provided in Table 4.2

Table 4.2 U.S. Federal Corporate Income Tax Rates, Effective 1997.

Over	But Not Over	Tax	Of the Amount Over
$ 0	$ 50,000	15%	$ 0
$ 50,000	$ 75,000	$ 7,500 + 25%	$ 50,000
$ 75,000	$ 100,000	$ 13,750 + 34%	$ 75,000
$ 100,000	$ 335,000	$ 22,250 + 39%	$ 100,000
$ 335,000	$ 10,000,000	$ 113,900 + 34%	$ 335,000
$ 10,000,000	$ 15,000,000	$ 3,400,000 + 35%	$ 10,000,000
$ 15,000,000	$ 18,333,333	$ 5,150,000 + 38%	$ 15,000,000
$ 18,333,333	$ ———	35%	———

Source: Internal Revenue Service, U.S. Corporation Income Tax, Form 1120

If the above schedule makes no sense to you, you are among the millions of other people to whom it makes no sense. But your authors are not kidding. This is actually the corporate income tax schedule in effect at the time of the writing of this book. There is no economic model driving this schedule. Rather, it is the result of political logrolling within the Congress and the executive branch with additional "foolish powder" thrown in by the IRS. If one finds this schedule unappealing, he/she should not be too concerned. Another one, probably more arcane and complicated, will spew forth in new legislation which is on the drawing board as this is written. One of the verities of the tax rules is: By the time you have learned the rules, the rules will have changed. In its infinite wisdom, Congress manages to make minor changes in the tax rules almost every year and major ones every four or five years. The cost of understanding and complying with ever-changing and sometimes even incomprehensible tax rules is undoubted one of the biggest burdens faced by American business, especially small business. One can immediately see why our tax system is a clear and obvious impediment to both production and productivity.

Interestingly, the shrewd entrepreneur may have observed that small business has been singled out to pay the highest of all marginal brackets. A typical business grossing a couple of million dollars in sales might well earn between $100,000 and $335,000. This company would be subject to the highest marginal bracket of 39% — even higher than the top bracket paid by large corporations (who, of course, have political action committees and contribute big money to the Members of Congress who write the tax laws). Unfortunately, it is just those smaller enterprises that are now generating most of the job growth in the United States, despite being over regulated and over taxed! The argument is made that the higher brackets are justifiable because of the lower brackets enjoyed at income below $100,000. That argument makes sense for a system where proportional taxation is adopted, but it does not make sense under a system of progressive taxation.

The shrewd entrepreneur may also now be wondering why all corporations do not subdivide themselves into many different corporations to take advantage of the preferential tax rate on the first $50,000 or $75,000 of income. The answer is that some do, although the advantages may not be as great as they seem. The Internal Revenue Code defines a control group of corporations as (very roughly) those which are owned 80 percent or more in common. If such a controlled group elects to file separate returns for each corporation, it is entitled to one $50,000, and one $75,000 taxable income bracket amount. It must allocate these among the various corporations such that there is only one opportunity to have income taxed at the lower rates. In addition, by not filing a consolidated return, the group loses the opportunity to offset the losses or loss carry forwards of one member against the gains of another. Further, affiliated corporations filing consolidated returns are allowed a 100 percent exclusion of dividends paid from one member to another, while only 70 percent may be excluded if separate returns are filed. Thus, most control group corporations elect to file consolidated returns.

From a tax viewpoint, the proportionate share of income from a proprietorship or partnership is included in full on each taxpayer's return, while the corporation pays taxes on its own income and its stockholders pay taxes on the dividends which they receive. It should be noted, however, that Subchapter S of the Code allows corporations with 75 or fewer shareholders, if they meet certain other conditions, to be taxed as partnerships. This arrangement has the disadvantage of making each owner pay taxes at his personal rate on his full share of corporate income, instead of on just the amount distributed as dividends. On the other hand, it does eliminate the double taxation of income and the possibility of an accumulated earnings tax (see below). Making a Subchapter S election has several advantages over being an unincorporated organization. Aside from the limited liability and ease of ownership transfer, it is possible to pass through to the stockholders the operating losses and capital gains of the corporation and, importantly, to deduct various fringe benefits (pension, medical, profit-sharing) which an unincorporated business often may not deduct.

Since the tax rates for individuals now go as high as over 40 percent, another question that might arise concerns the use of a corporate "shell" by high-bracket taxpayers to avoid taxes. The IRS has several tools to prevent this. In the first place, if a company is owned and controlled by a few people (closely-held) and receives most of its income in the form of interest, dividends, royalties, etc., it may be classified as a personal holding company and be subject to a flat tax of 39.6 percent on the amount of personal holding company income not paid out in dividends to stockholders. Even if a company is involved in a trade or business, it may be subject to penalty if it fails to pay dividends in order to avoid a tax liability for its stockholders. If such a company accumulates earnings beyond the reasonable needs of the business for the purpose of avoiding taxes on its stockholders, it may be subject to a tax of 39.6 percent on the amount retained beyond $250,000. In practice, this law is usually applied only to "closely held" corporations which are, in effect, personal holding companies in disguise.

There are a number of tax implications for the operation of a business that may be derived from the above analysis. Several have already been suggested. For example, the entrepreneur may find debt a more attractive source of funding than equity because interest is a deductible expense but dividends paid on common and preferred stock are not. In addition, since dividends are taxable to stockholders but earnings retained are not, there is a definite advantage to retaining earnings for new investment rather than paying dividends and attempting to issue new stock. Even if the retention results in a higher value for the stock, the stockholder is taxed at more favorable personal capital gains rates (a maximum of 20% for securities held for 18 months or longer versus personal rates that can exceed 40%) and only when he/she sells the stock. A major goal in dealing with the Internal Revenue Service is to put all possible expenses into the current period, so that taxable income is lower. Hence, taxes are reduced. One should not adopt the view that taxes will have to be paid sooner or later so they might as well be paid now. Money has time value, so the longer the payment of taxes may be deferred, the longer one is able to use the money. If the entrepreneur can earn a 10 percent rate of interest on his/her money and it is possible to defer the payment of $1 in taxes for a year, the tax bill has been effectively cut to $.91.

4.6 Business Depreciation

The models of equations (4.1) - (4.13) also consider but do not fully develop the role depreciation plays in production decisions. In our earlier example with Mr. Smith, depreciation was ignored because we assumed that Smith hired (leased) his plant and equipment. As a matter of economic efficiency this is probably a wise thing for Mr. Smith to do since it conserves the amount of scarce funding that either he or a venture capitalist must invest in the business. Plant and equipment purchases typically require large amounts of capital, and the entrepreneur may have to give the venture capitalist a handsome return (say 25 percent or more) to raise the funds to acquire plant and equipment. We shall return to this point below.

At some point, however, the entrepreneur may decide to purchase rather than lease his/her plant and equipment. This may be of necessity if leasing is unavailable. It may be a proper economic choice once the business is generating earnings and the investors wish to reinvest those earnings back into the business albeit at returns probably below those obtained from the pure entrepreneurial investment. (See discussion in section 4.8 below). In our example of Mr. Smith, let us suppose that he has decided to purchase rather than lease $500,000 worth of plant and equipment. Notice that this is $400,000 above the original advance lease payment he planned to make. Thus, an additional $400,000 in capital would have to be raised. In addition, we now also have the question of calculating how to expense the plant and equipment Mr. Smith has purchased. We need to do this to determine net earnings. Furthermore, the tax collector will allow us to deduct these expenses (at rates provided by the tax collector), thus reducing Mr. Smith's tax liability. At this juncture, the means of calculating depreciation becomes a matter of deciding the purpose for which we use the depreciation figure. If we wish to determine "true" economic earnings, the real physical (value) depreciation of the plant and equipment should be determined. This is purportedly what is done when "accounting" income is determined, although there are skeptics who believe accounting depreciation is just about as arbitrary as tax depreciation (see discussion below). We might review some of the accounting methods of depreciation in any case. There are essentially four accounting methods to depreciate plant and equipment. They include the following:

1. *Straight-line Method.* The cost or other basis of the property, less salvage value, is allocated evenly over the remaining useful life of the property. Salvage values which are less than 10 percent of the total value on personal property having a three-year life or more is sometimes ignored.

2. *Declining Balance Method.*

a. Double declining balance. Depreciation at twice the straight line rate is allocated to the remaining value of the asset, unadjusted for salvage. The company may switch to straight line at any time during the life of the asset. This method usually applies to new or rebuilt property with at least a three-year life.

b. Limited declining balance. Depreciation is allocated at 1-1/2 times the straight line rate. This method is often used for used tangible property with a three-year life or more.

3. *Sum-of-the-years digits Method.* Cost or other basis, less salvage, is allocated according to a fraction the numerator of which is the number of years' useful life remaining and the denominator of which is the sum of the numbers representing the number of years of useful life of the property. It is generally applied to the same type of property as double declining balance.

4. *Units of Production Method.* The difference between cost and salvage is allocated by a fraction given by the units produced during an accounting period divided by the number of estimated units to be produced over the useful life of the asset.

To illustrate the more common methods, let us suppose that Mr. Smith purchases plant and equipment for $500,000, that such plant and equipment has a 5-year useful life and a nominal salvage value at the end of its life. Depreciation might be determined as in Table 4.3.

Table 4.3 Illustration of Various Methods of Accounting Depreciation.

Year	Straight-Line	DDB	S of YD
1	$100,000	$200,000	$166,667
2	100,000	120,000	133,333
3	100,000	100,000	100,000
4	100,000	80,000	66,667
5	100,000	-0-	33,333
Total	500,000	500,000	500,000

For tax purposes, there are at least 100 different ways the same plant and equipment might be depreciated depending on when such plant and equipment was purchased. It seems that every time Congress passes another tax law, a new set of depreciation schedules is placed in effect. One possible schedule that is effective as of this writing is provided in Table 4.4.

It should be apparent that the accelerated accounting methods and the one illustrated in Table 4.4 allocate a greater part of the depreciation expense to the earlier years. This will result in income being reduced in the early years of plant and equipment ownership. From a tax standpoint, the plant and equipment have already been paid for and this expense allocation is merely a bookkeeping exercise. Nevertheless, the allocation reduces taxable income and thus reduces taxes in the earlier years of ownership. It may be argued that, as long as a firm continues to grow and buy new assets, it may never need to worry about the higher taxes in later years when the accelerated methods provide lower depreciation charges because there will be new assets to depreciate and shield income from taxation.

Given the schedules in Tables 4.3 and 4.4, we may compute book and tax depreciation for Mr. Smith's plant and equipment. Assuming a five year life for Mr. Smith's plant and equipment, and assuming he uses straight line depreciation for book purposes, his depreciation in the first year of ownership would be $100,000 (see Table 4.3). For tax purposes, depreciation would be: (.2) × ($500,000) = $100,000. It is coincidental that the two numbers are the same. (The tax table uses a "half year" convention and double declining balance depreciation. Thus, for the first year, a 40% depreciation rate is cut in half to 20%.) Given this number, we may determine accounting and taxable income for Mr. Smith (see Table 4.5) assuming our previous calculations about Mr. Smith's sales and other costs.

Suppose Mr. Smith operates his business as Smith International, Inc. and is taxed as a Subchapter C corporation. Smith International would pay federal income taxes of $22,250 (see Table 4.2). It would have accounting and after-tax income of: $100,000 - $22,250 = $77,750. (The two are the same only because depreciation is the same for both).

Table 4.4 Illustration of Depreciation Allowed for U.S. Federal Income Tax Determination Purposes.				
Year	3 Year Recovery	5 Year Recovery	7 Year Recovery	10 Year Recovery
1	33.33%	20.00%	14.29%	10.00%
2	44.45	32.00	24.49	18.00
3	14.81	19.20	17.49	14.40
4	7.41	11.52	12.49	11.52
5	—	11.52	8.93	9.22
6	—	5.76	8.92	7.37
7	—	—	8.93	6.55
8	—	—	4.46	6.55

Source: Internal Revenue Service, U.S. Corporation Income Tax, Form 1120

Table 4.5 A Hypothetical Pre-Tax Statement of Income.	
Sales	\$500,000
Cost of Goods Sold	
Wages	\$100,000
Materials	100,000
Depreciation	100,000
Total Cost of Goods Sold	$< 300,000 >$
Gross Profit	200,000
Interest Expense	$< 100,000 >$
Income Before Tax	\$100,000

The following is also assumed: (1) The cash, receivables, and inventory requirements of the business are those previously described for Mr. Smith. (2) The employee training program is deemed to have continuing value and is therefore not depreciable and cannot be expensed. (3) The company can get trade credit at no cost from its suppliers equal to its inventory purchases. (4) The venture capitalist supplies \$500,000 in debt and earns 20% interest on his/her funds. (5) The balance of the financing (\$400,000) comes from Mr. Smith, the entrepreneur. Given these assumptions, the balance sheet described in Table 4.6 may be constructed. Further, given the above assumptions, we may invoke equation (4.1):

$$W = (1/.25)(77,750) - \$400,000 = -\$89,000$$

Table 4.6 A Hypothetical Balance Sheet.			
Assets:		Liabilities:	
Cash	$150,000	Accounts Payable	$100,000
Receivables	200,000		
Inventory	100,000	Long-Term Debt	500,000
Total Current	450,000		
Fixed Assets:			
Training	50,000	Common Stock	400,000
P&E	500,000		
Total Fixed	550,000		
Total	$1,000,000	Total	$1,000,000

Thus, Smith would have a negative net value for his enterprise. Remember that when we first invoked equation (4.1), the net value of the enterprise to Smith was +$300,000. The change to a negative value is due to three changes in assumptions: First, Smith has decided to purchase his plant and equipment and therefore has to invest $300,000 more of his own money into the business; second, Smith would have had to invest $400,000 more, but he was able to get his trade creditors to finance his inventory at no cost; and third, we now include the fact that Smith has to pay U.S. federal income taxes. This is not to say that Smith's business is not profitable. He does earn an after-tax profit of $77,750. The problem is that this return is not sufficient to justify the risk Smith has assumed. A $77,750 return on a $400,000 investment is: (77,750)/(400,000) = 19.4%, where Smith has determined that he needs a 25% return. How can Smith make his business more profitable? Are there ways to improve efficiency? Can his productivity be improved? All of these questions are similar in nature and we shall address them in the next section.

4.7 Enhancing Productivity

There are many ways for a business to improve its productivity (and, hence, its efficiency and profitability). A complete review of the optimization model presented in equations (4.1) - (4.13) may be in order. The entrepreneur may have miscalculated in any number of places. First, are the optimal sales levels correct? Can more sales and production be achieved with less than commensurate increases in costs? Smith assumes he can sell 100,000 units of his product at $5 per unit. Can he charge more without negatively effecting demand? If he does charge more, will he still make more profit even though demand may decline somewhat? These are questions typically raised in price theory courses in economics and require an analysis that is beyond the scope of this book. Many readers will already have addressed these issues in other reading they have done or in courses they have taken. For those who would like to learn more, see any basic managerial economics text.

Second, can costs be reduced? Assuming selling 100,000 units of output at $5 per unit is optimal, are there ways to reduce labor costs? How about materials costs? If we assume we are paying fair market wages and fair market prices for our materials, we may not be able to reduce wage rates or unit costs for materials, but we may find ways to use less labor and less materials for each final unit of output we make. Waste and poor quality are often culprits in causing cost inefficiency, and we should look for ways to reduce waste and improve our quality control standards. Chapter 8 in this book is specifically devoted to introducing methods to accomplish this objective, and the reader is advised to study this material carefully.

Third, can we reduce our tax expenses? It is often said that a good tax accountant is worth more than a production efficiency expert. It is sad but true that controlling the tax costs may be even more important than operating more efficiently. This is because a dollar of taxes saved is a full dollar whereas a dollar of costs saved must be shared (at up to 39% — see Table 4.2) with the tax collector! Although the tax code is arbitrary and capricious, the entrepreneur must be aware of its features and must learn how to deal with it. Most of us cringe at the thought of spending many hours (and dollars) just to beat the tax collector (since the result is to waste resources that could be usefully employed elsewhere) but we have no choice. As long as our government is run by lawyers and tax accountants, which it very definitely is, no business person can afford to ignore creative ways to reduce taxes.

Fourth, can we make our investment more efficient? One of the assumption changes that caused the net value of Mr. Smith's business to become negative was that of purchasing rather than leasing the firm's plant and equipment. This decision caused Mr. Smith to have to invest an additional $300,000 in the business. Although he earned a positive return on this investment, it was insufficient to cover his risk opportunity cost.

Fifth, can we finance our investment more cheaply? Are there ways for us to reduce (perhaps to zero) the amount of capital the entrepreneur has to invest? Have we obtained the best terms from venture capitalists? Can we secure debt (perhaps from a bank or other source) on better terms than from a venture capitalist? Mr. Smith has been able to get his suppliers to provide him financing for his inventory at no specific cost. This is not unusual, incidentally, if the suppliers really want your business. Mechanically speaking, they really do not finance your inventory, they simply provide extended terms for payment (often at no charge).

At this juncture, Smith might reconsider his decision to purchase rather than lease his plant and equipment. Returning to the calculations for his original decision, we find that, coincidentally, his first year lease cost of $100,000 was equal to the first year depreciation charge. Thus, Smith International's pre-tax income based on ownership of plant and equipment would remain at $100,000 if he leased. After-tax profit would remain at $77,750. Nevertheless, Smith only has to invest $100,000 now. Invoking equation (4.1), we find:

$$W = (1/.25)(77,750) - \$100,000 = \$211,000$$

Thus, even after paying U.S. federal corporate income taxes, Smith can still have a business with a net value of $211,000.

4.8 Conclusions

The models presented in this chapter provide the optimal production, investment, and financing decisions for the entrepreneur. When real world issues such as taxation are added to the models, we can get a fairly clear picture of the determinants that can be influenced (manipulated) to get greater production and productivity at the entrepreneurial level. The models presented provide only a glimpse into some of the areas that are explored in greater depth in the chapters to follow. Debt financing is also ignored in our entrepreneurial model, and this subject will be dealt with in more detail in Chapters 5-7.

Although the debt /equity tradeoff and optimal debt to equity ratios are featured in corporation finance theory, debt financing is not really a major option for the entrepreneur. To the extent that the entrepreneur borrows money, he/she must personally guarantee payment. As such, this is really a formed of disguised equity capital. Similarly, although the venture capitalist's investment may take the form of debt (say, for tax reasons), it also remains essentially a form of equity capital. Finally, the model does not formally deal with entrepreneurial whim and fancy. Variables designed to take into account the non-economic but nevertheless important entrepreneurial characteristics discussed above will have to be incorporated into any complete production model of the entrepreneurial firm. Alas, this subject is beyond the scope of this book.

References

[1] Amit, R., Glosten, L.R., and Muller, E., "Does Venture Capital Foster the Most Promising Entrepreneurial Firms?" *California Management Review*, Spring 1990, pp. 102- 111.

[2] Baumol, W.J. "Entrepreneurship in Economic Theory," *American Economic Review*, May 1968, pp. 64-71.

[3] Berle, A.A. and Means, G.C., *The Modern Corporation and Private Property*, New York: Macmillan, 1932.

[4] Boyatzis, R.E., *A Two-Factor Theory of Affiliation Motivation*, Cambridge: Harvard Univ. Dissertation., 1972.

[5] Cole, A.H., "The Entrepreneur: Introductory Remarks," *American Economic Review*, May 1968, pp. 60-63.

[6] Collins, O.F. and Moore, D.G. with Unwalla, D.B., *The Enterprising Man*, Lansing: M.S.U. Business Studies, 1964.

[7] CCH Tax Law Editors, *U.S. Master Tax Guide*, 79th edition, Chicago: CCH, Incorporated, 1996.

[8] Findlay, M.C. and Williams, E.E., *An Integrated Analysis for Managerial Finance*, Englewood Cliffs: Prentice Hall, 1970.

[9] Findlay, M.C. and Williams, E.E., "Capital Allocation and the Nature of Ownership Equities," *Financial Management*, Summer 1972, pp. 68-72.

[10] Findlay, M.C. and Williams, E.E., "Owners' Surplus, Market Equilibrium, and the Marginal Efficiency of Capital," *Journal of Business Finance and Accounting*, Spring 1979, pp. 17-36.

[11] Findlay, M.C. and Williams, E.E., "A Positivist Evaluation of the New Finance," *Financial Management*, Summer 1980, pp. 7-17.

[12] Findlay, M.C. and Williams, E.E., "Financial Theory and Political Reality under Fundamental Uncertainty," *Journal of Post Keynesian Economics*, Summer 1981, pp. 528- 544.

[13] Findlay, M.C. and Williams, E.E., "A Post Keynesian View of Modern Financial Economics: In Search of Alternative Paradigms, *Journal of Business Finance and Accounting*, Spring 1985, pp. 1-18.

[14] Findlay, M.C. and Williams, E.E., "Better Betas Didn't Help the Boat People," *Journal of Portfolio Management*, Fall 1986, pp. 4-9.

[15] Fried, J., "Financial Theory and the Theory of Investment," *Journal of Post Keynesian Economics*, Summer 1992, pp. 465-481.

[16] Giacalone, J.A., "Entrepreneurial Theory and American Business History: A Survey," *Review of Social Economy*, September 1968, pp. 156-167.

[17] Gordon, M.J., "Neoclassical and a Post Keynesian Theory of Investment," *Journal of Post Keynesian Economics*, Summer 1992, pp. 425-443.

[18] Hertz, D., "Risk Analysis in Capital Investment," *Harvard Business Review*, January-February 1964, pp. 95-106.

[19] Kirzner, I., *Competition and Entrepreneurship*, Chicago: Univ. of Chicago Press, 1973.

[20] Keynes, J.M., *The General Theory of Employment, Interest, and Money*, New York: Harcourt Brace Jovanovich, 1936. *Journal of Finance*, September 1983, pp. 911-922.

[21] Liebenstein, H., "Entrepreneurship and Development," *American Economic Review*, May 1968, pp. 72-83.

[22] Liles, P., *New Business Ventures and the Entrepreneur*, Homewood, Ill.: Richard D. Irwin, 1974.

[23] Magee, M., "How to Use Decision Trees in Capital Investment," *Harvard Business Review*, September-October 1964, pp. 79-96.

[24] Maslow, A.H., *Motivation and Personality*, New York: Harper & Row, 1954.

[25] McClelland, D.C., *Power: The Inner Experience*, New York: Irvington Publishers, 1975.

[26] McClelland, D.C., *The Achieving Society*, Revised Edition, New York: Irvington Publishers, 1976.

[27] McClelland, D.C., Atkinson, J.W., Clark, R.A., and Lowell, E.L., *The Achievement Motive*, Revised Edition, New York: Irvington Publishers, 1976.

[28] Ross, S.A., Westerfield, R.W., and Jaffe, J.F., *Corporate Finance*, Fourth Edition, Homewood: Richard D. Irwin, 1996.

[29] Schumpeter, J., *The Theory of Economic Development*, Cambridge: Harvard Univ. Press, 1934.

[30] Solow, R.M., "Technical Change and the Aggregate Production Function," *Review of Economics and Statistics*, August, 1957, pp. 312-320.

[31] Soltow, J.H., "The Entrepreneur in Economic History," *American Economic Review*, May 1968, pp. 84-92.

[32] Vickers, D., *The Theory of the Firm: Production, Capital, and Finance*, New York: McGraw-Hill, 1968.

[33] Williams, E.E., "Cost of Capital Functions and the Firm's Optimal Level of Gearing," *Journal of Business Finance*, Summer 1972, pp. 78-83.

[34] Williams, E.E., "Innovation, Entrepreneurship and Brain Functioning," in Vesper, K., *Frontiers of Entrepreneurship Research*, Wellesley. Mass.: Center for Entrepreneurial Studies, 1981.

[35] Williams, E.E., "Entrepreneurship, Innovation, and Economic Growth," *Technovation*, February 1983, pp. 3-15.

[36] Williams, E.E., "The Role of 'Whim and Fancy' in Economics: An Essay in Honour of Paul Davidson," in Arestis, P. *Employment, Economic Growth and the Tyranny of the Market*, Vol. Two, Cheltenham: Edward Elgar, 1996, pp. 19-36.

[37] Williams, E.E. and Findlay, M.C., "A Reconsideration of the Rationality Postulate: 'Right Hemisphere Thinking' in Economics," *The American Journal of Economics and Sociology*, January 1981, pp. 17-36.

[38] Williams, E.E. and Findlay, M.C.,"Is Common Stock Obsolete?" *Abacus*, June 1983, pp. 39-55.

[39] Williams, E.E. and Findlay, M.C., "Corporate Governance: A Problem of Hierarchies and Self Interest," *The American Journal of Economics and Sociology*, January 1984, pp. 19-36.

[40] Williams, E.E. and Findlay, M.C., "Risk and the Role of Failed Expectations in an Uncertain World," *Journal of Post Keynesian Economics*, Fall 1986, pp. 32-46.

[41] Williams, E.E. and Findlay, M.C., "Toward a Positive Theory of Corporate Financial Policy," *Abacus*, September 1987, pp. 107-121.

[42] Williams, E.E. and Manzo, S.E., *Business Planning for the Entrepreneur*, New York: Van Nostrand, 1983.

[43] Williams, E.E. and Siok, R.B., "The Marginal Productivity of Money Capital, Simultaneous Solutions, and the Optimal Structure

of the Firm," *Journal of Business Finance*, Winter 1972, pp. 53-57.

[44] Winter, D.G., *The Power Motive*, New York: The Free Press, 1973.

[45] Wiseman, T., *The Money Motive*, New York: Random House, 1974.

Problems

Problem 4.1 One might conclude from the example in the text that leasing is always a superior choice to ownership. That is not always the case. Suppose a bank would be willing to finance the equipment to Mr. Smith at an interest rate of 8%. How would that change the results?

Problem 4.2 Would your answer in problem 4.1 above depend upon whether or not Mr. Smith had to personally guarantee the bank debt?

Problem 4.3 Assume the following: p = \$10; Q = \$100,000; ρ = 50%; r_{vc} = 30%; E = \$10,000; k_{vc} = \$200,000; k_1K = \$100,000; k_2L = \$10,000. Determine $g(Q)$.

Problem 4.4 Interpret the meaning of each variable in problem 4.3.

Problem 4.5 Determine W for the assumptions in problem 4.3 if $\gamma_1 K$ = \$10,000 and $\gamma_2 L = .5\ pQ$.

Problem 4.6 Interpret the meaning of $\gamma_1 K$ and $\gamma_2 L$ in problem 4.5.

Problem 4.7 Interpret the meaning of W in problem 4.5.

Problem 4.8 Prepare a pre-tax statement of income and balance sheet for the facts given in problems 4.3-4.7 above.

Problem 4.9 The data described in problems 4.3-4.8 above are for a U.S. corporation owned by an entrepreneur named Brown. Using the corporate tax rates provided in Table 4.2, calculate the U.S. federal income tax due from this corporation.

Problem 4.10 Recalculate W for Mrs. Brown in problem 4.9 assuming her corporation must pay U.S. income taxes.

Problem 4.11 How do you account for the decline in W in problem 4.10 above?

Chapter 5

Preparing a Business Plan

5.1 Introduction

In the previous chapter, the broad outline of a theory of the entrepreneurial firm was presented. A concrete example was also developed to identify the key variables that go into entrepreneurial decision making. These variables are frequently made specific in a business plan, and the purpose of this chapter is to provide the entrepreneur with a step-by-step guide, setting the foundation for writing a business plan. Each of these initial steps must be taken before an actual plan can be prepared. In Chapter 6, we will build upon the steps set forth below in order to create an actual plan.

In this chapter, a continuous example will be portrayed. By illustrating the details of plan preparation with a single example, one will see how a plan should be done from start to finish. The company chosen is a service business that is relatively easy to understand operationally. Our reason for selecting this kind of enterprise is so that we may discuss the basics of preparing the business plan without getting lost in minor details that would be of interest to only one industry or kind business. Of course, detail knowledge of the specific characteristics of an enterprise is a necessary requirement for preparing a good plan, but there are too many types of businesses with unique features to illustrate even a few in a short, concise treatment such as the one we present here. Nevertheless, the example we have chosen perfectly reflects the economic nature of that business (a funeral home), and it should not be at all difficult for the entrepreneur to take the analysis and expand or change it where necessary for his or her own case. Needless to say, plans will vary depending upon the nature of the business involved, the age of the business, and the purposes for which the plan is being prepared. In the example employed in this book, it is assumed that the plan is for a new enterprise. The procedure for planning for an on-going enterprise would not be different, however.

Our example will be an entrepreneur by the name of Ben Jackson who is contemplating establishing a new business. He is 35 years old and has spent the past thirteen years as a funeral director in New York and New Jersey. Given his experience and a "burning desire" to be the proprietor of his own business, he has begun the preparation of a business plan to determine whether the new venture makes economic sense. He intends to prepare a complete plan to assist him and his future employees guide the enterprise from its initiation through its first year and then on to the next three years of operations. The complete plan will then be summarized in a financing plan which will be used to raise the funds required to get the business started and see it through its first four years.

In early 1997, Ben began contemplating opening a business in Wesson, New Jersey, which is located north of Philadelphia just east of the Pennsylvania state line. His choice of location was based partly on his personal desire to live in a smaller town and partly on his belief that a new funeral home could be successful in Wesson. In making the location decision, it occurred to Ben that he was already in the process of planning. In fact, the process had actually started from the point that he decided to establish a new funeral concern.

5.2 Step One: Statement of Enterprise Mission

There has to be a reason for a business to exist. For most businesses, there are probably a number of reasons that they exist. For many entrepreneurs, a business represents a means of self expression. It allows the entrepreneur a creative opportunity "to do your own thing." The business thus provides an important psychological raison d'etre. Interestingly, as we saw in the previous chapter, this motivation for owning and operating an enterprise may be more important than the more obvious one: to make money. Nevertheless, making a profit usually plays a role in the decision to be in business, and few entities can exist for long if they do not become profitable at some point. There are many other explanations for the existence of a business as well, and it is critically important for the entrepreneur to ask from the start just *why* he or she wants to be in business.

The desire to have a business for whatever reason is not sufficient in and of itself to explain the justification for an enterprise. There also has to be an economic "demand" before a firm can survive. That is, the business must supply products or services that people will buy in sufficient quantity to justify the cost of producing those goods or services. The entrepreneur who says, "I want to be in the hobby shop business in Podunkville because I want 'to do my own thing' and I like the climate in Podunkville," may not be in business long if nobody in town wants to buy model airplanes and other products in the hobby shop line. On the other hand, there are many businesses that come into being because there was a real need for specific goods or services, and some smart entrepreneur came along to establish a firm to provide them.

The first step in business planning is the delineation of the reasons a given firm should exist. These reasons should be spelled out in a short, one- or two-sentence narrative statement (called the *Enterprise Mission*) that reflects the motivations of both the entrepreneur who creates (or sustains) the entity and the market which will be served by it (and hence will pay money for its products or services).

To continue with our example, entrepreneur Ben Jackson has given serious thought to the mission of his proposed new business. He has determined that there are two principal reasons that he wants to be in business for himself. First, he wants to have the freedom to determine how he lives his life. Thus far, while working for other people, his lifestyle and even the timing of his rising in the morning and going to bed in the evening has been determined by someone else. He would like to decide these things for himself in the future. Second, Ben wants to be financially independent. His first personal goal is to reach a net worth of at least $250,000 before he is 40 years old (five years hence).

Based upon his experience, Ben has also considered what the public wants from a funeral service firm. He know that in time of personal bereavement the family needs assistance and services of a professional caliber, offered in dignified facilities and manner. He also knows that many people feel very vulnerable when dealing with funeral homes and funeral directors. They fear being "ripped off," yet few people would want to take care of many of the unpleasant tasks that are handled by the mortuary establishment. Thus, Ben has decided that he must build a reputation as an honorable and ethical businessman in order to gain the trust of his community.

> *Mission.* To provide the Wesson area community with the highest quality funeral home facilities and services, while permitting the proprietor of the business to achieve personal and financial independence and pride in a sensitive service well performed.

5.3 Step Two: Definition of Business

It might seem like a simple enough matter to define what a business does, but is it really so easy? Years ago, Santa Fe Industries (now Burlington Northern/Santa Fe) considered itself to be a railroad. Its name, the Atchison, Topeka, and Santa Fe Railway Company, signified that the firm carried people and freight by railway over given routes. Later, the AT&SF began to think of itself not as just a railroad but as a transportation company. The Santa Fe was in the business of transporting people and commodities. This broader definition encouraged the development of a range of transportation services to include trucking and pipelines. Santa Fe Industries became a diversified company active in four major business area: transportation, natural resources, forest products, and real estate and construction.

The business definition should be broad enough to stimulate thinking and not constrain creativity but narrow enough to provide direction. After the merger with Burlington Northern, several of the diverse activities of the Santa Fe were scaled back or sold, illustrating the point that the business definition can be too broad. As a further example, it might be useful for an "oil" company to consider itself as an energy concern. Most major "oil" companies in the United States now deem themselves to be suppliers of all forms of energy and are either providing or are exploring the potential of supplying oil, gas, coal, solar energy, and other power sources. As business has become more complex and competitive in recent years, older definitions of businesses have become broader. Banks, for example, have established holding companies and are becoming general financial service firms. Newspapers are really in the communications business, and stockbrokers are specialized financial service concerns. Interestingly, it is those industries where broader business definitions have been employed that have demonstrated the most growth and development. Less imaginative industries (steel, for example) that cling to the definitions more or less established around the turn of the twentieth century have show less growth and many have entered a stage of absolute decline.

Years ago, cabinet makers began making specialty boxes (called coffins then) for burying the dead. This was a side activity that merely complemented the cabinet maker's other carpentry products. After a time, some cabinet makers began to concentrate exclusively on making burial boxes, and by the mid-nineteenth century, individuals were setting up businesses to "undertake" to handle all the unpleasant details associated with the care and burial of the dead. These undertaking concerns found a demand for products and services in addition to burial boxes, and by the turn of the twentieth century funeral "parlors" were becoming common. They provided for the removal and transportation of the dead, cosmetology and embalming services, and a location to hold a funeral service. Modern funeral directors have come to realize that their principal role is not merely caring of the dead but tending to the needs of the family and friends of the dead person. Thus, services ranging from writing obituaries and helping the family with insurance and social security claims, to providing an on-the-premises psychologist who specializes in grief therapy, are becoming increasingly common. Our entrepreneur Ben Jackson is aware of the history and development of his industry and feels that anything less that a full-service funeral home would be unsuccessful. He is also aware of a countertrend toward very simple memorial services where the body is cremated and only a limited range of merchandise and services are demanded. In some communities (large cities, the West Coast, etc.), a limited service firm might be successful. He believes such a firm would not do well in the market he plans to enter.

> *Definition.* The Jackson Funeral Home will be a full-service mortuary providing services and merchandise re-

lated to the care and disposition of the dead and assistance to their families in area surrounding Wesson, New Jersey.

5.4 Step Three: Identification of the Business Opportunity

Once the entrepreneur has stated the mission of and defined his or her business, there must be confirmation that there is a need for the enterprise. Thus, in the case of a new entity, the entrepreneur should spell out why the proposed firm should be started, what unique niche it will fill, and why someone else has not already done the same thing. For an existing entity, the entrepreneur should detail why the firm was needed originally, what niche it has been filling, and what (if any) competition has arisen and why. The initial formulation of a market analysis (which will later be incorporated into the business plan as part of the marketing plan and strategy) should be made. The entrepreneur may perform this task or engage a market analysis firm to handle the project. In any event, certain key economic, geographic, demographic, and other data will be required in the preparation of the market analysis.

Ben Jackson has spent several months analyzing the market for funeral services in the greater Wesson area. He has prepared a "pin map" illustrating the residence locations of those dying in the city. The map identifies which of the existing funeral homes in Wesson handled each service for the past four years. He also hired a market research firm to do a demographic study of the market area in question. The report of Market Analysis, Inc., is shown in Figure 5.1. Ben has concluded that there is a definite need for a new funeral firm in Wesson to replace the old Second Avenue Mortuary (see discussion in Figure 5.1). He believes a minimum of 100 services could be secured (only a 3.3% share of the total market) with no marketing effort and that figure could double over the next decade if a consistent effort were made to appeal to families who presently employ the services of other funeral directors in the city.

Report of Market Analysis, Inc. to Mr. Ben Jackson

The city of Wesson is located in New Jersey north of Philadelphia and east of the Pennsylvania state line. The median income in the city has risen from $25,200 per year in 1991 to $30,200 per year in 1996. The recorded population estimates for the city are as follows:

Table 5.1a. Market Analysis.

Year	Population Estimates
1993	320,000
1994	318,000
1995	315,000
1996	310,000

The slight decline in population reflects a migration to the suburbs over the past 6 years. Most of the migration has been to the north and northwest, outside the Wesson city limits and is thus not reflected in the figures. Overall population of the county is approximately 425,000. The northwest area has been growing at a rate exceeding the losses from Wesson. Furthermore, whereas the median income within the city is lower than the national average, these newer suburbs are much more affluent.

Our survey indicates, however, that the people who proportionately spend the most on funerals, nationally, are not the wealthiest. The distribution for sales of services by income level is skewed below the national income average. Of additional interest is our finding that the death rate within the city is higher than the national average: 10 deaths per thousand in 1993, down to 9.8 deaths per thousand in 1996. These figures reflect the same trend, however, as national statistics toward a lower death rate per thousand over the last few years.

Table 5.1b. Wesson Mortality Statistics.

Year	Deaths
1993	3,200
1994	3,120
1995	3,092
1996	3,038

There are no funeral sales figures available for the northern areas as yet, but only 2 funeral homes are operating there at the moment.

Conclusions drawn are that the migrating and new population influxes to the north and northwest are middle class, more affluent families. In contrast, it would seem from the higher than average death rates, that the city of Wesson has an older, more established population with slightly lower income base. Wesson currently has a predominantly Christian population with 65% of these persons being Protestant and 35% Catholic. Approximately, 30% of the city is African-American.

Although the central downtown area has deteriorated in recent years, and is predominantly African-American, real estate values in the past six months have risen. There are isolated instances of old Victorian houses being rehabilitated within the city because they have been available at bargain prices. There appears to be little concern by these returning families about the condition of the homes or the minority dominance in the neighborhoods.

The funeral home businesses in Wesson are all locally owned and operated. Two have been in business nearly 50 years; and one (The Wesson Mortuary) is clearly the superior location in the city, as supported by both the sales figures among the competitors and by several interviews we conducted with local civic leaders.

These are currently 12 funeral homes operating in Wesson, down from 13 last year. Three of these funeral homes serve the African-American community primarily. As mentioned, not included in the total are two additional funeral homes opened in the northern area within the past year.

An analysis of the pin map supplied to us by Mr. B. Jackson suggests the possible need for a new funeral location to replace the mortuary that closed last year. That firm was located on Second Avenue, downtown, and served an increasingly elderly market. The business did not fail, but was closed by the widow of the former owner. It is our understanding that the property and physical location can be purchased. In past years, the Second Avenue Mortuary handled about 100 services per year with no marketing effort. Surveys indicate that families selected Second Avenue principally because of its convenient location.

Figure 5.1. A Market Research Report.

5.5 Step Four: Specification of External Variables

The next step in laying the foundation for writing the formal business plan is to specify those factors outside the control of the business that will affect its success. Current data about these variables should be collected and analyzed.

Where do you get information about external (exogenous) variables? Probably the most widely discussed external variable is the Gross Domestic Product. Nevertheless, most businesses are not big enough to be directly influenced by GDP (see discussion in Chapter 2). General Motors may worry when GDP is down 5%, but there are many other economic, demographic, and social statistics that may be more important to the average business. Many of these data are available in numerous government publications which are reasonably priced. Most of these publications are available in U.S. Government Book Stores that are located throughout the country. These stores have practically everything the government prints.

A very important source in the *Statistical Abstract.* This is an excellent compilation of data in simplified, abstract form; and it also contains references which indicate the source of original information. The *Statistical Abstract* is published annually and costs about $40 in paperback. It has a wide variety of factual and useful statistical information.

Every five years a *Census of Business* is taken covering sales, employees, payroll, etc., of almost every category of business. Censuses are available for many years past and thus can provide information regarding long-run trends for various types of businesses. Similarly, the use of data from the demographic census taken each decade may be useful. For many businesses, demographic factors (such as population, age groupings, income levels, etc.) are important and this type of information can be obtained for small areas called "census tracts." Also, the local Chamber of Commerce is frequently an excellent source of economic, statistical, and other information, and many of the larger banks have substantial data files as well.

Another recommended source is the *U.S. Industrial Outlook*, an annual publication of the Department of Commerce which examines practically every industry in the U.S. and makes economic projections. *The Economic Report of the President* is required reading for those who need such economic data as GDP, consumer price indexes, interest rates, etc. The Small Business Administration is yet another source of information. They supply free or at nominal cost) booklets on everything from how to establish an accounting system for your firm to how to price your product. Some of these publications are limited in scope and detail, but they are worth having. The Internal Revenue Service and the various state comptroller's offices also can be sources of information. They publish tax guide materials and provide tax assistance to businesses.

The *Wall Street Journal* is an outstanding source of current information on national and international problems and trends affecting business. Other excellent publications are *Business Week*, *Forbes*, and *Fortune*. *The Economist* is an important international publication, and it is worth reading for the perspective it provides on international issues as well as on events in the United States. Years ago what happened in certain distant countries like Iraq did not make too much difference to us, but they do now. There are all kinds of international dislocations and problems than can affect your business.

Obviously a businessperson cannot absorb all the information and knowledge available in these multiple sources. However, the well informed entrepreneur must learn what to read and how to read it quickly to get information that may have an impact on his business. This is integral to planning and to managing an enterprise. Many of the dreams, ideas, and thoughts for new businesses probably incubated from something read by an entrepreneur.

In analyzing the Jackson Funeral Home opportunity, Ben Jackson considered the major external variables that might affect his business. The report of Market Analysis, Inc. suggested that certain economic, demographic, social, and competitive variables might be significant. Among these were: (1) the median income levels of families residing in Wesson, (2) total population and population movements in Wesson, (3) the mortality rate and absolute number of deaths in Wesson, (4) the religious and ethnic mix of the population, and (5) the number and location of other funeral homes in Wesson. The report provided specific data about these variables for the four previous years. The next step in preparing the business plan will be to project values for the major variables for the forthcoming years.

There is an additional major category of variables that must be considered at least qualitatively; that is, the activities and policies of various governmental regulatory entities. The funeral home business is specifically regulated by the states, and most states license funeral directors and embalmers before they can practice. Ben Jackson is licensed in New Jersey and anticipates no difficulties in complying with any state regulations that might be imposed. The federal government is also interested in the business practices of funeral homes. The Federal Trade Commission has investigated the industry and found that some funeral homes engage in "unfair and deceptive" practices. Ben has read in the numerous trade magazines that he receives that the FTC has issued a Rule that allows the federal government to determine how he could establish his prices, what kind of caskets he would have to offer to his customers, whether or not he could embalm and under what circumstances, and a host of other red-tape-type regulations that have come to characterize much of the federal regulatory apparatus over the past several decades. Ben is convinced that such federal intrusion is generally unnecessary and unwarranted since state regulation exists to determine when a licensee has been unscrupulous and to discipline him accordingly. Ben also believes that many Americans are fed up with the intrusion of the federal government in their lives. He agrees with a spokesman from a major funeral home trade association who has said, "The FTC Rule should have no perceptible impact on the operation of legitimate American funeral homes." Thus, Ben is making no provision in his business plan for the regulation of his business by the federal government. Should political conditions change and should it appear that the recent conservative trend evidenced in the United States may be arrested, Ben has decided that he may have to adjust his plan. He foresees no major difficulties with complying with any reasonable regulations, although he would expect to pass along to the customer any cost increases that might be associated with complying with federal regulations.

5.6 Step Five: Making Critical Assumptions

Once the significant external variables have been determined and the pertinent sources of information have been located, it is necessary to make specific assumptions about each variable and project values for each period in the planning horizon. Ordinarily, this is the most difficult part of planning. Nevertheless, the major factors must be identified, and using whatever data that can be reasonably collected (plus the good judgment of the entrepreneur), an assumption should be made about each one.

To whatever extent possible, the entrepreneur should employ projections that have already been made by experts in the field in question, although these might be tempered with his or her own view of the situation. For example, if macroeconomic statistics are important external data to a given industry, the forecasts of various economists might be used as a starting point for projections. Forecasts of GDP, consumer prices, interest rates, and other such economic data are made by many economists and appear regularly in business publications. It is, of course, true that economists are frequently wrong and they often disagree violently among themselves about what is going to happen in the future (and what is happening now, for that matter), but their professional views are probably sounder than the seat-of-the-pants prognostication of the entrepreneur who has never read an economics text. Nevertheless, judgment should play the deciding role, and the entrepreneur has to feel convinced that the position of the experts fits his or her own situation and is pertinent.

Forecasts are provided by many governmental agencies for all sorts of data. The *U.S. Industrial Outlook* has previously been referred to as a useful source. In addition, the U.S. Department of Labor also provides helpful projections on data such as labor force and price trends. For the smaller concern operating in a limited area, however, forecasts on a national basis may be of little value and local economic factors should be assessed. Fortunately, most of the banks and the Chambers of Commerce in the larger cities maintain data files and projections on important economic, demographic, and competitive conditions in their communities. The entrepreneur should consult these sources in preparing projections.

Finally, the entrepreneur does not have to reinvent the wheel when preparing a business plan. There are a number of consultants and professional data analysis firms that specialize in gathering information and making projections about essential statistical series. The entrepreneur might find that spending two or three thousand dollars to get an outsider to help him analyze the exogenous variables affecting his business is an excellent investment. It might cost far more in time if one tried to do the same thing, assuming one had the expertise in the first place. Also, do not overlook the possibility of hiring a professor from a nearby university economics department or business school as a consultant. While the days when these professionals would work for practically the minimum wage are behind us, most of them have their overhead (offices, secretaries, etc.) already covered and can provide exceptional services for reasonable fees. For those entrepreneurs who are statistically inclined and sufficiently ambitions, Chapter 8 in this book provides a practicum in forecasting.

Ben Jackson has decided that a four-year time horizon will be the appropriate planning period for his new business. With this in mind, he has reviewed the pertinent data series gathered for him by Market Analysis, Inc. The most important information relates to the expected demand for his services, and population and mortality statistics are those most germane to project such demand. He has summarized these data as shown in Table 5.2.

Table 5.2. General Demographic Data.

Year	Population	Number of Mortalities	Mortality Rate (per thousand)
1993	320,000	3,200	10.0
1994	318,000	3,120	9.8
1995	315,000	3,092	9.8
1996	310,000	3,038	9.8

Ben also knows, however, that funeral services are provided along ethnic and racial lines. Although no ethical (or profit-oriented) funeral home would discriminate against a family on racial or religious grounds, it is usually the case that White Protestants use one funeral home, Black Protestants another, White Catholics still another, and Jewish people still another. In very large cities, such as New York, the specialization may get even more pronounced with one funeral home catering to Orthodox Jews while another handles primarily Conservative and Reformed congregations. Ben is a White Presbyterian and believes that most of his business will come from White Protestants although he may get some business from White Catholics. He expects his African-American and Jewish clientele to be nominal. Given this added information, Ben has asked Market

Analysis, Inc., to investigate the demographic characteristics in the seven census tracts falling within a three-mile radius of the proposed location of the Jackson Funeral Home on Second Avenue. The material in Table 5.3 was subsequently supplied.

These data suggest that the overall population in the determined market area has declined slightly over the past four years (by 3.5%), but the percentage of Protestant and Catholic Whites has risen (from 84.4% to 84.9%). Thus, the population of the determined market has declined by a smaller percentage (3.0%) than the population as a whole.

Table 5.3. Specific Demographic Data.

Year	Population	Protestant Whites	Catholic Whites	Other
1993	31,500	20,200	6,400	4,900
1994	31,300	20,100	6,300	4,900
1995	30,498	19,603	6,212	4,683
1996	30,400	19,600	6,200	4,600

Next, Ben asked Market Analysis, Inc., to analyze the age structure of the population in the seven census tracts. Since the death rate among the elderly is far higher than for younger people, he deemed such data to be highly significant. It was determined that over half of the population in the area in question was over age fifty and that 20% were above age sixty-five. This is much higher than the aggregate U.S. statistic and somewhat higher than the aggregate Wesson figure. Interestingly, it turned out that although only about 10% of Wesson's population lived in the seven census tracts in question, 15% of the population over age sixty-five lived there, and 21% of White Protestants and Catholics over age sixty-five were residents of the area.

The final step in the demographic analysis was to examine the mortality statistics for the seven census tracts. It was not possible to break these data down along racial and religious lines, but it was possible to determine the number of services handled by the old Second Avenue Mortuary and compare this figure with the total number of mortalities (see Tables 5.4 and 5.5).

Table 5.4. General Mortality Data.			
Year	Population	Number of Mortalities	Mortality Rate (per thousand)
1993	31,500	397	12.6
1995	31,300	388	12.4
1995	30,498	369	12.1
1996	30,400	374	12.3

Table 5.5. Specific Mortality Data. and Market Share			
Year	Number of Mortalities	Services Handled by Second Avenue	Percentage
1993	397	126	31.7
1994	388	110	28.4
1995	369	98	26.6
1996	374	no longer in business	—

Given these data, Market Analysis, Inc. has projected the potential total market and the possible share that Jackson might hope to attain over the next four years. It was assumed that the small population decline would continue and that the mortality rate would stabilize at around 12.2 per thousand. These data are shown in Table 5.6.

Table 5.6. Relevant Market for 1997-2001.					
Year	Population	Mortality Rate (per thousand)	Mortalities	Percentage Handled by Jackson	Case Volume Expected by Jackson
1997	30,350	12.2	370	—	—
1998	30,300	12.2	370	25.0	93
1999	30,200	12.2	368	27.0	99
2000	30,100	12.2	367	30.0	110
2001	30,000	12.2	366	35.0	128

*Year in progress.

Ben considered the other major external variables that might be significant to his business and determined that income levels and the consumer price index (CPI) might influence what families were willing to spend on funeral services. He also gathered data from the leading trade association in his business to find out what the trend in per service expenditures had been for the most recent four-year period that data were available. The figures in Table 5.7 were compiled.

Table 5.7. Pertinent Economic Data for 1993-1996.

Year	Median Family Income	Consumer Price Index (All Items)	Per Service Funeral Expenditures
1993	27,640	144.5	4,412
1994	29,966	148.2	4,544
1995	31,023	152.4	4,690
1996	32,384	156.2	4,821

Market Analysis, Inc., was consulted as to guidance in forecasting what the per service expenditures will be from 1997-2001. They informed Ben that there was a correlation between per service expenditure (PSE) and median family income (MFI). They carried out a least squares fit (how to do this is discussed in Chapter 8 but the software to do so is a part of almost every practical software package for data analysis), that is, they found a_0 and a_1 which minimize

$$\sum_{j=1993}^{1996} [PSE(j) - (a_0 + a_1 MFI(j))]^2 \tag{5.1}$$

and proudly presented Ben with the following as a means of forecasting PSE in the out years

$$PSE = 1948 + .0885 \times MFI \tag{5.2}$$

Ben asked whether it was not also possible to obtain a fit of PSE as a linear function of the Consumer Price Index. Market Analysis cheerfully obliged using a similar least squares analysis obtaining an alternative prediction equation

$$PSE = -634.63 + 34.93 \times CPI \tag{5.3}$$

But could not both MFI and CPI be used as prediction variables? Indeed they can. So Market Analysis used least squares to find a_0,a_1 and a_2 to minimize

$$\sum_{j=1993}^{1996} [PSE(j) - (a_0 + a_1 MFI(j) + a_2 CPI(j))]^2 \tag{5.4}$$

Their ultimate forecast model, then, was

$$PSE = -492.85 + .0050 \times MFI + 32.98 \times CPI \qquad (5.5)$$

Ben is no statistician, but he has fair amount of common sense, and he is not very comfortable over the fact that the three models seem to jump around a great deal. For example, the constant terms in the three models are 1948, -634.63, and -492.85. Furthermore, the coefficient of the MFI term in the first model is .0885, and in the third it is .005. He is not particularly comfortable in using any of the three models for forecasting purposes. Generally speaking, a model at variance with common sense should cause us to recheck whether the model might simply be, somehow, wrong. Let us examine a three dimensional scatterplot of the data in Table 5.7 in Figure 5.2.

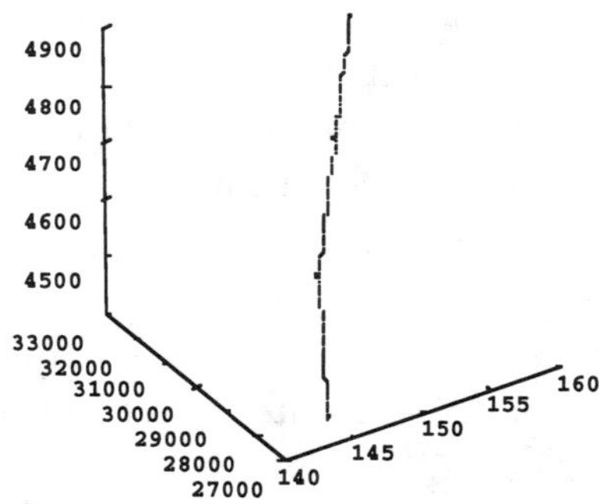

Figure 5.2 PSE vs, MFI and CPI, 1993-1996.

As we use line segments to connect data points in the scattergram, we note departures from the linear model, but these do not seem to be serious departures from the model. If we take a cloud of points which nearly lie on a straight line, we can attempt to rotate the axes until we see, very nearly, just a point. Using rotation techniques generally available in statistical software packages such as SYSTAT, SPSS and DATADESK, we note that the data can be brought to the representation in Figure 5.3. We observe that if the data truly lie on a line, then by rotations, we will be able to bring them to a single point. We have nearly achieved this in Figure 5.3. The linear model is fairly accurate.

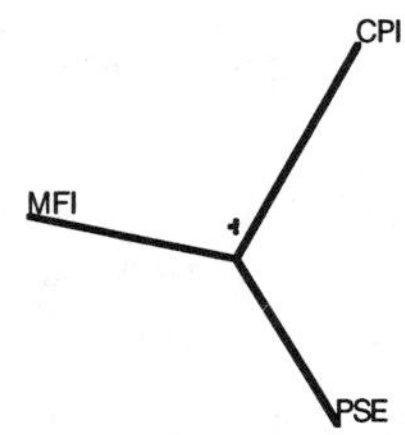

Figure 5.3. Rotated PSE vs. MFI and CPI, 1993-1996.

Let us consider graphing MFI and CPI. We do this in Figure 5.4. Obviously, there is a very strong relationship between MFI and CPI. This is part of the reason for things jumping around as we go from one graph to the next. The least squares fitting is at a loss whether to put weight on MFI or on CPI, since they are, in fact, close to be linearly transformed values of each other. Still, perhaps Ben has something to show for his fees paid to Market Analysis, Inc. He probably can forecast PSE rather well as a function of MFI and CPI.

One small problem remains, however. How is Ben to know the value of the mean family income or the consumer price index two years, say, in the future? An excellent question. Ben has not been totally successful in his selection of a consulting firm. They have committed a rather characteristic consultant's faux pas: they have provided a forecast assuming things known that cannot be assumed to be known. Ben is probably more likely to have a gut feeling as to the PSE in two years than he is to know what the CPI will be at that time.

Still, Ben recalls that there is strong indication of a relationship between the CPI and the PSE. The naive estimate for the CPI j years from now is

$$CPI(j) = CPI(0) \times (1 + r)^j \tag{5.6}$$

where r is the rate of inflation. Now taking logarithms of both sides, we have

$$\log[CPI(j)] = \log[CPI(0)] + j \log[1 + r] \tag{5.7}$$

in other words, a linear relationship between the logarithm of the CPI and the time variable j. Ben decides to plot the logarithm of the PSE versus time. We show this plot in Figure 5.5.

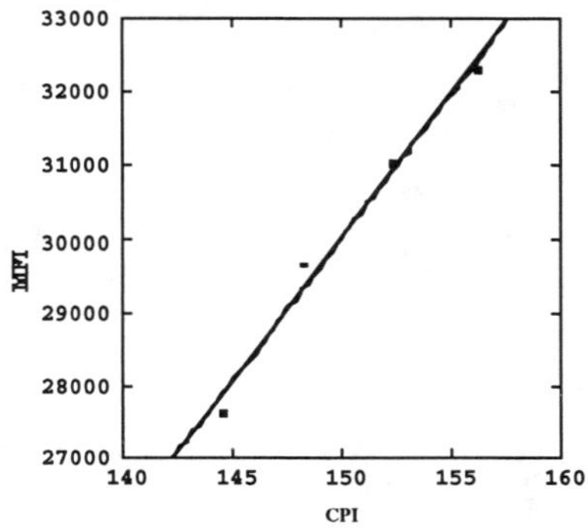

Figure 5.4. MFI **vs.** CPI**, 1993-1996.**

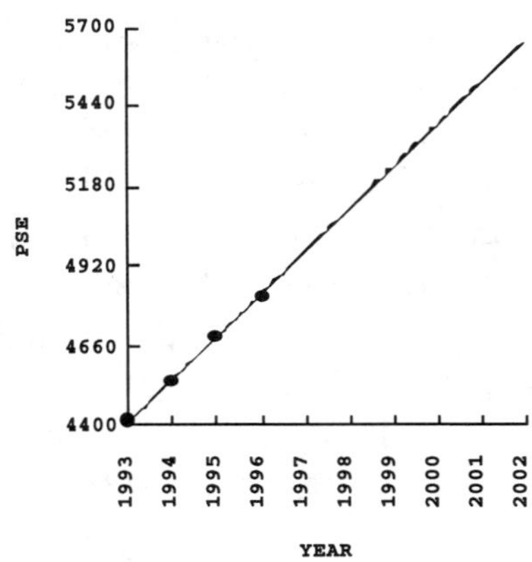

Figure 5.5. PSE **vs. Year, 1993-1996.**

Empirical extrapolation is generally most satisfactory when it can be done along a straight line. In this case, the straight line in Figure 5.5 corresponds very nearly to

$$\log[PSE(j - 1996)] = \log[4821] + 1.03 \times (j - 1996) \tag{5.8}$$

or, equivalently to

$$PSE(j - 1996) = 4821 \exp[1.03(j - 1996)] \tag{5.9}$$

This gives the per service expenditure forecasts for the next five years as follows

Year	PSE
1997	4,966
1998	5,115
1999	5,268
2000	5,426
2001	5,589

Once again, we note that if we have compound growth according to the law

$$P(t) = P(0)(1. + .03)^t \tag{5.10}$$

then taking logarithms of both sides of (5.10), we have

$$\log(P(t)) = \log(P(0)) + t \log(1.03) \tag{5.11}$$

We note that (5.12) is linear in t. Put another way, PSE is growing by a compounded rate of about 3% per year.

Let us review the forecasting strategy Ben finally used. First of all, we recall that he was working with a rather short time series—only four points in sequence. Next, we observe that he decided not to regress PSE on variables whose values were themselves as unknown as PSE itself. He saw, by plotting the logarithm of PSE versus time, that PSE was indeed growing exponentially. He used this information to extrapolate along a straight line in $\log PSE$ versus time to forecast the value of PSE for the next five years. How much confidence can Ben have in his forecast? That is not easy to say, due, in part, to the small number of data points involved. There is also the fact that economic time series are notorious in that the underlying model frequently is subjected to shocks which change, sometimes intermittently, sometimes persistently, the form of the mechanism generating the data. Ben is somewhat comforted by the fact that the logarithm of his PSE data plotted against time is very close to linear. And then there is the fact that there is some inelasticity in what people are willing to spend on a funeral. If Ben is careful, he will probably not be far off the mark to use his log linear model.

Ben's situation was fairly typical for a startup entrepreneur. First of all, he had a very limited amount of data. Secondly, his consultants served him ill with models which implicitly assumed information not likely to be available prospectively. Thirdly, he was able to cope with a fairly simple model. What is unusual about Ben is that he had enough modeling ability to survive his own consultants and come up with a reasonable solution himself. Unfortunately, in the real world, Ben would likely trust in the bad advice of his consultants. One of the purposes of this book is to demonstrate that generally there are ways to analyze skimpy data simply and with some confidence. It is easier to teach an entrepreneur to model for forecasting purposes than it is to teach most consultants the essential details of a business opportunity.

5.7 Step Six: Pinpointing Success Determinants

The next step in laying the foundation for writing the formal business plan is to pinpoint the important internal variables that affect successful performance. What are the major factors? For some firms, the growth rate of sales will be the most important element. These enterprises usually have some degree of control over the market in which they participate, and an aggressive advertising and sales promotion program may be the key to success. Other companies face a more competitive situation where they may be unable to secure a larger market share by adopting an aggressive selling strategy. These firms may even have their prices set by a market dominated by larger competitors or customers who may be able to dictate terms. The major success determinants for such entities may be those relating to cost control and efficiency.

Each particular business will have its unique mix of key internal variables. For manufacturing firms, turnovers, rejects, machine downtime, and capacity may be quite important. For service entities, labor costs, account collection, and overhead control may be significant. Retail concerns usually must be very aware of markups, inventory management, and promotional techniques. Businesses of all kinds with high fixed cost levels must be knowledgeable of their cost structure and the dollar and unit break-even points.

There are a number of variables which influence the riskiness of the total enterprise. The most significant of these variables is the predictability of a firm's revenues. If the entrepreneur knows with a high degree of confidence the level of sales for a number of years in advance, the planning process is facilitated. Furthermore, knowledge of future revenues allows the entrepreneur to arrange disbursements without fear of possible financial embarrassment. Although a firm's revenue pattern may be highly volatile over time, if the nature of the volatility is known with certainty, the planning process can reduce the impact of fluctuations. On the other hand, if revenues are volatile and unpredictable, no amount of planning can abate the consequences of volatility.

A volatile sales pattern implies a highly uncertain flow of cash into the firm. This is disadvantageous for two reasons: (1) a risky pattern of cash inflows may reduce the ability of the firm to meet its cash payment obligations, and (2) a risky pattern of cash inflows will generally result in an unstable pattern of net income. In the first instance, risky cash inflows increase the possibility of insolvency; in the second, they may reduce the value of the business.

Although the most important determinant of the riskiness of an enterprise is the predictability of its revenues, there are other variables which may magnify the impact of a volatile cash inflow pattern. One such variable is the degree of *operating leverage* characteristic of the firm. A firm possessing a high degree of operating leverage is characterized by high operating fixed costs. Operating fixed costs include such items as depreciation, overhead, permanent salaries, etc. The presence of high operating fixed costs may increase the possibility of insolvency, since fixed costs do not vary with output, and will increase the volatility of earnings. (Noncash charges, such as depreciation, may influence the volatility of earnings, but they will not increase the probability of the firm's running short of cash.)

Let us assume a business faced with the following set of sales possibilities:

	Sales
Maximum expectation	$150,000
Most likely expectation	100,000
Minimum expectation	50,000

Let us further assume that the business has a *variable cost ratio* (variable cost/sales) of 0.8 and operating fixed costs of $20,000. In the best of all possible worlds, where sales are $150,000, the firm's income statement would be as follows:

Sales		$150,000
Variable costs	$120,000	
Operating fixed costs	20,000	140,000
Earnings		$10,000

If sales are only $100,000, however, the business just breaks even:

Sales		$100,000
Variable costs	$80,000	
Operating fixed costs	20,000	100,000
Earnings		$ 0

In the worst of all possible worlds, where sales are $50,000:

Sales		$50,000
Variable costs	$40,000	
Operating fixed costs	20,000	60,000
Earnings		($ 10,000)

Thus, the presence of operating fixed costs in the third instance would result in a net loss for the firm.

Operating leverage is frequently examined in terms of *break-even analysis.* The break-even point is defined as that level of sales where revenues exactly equal expenses. Fixed costs play a crucial role in break-even analysis, since a firm with no fixed costs would have a break-even sales point of zero. The variable cost ratio is also significant, since a firm's contribution to fixed costs (and profit beyond the break-even point) depends on how much of an extra dollar of sales must go to meet variable costs. In the above example, the variable cost ratio is 0.8. Thus every additional sales dollar provides a $0.20 contribution to fixed costs and profit. In the case of a fixed cost level of $20,000, sales must be $100,000 to break even. Every dollar of sales less than $100,000 means a loss of $0.20. On the other hand, every dollar of sales over $100,000 means a profit of $0.20. These relationships are described in the following equation:

$$S_b = \frac{FC}{1 - \frac{VC}{S}} \tag{5.12}$$

where:

S_b is break-even sales
FC is the value of operating fixed costs
VC is the variable cost per unit of sales
S is the selling price per unit

It is unnecessary to know the break-even volume in terms of units for most purposes. In the variable cost ratio, the unit expression drops out. Thus, if the selling price is $10 per unit and the variable cost per unit is $8, the VC ratio 0.8. This ratio could also have been determined from an income statement by comparing total variable costs to total sales.

In order to explore the impact of operating leverage on the riskiness of the enterprise a bit further, let us consider another example. Assume that a firm has a high degree of operating leverage. Let $VC/S = 0.2$ and operating fixed costs equal $80,000. The break-even point for this entity would be

$$S_b = \frac{\$80,000}{1 - 0.2} = \$100,000 \tag{5.13}$$

Thus, the break-even point for this firm is that same as for the company in the previous example. The firms are distinctly different, however, in that the latter firm is far more leveraged operationally. Let us assume several possible sales levels with the ensuing income statements for the latter enterprise:

Sales	$120,000	$140,000	$160,000
VC	24,000	28,000	32,000
FC	80,000	80,000	80,000
Earnings	$16,000	$32,000	$48,000

Let us further assume that $140,000 is the expected sales figure but that there is a possibility that sales could be $120,000 or $160,000. If sales turned out to be $160,000, actual sales would have exceeded expected sales by $20,000, or $20,000/$140,000 = 14.3%. Earnings, however, would have been $16,000 larger, or $16,000/$32,000 = 50%! This percentage difference in earnings, given any change in sales, is the essence of operating leverage. Leverage may also work unfavorably. Had sales been 14.3% under the estimate ($120,000 instead of

\$140,000), earnings would have been cut in half! These examples illustrate the effects of operating leverage given differences in actual sales from expected sales. Similar examples could illustrate changes in earnings given changes in actual sales over time. Of course, if these sales changes were known with certainty, the earnings stream could also be predicted with certainty.

Returning to our initial example where VC/S=0.8 and operating fixed costs are \$20,000, let us assume a profit of \$32,000 as in the previous case. The projected income statement would be:

Sales	\$260,000
VC	208,000
FC	20,000
Earnings	\$32,000

Now, let us vary sales positively and negatively by 14.3% as in the previous example (14.3% × \$260,000 = \$37,200):

Sales	\$222,800	\$260,000	\$297,200
VC	178,240	208,000	237,760
FC	20,000	20,000	20,000
Earnings	\$24,560	\$32,000	\$39,440

The change in earnings, given a sales change of 14.3%, is \$7,440, or \$7,440/\$32,000= 23.3%. Thus, the leverage factor is roughly half of that in the previous case.

Ben Jackson's basic knowledge of funeral home operations has enabled him to determine the important internal economic variables that will spell success or failure for his new venture. Despite the fact that a funeral home is essentially a service business and most service businesses require only a small investment and hence have a low level of fixed costs (and hence a low break-even point), the large investment required to operate a funeral establishment means that it will typically have a low variable cost-to-sales ratio and a high level of fixed costs. Most funeral homes also have substantial excess capacity which must be maintained to meet peak-load periods of demand. Salaries, which for all intents and purposes are a fixed cost for a funeral home, are usually the most significant expense item. Ben has acquired data from his trade association which indicate that about 40% of the revenues of American funeral homes are spent on wages and salaries. Facility expenses (rent, taxes, depreciation, interest, utilities, maintenance, etc.) account for another 15%, while vehicles (lease costs, depreciation, interest, maintenance, gasoline, etc.) require about 12%. The most important variable cost item is casket merchandise, and this expense accounts for about 18% of the funeral revenue dollar. Thus, a typical common-size (percentage of sales) income statement for a funeral home would appear as follows:

Revenues		100%
Variable costs		
Merchandise	18%	
Fixed costs		
Salaries	40%	
Facilities	15%	
Vehicles	12%	
Total costs		85%
Profit before income tax		15%

The variable cost ratio for the typical establishment would then be:

$$VC/S = 18/100 = 0.18 \qquad (5.14)$$

and the break-even point would depend on the overall level of fixed costs.

Of course, fixed costs are only fixed in the short-run and for a range of volume. For example, it might be possible to handle between 0 and 200 services with a location of a given size, with a given number of employees and with a given number of vehicles. In the volume range from 200 to 500 services, a larger location, more people, and additional vehicles might be required. All businesses are similar in this respect in that fixed costs *may vary* as the size of the operation increases. Thus it is important to determine the *relevant range* of business volume anticipated in preparing any plan. Obviously, because of the high fixed cost nature of the funeral business, volume becomes a key success variable in determining profitability. Large locations may spread fixed costs over more cases and thus get increasing income per dollar of revenue and invested capital. Ben Jackson considers his proposed location to be "typical" since his volume expectations are in line with those of the nation as a whole. Trade statistics indicate that the "average" American funeral home handles approximately 140 services annually, and the common-size income statement previously outlined is for a firm doing about this volume of business.

Although the level of fixed costs for the typical funeral home is high, this does not necessarily imply that funeral homes have a high degree of operating leverage. Actually, the contrary is true. Cash flows in the industry are stable due to the nature of the business, and bankruptcy is very rare. According to Dun & Bradstreet, funeral homes have a consistent record of suffering the fewest failures of any business in the United States.

5.8 Step Seven: Outlining Major Strengths

The entrepreneur should next outline the major strengths of the venture idea which will provide the basis for success. What are the strengths? For some businesses, it will be the provision of a new product that has no competitive alternative. For others, it will be selling a product similar to others on the market for a lower price. For yet others, better service or a higher quality product will be the major strength of the endeavor.

The entrepreneur may be a key asset to the business. His or her knowledge, expertise, and overall "get-up-and-go" may be the most important success ingredient to the enterprise. In other cases, it may be the lack of expertise or entrepreneurship displayed by the competition that provides the principal strength of a venture. In a typical situation, the established firms tend to get conservative and fat and lazy, thereby opening up an opportunity for someone else who will go that extra mile to provide better service or a superior product.

Occasionally, the marketing strategy of the entrepreneur will be the principal strength. The entrepreneur (or those employed by the entrepreneur) may have prepared a superb advertising program or lined-up a larger network of distributors or carved out a unique niche in a highly specialized market. Location will sometimes play a role here. As in real estate acquisition, there used to be an old saying in marketing that there are three reasons for the success of a retail establishment: location, location, and location.

Other strengths may be found in the following: (1)the financial capacity of the enterprise, (2) the ability of the entity to grant credit terms to customers, (3) the lack of indebtedness or other fixed obligations of the business, (4) the cost effectiveness and efficiency of the plant and equipment, (5) the age of the plant and equipment, (6) the employees who work for the firm, (7) the lack of a union among the employees, (8) existing contracts or the promise of contracts from major customers, (9) the financial condition of the clients of the business, and (10) the general economic climate at the time the planning period begins.

Of course, each situation will be different and the strengths for one situation will not apply to another. Nevertheless, the entrepreneur should be quite careful in outlining existing and potential strengths. They will quite literally explain whether or not the business will succeed.

Ben Jackson has thought about the conceivable major strengths of his proposed new business. In order of importance, he has listed the following:

1. Location. The Jackson Funeral Home will be conveniently located on Second Avenue in a building that was formerly a reasonably successful funeral home.

2. Service. The Jackson Funeral Home will offer a full line of funeral merchandise (caskets, grave vaults, clothing, etc.) and will strive to offer the best service available in Wesson.

3. Price. The Jackson Funeral Home will price its merchandise and service to offer the best value in Wesson. The principal clientele of the firm will be elderly people with limited wealth. The families of these people should appreciate being able to get the best in quality for a reasonable price.

4. Building. The old Second Avenue Mortuary building will be completely remodeled to reflect an image of quality yet not opulence.

5. Employees. The Jackson Funeral Home will not be unionized. Employees will be personally selected by Ben Jackson from the most dependable people he has worked with throughout New Jersey and New York.

5.9 Step Eight: Outlining Major Weaknesses

The final step prior to the actual preparation of the planning documents is to outline the major weaknesses of the business that may cause it to fail. In many respects, outlining weaknesses is the reverse of outlining the strengths. Is the product or service not really very much differentiated from other products or services on the market? This may be a fatal weakness. Is the competition so severe that it may be difficult to carve out a unique niche in the market? This also may be a key weakness. Is it impossible to find just the right location? For a business that sells to the general public, this may be very significant.

For many new enterprises, the major weaknesses revolve around the lack of longevity of the firm. People simply do not know you are in business. This can be overcome in some instances by an aggressive marketing strategy, but it still takes time for the customer list to be developed. Building relationships with suppliers can also take time (and be costly) as older customers get preferred treatment at the expense of the new entrepreneur. Similarly, the employees of the new enterprise may not be as skilled or experienced, at least initially, and this may lead to production, delivery, or selling errors. Over time, these problems can be remedied, but the firm has to have the financial resources to stay in business in the meanwhile.

Financial factors are often among the major weaknesses of the new enterprise. The firm may be undercapitalized and the financial needs of the business may have been seriously understated by the optimistic entrepreneur who was positive the firm would cross the break-even point during the second month of operations. The firm may have been started with a lot of borrowed money, and simply paying interest on the debt may be a problem. It may be difficult for the new business to get credit, and even suppliers may put the new enterprise on a C.O.D. basis until it has been in business for a while. Once again, each situation will be unique and the major weaknesses of one may not be at all applicable to another. Complete candor in analyzing the possible weaknesses of the new venture idea may be the most important element in preparing the business plan.

Like most entrepreneurs, Ben Jackson does not like to think about the possibility that his new business will not be successful. Nevertheless, in being honest with himself and his financial backers, Ben has outlined the potential problem areas that he must face. Pinpointing these areas of weakness not only gives Ben a better idea about his chances for success, it also makes it possible for him to concentrate on curing any weaknesses that might exist. In order of importance, he has listed the following:

1. Nature of business. It typically takes a long time for a new funeral home to become established in the eyes of the community. Some businesses require months before they handle even a few services, and it may take years for a new location to become profitable.

2. Marketing strategy. It is difficult to market funerals. The nature of the service limits the effectiveness of the usual techniques such as a grand-opening sale or extensive advertising. Price cutting also does not work ordinarily, since people are not likely to buy a funeral simply because it has been marked down in price.

3. Competition. There are currently twelve funeral homes in Wesson. Although it appears that the market could support another one (particularly in the location that has been selected for the Jackson Funeral Home), competition would remain keen. Two competitors have been in business for over fifty years, and The Wesson Mortuary is clearly thought by almost everyone to be the prestige "carriage-trade" operation in the city. It is also the fastest growing business. Fortunately, it is located eight miles from the proposed site of the Jackson Funeral Home.

4. Market size. The population of Wesson has been decreasing in recent years and the death rate has been declining. As a result, the overall size of the market has been diminishing slightly.

5. Financing. Ben Jackson only has a limited amount of personal savings to invest in the business. Given what it will take to get the business started and sustained for the first year, additional funds will have to be borrowed or equity partners will have to be found.

5.10 Summary and Conclusions

The initial steps in setting the foundation for the complete business plan are critical to the plan's development. These steps provide the information and basis upon which the complete plan is built and help determine the degree of success the venture will have.

By way of a practical example, this chapter has demonstrated the thinking, actions, and analysis an entrepreneur should initially follow in developing a business plan. The critical steps include: (1) delineating the reasons and motivation for the entrepreneur to go into business (resulting in a statement of the mission of the business); (2) describing the history of the industry (leading to the definition of the business); (3) identifying the business opportunity (market analysis); (4) specifying the external variables affecting the enterprise; (5) making critical assumptions about the variables and projecting values for them over the planning period; (6) pinpointing success determinants and projecting values for the internal variables that will affect success; (7) outlining major strengths; and (8) outlining major weaknesses.

With these initial steps completed, we are now ready to proceed to the preparation of the complete plan.

References

[1] Collins, O., and Moore, G., *The Organization Makers,* New York: Appleton-Century-Crofts, 1970.

[2] Findlay, M. C., III, and Williams, E.E., *An Integrated Analysis for Managerial Finance*, Englewood Cliffs: Prentice-Hall, Inc., 1970.

[3] Hoad, W.M. and Rosko, P., *Management Factors Contributing to the Success and Failure of New Small Manufacturers*, Ann Arbor: Bureau of Business Research, University of Michigan, 1964.

[4] Liles, P.R., *New Business Ventures and the Entrepreneur*, Homewood, Illinois: Richard D. Irwin, Inc., First Edition, 1974.

[5] Mayer, K.B., and Goldstein, S., *The First Two Years: Problems of Small Firm Growth and Survival*, Washington, D.C.: Small Business Administration, U.S. Government Printing Office, 1961.

[6] McClelland, D., *The Achieving Society*, Princeton: Van Nostrand, 1961.

[7] McGuire, J.W., *Factors Affecting the Growth of Manufacturing Firms.* Seattle: School of Business, University of Washington, March, 1963.

[8] Schumpeter, J.A., *The Theory of Economic Development*, Cambridge, Massachusetts: Harvard University Press, 1934.

[9] Stevenson, H., Roberts, M.J., and Grosbeck, H.I., *New Business Ventures and the Entrepreneur*, McGraw Irwin, Fourth Edition, 1994.

[10] Williams, E.E. and Manzo, S.E., *Business Planning for the Entrepreneur*, New York: Van Nostrand, 1983.

[11] Williams, E.E. and Thompson, J.R., *The Economics of Production and Productivity: A Modeling Approach*, Austin: Capital Book Company, 1996.

[12] Woodruff, A.M. and Alexander, T.G., *Success and Failure in Small Manufacturing*, Pittsburgh: University of Pittsburgh Press, 1958.

[13] Woodworth, R.T., et al, *The Entrepreneurial Process and the Role of Accountants, Bankers and Lawyers*, Seattle: School of Business, University of Washington, 1969.

Chapter 6

The Structure of a Complete Plan

6.1 Introduction

Once the planning steps have been accomplished, it is possible to begin preparing the plan itself. It should be remembered that the planning process in general, and writing a business plan in particular, involve a number of iterative procedures that may have to be repeated a number of times before the final plan is ready. Thus, the document itself is the result of conceivably numerous trials and reworkings from the original planning draft. In this chapter, we shall work through an entire iteration of our continuous example (the Jackson Funeral Home) so that all phases of the mechanics of preparation may be illustrated.

We begin the analysis with the finished product and from this we work back to see how each part of the plan is done. The following is a recommended outline for a complete plan. This is the document that the entrepreneur will use in actually managing the enterprise. The starred sections of the outline would also appear in the summary (financing) plan that would be presented to bankers, venture capitalists, or other potential investors.

1. Executive Summary*
    A. A one-paragraph statement about the nature of the business.
    B. A one-paragraph rationale for the existence of the business.
    C. A brief statement about the financing required.
    D. Key characteristics of the industry.
    E. Structure and important features of the company.

II. Complete Analysis of the Industry*

III. Form and Organizational Structure of the Company*

IV. *Pro Forma* Financial Statements*
    A. Balance sheet at inception
    B. Income, cash flow, and balance sheet *pro forma* statements over the planning horizon.

V. The Strategic Plan
    A. Statement of the enterprise mission.
    B. Definition of the business.
    C. Specific enterprise goals.
    D. Enterprise strategies.
    E. Statement of planning premises.
    F. Strategic long-range plan objectives.
        1. Sales, cost, and profit projections.
        2. Major capital additions (plant, equipment, etc.)
        3. Cash flow and financing.
        4. Personnel requirements.

VI. The Operating Plan
    A. Marketing (sales) plan.
    B. Production plan.
    C. Various expense plans.
    D. Operating income plan.
    E. Cash flow and cash balance plans.
    F. Planned balance sheet.
    G. Planned operating and financial ratios.

VII. Appendices*
    A. Pertinent contracts.
    B. Technical information.
    C. Other supporting data.

Much of the information called for in the outline will have been developed in the preparation steps already taken (see Chapter 5). For example, the statement about the nature of the business would have been analyzed in Step Two: Definition of the Business; the rationale for the existence of the business should have been addressed in Step Three: Identification of Opportunity; etc.

6.2 The Executive Summary

The executive summary should spell out in its first paragraph what the business is all about, who is involved, where it will be located (if that is a relevant concern), and why there is a need for the business to exist. The second paragraph should provide a succinct statement about the nature of the business. The third paragraph should describe what financing is required and what will be done with the funds raised. The remaining paragraphs should outline key characteristics of the industry in which the venture will participate (or in which it currently participates) and the venture itself. Two or three paragraphs should be devoted to summarizing the detailed industry analysis which will appear later in the business plan. This summary requires the entrepreneur to focus attention on the salient external variable that will influence his business (see discussion in Chapter 5). Next, key features of the specific venture should be discussed. Two or three paragraphs should be prepared to provide focus on the particular business envisaged and how the entity will be financed. The executive summary for the Jackson Funeral Home is presented below.

Executive Summary for the Jackson Funeral Home

The Jackson Funeral Home is being founded by Mr. Ben Jackson to fill the need for an additional funeral service location in Wesson, New Jersey. Presently, Wesson has twelve funeral homes, but there is a demand for another location to serve the increasingly elderly community that lives in the downtown part of the city [see the Report of Market Analysis, Inc. in the Appendix to this plan].

Funeral concerns provide two basic services to society: (1) Care of the dead, and (2) assistance to survivors. The means of caring for the dead depends on the customs, laws, and physical environment of a given culture. In the United States, most families employ the services of a funeral director to take charge of the details of providing such care. American funeral practice has evolved over the years to minimize the inconvenience of the living. Thus, the typical funeral home will also seek to assist the family in whatever way it can.

The estimated required investment to begin operations is $400,000. Mr. Jackson will invest $50,000 of his personal funds in the business and $150,000 will be borrowed from a local bank. The balance of $200,000 is solicited from an outside investor or venture capitalist who will lend the company $150,000 and who will acquire one-half of the corporation stock for the remaining $50,000 in equity.

The most recent U.S. Department of Commerce census data indicate that there are approximately 25,000 funeral home locations in the United States. The majority of these are owned and operated by families who have been in the funeral business for generations. Despite its fragmentation, the funeral service industry is an important economic market. Consumer expenditures on funerals and burials are estimate to exceed $8 billion per year.

The most important determinant of the demand for funerals is the number of deaths which occur in a given market area. For many years, the aggregate mortality rate in the United States has been declining. As demographers look to the Twenty-First Century, it becomes increasingly obvious that the death rate will rise dramatically as the age distribution of the population shifts in favor of the elderly.

Most funeral businesses are characterized by the existence of high levels of fixed costs and substantial excess capacity. Because of the high fixed cost nature of the business, volume becomes an important consideration in determining funeral home profitability. As a firm becomes larger, and moves to the positive side of the break-even point, small increases in case volume can produce substantial percentage increases in profitability. It is possible to handle 100, 150, or even 200 services for about the same level of fixed costs. Thus, the 200-case-volume firm will be much more profitable than the one doing half that amount of business.

The proposed Jackson Funeral Home plans to take advantage of the demographic trends that will be apparent in Wesson, New Jersey over the next few years. The population of Wesson is becoming increasingly aged, and there will clearly be an increase in the demand for the services of funeral directors as a result. The firm will begin operations with Mr. Ben Jackson and several assistants.

Mr. Jackson is licensed in both New Jersey and New York, and he will have other licensed professionals join him in the endeavor. Additional employees will include clerical receptionists who have funeral home experience and can help with family counselling and other matters.

There now exists a funeral home location on Second Avenue in Wesson that was closed with the death of its owner last year. The building is owned by the widow of the former owner who was physically unable to maintain operations of the business. She has been contacted, however, and has agreed to lease the land and building to Jackson Funeral Home, Inc. with a purchase option.

Jackson Funeral Home, Inc. is a corporation chartered in the state of New Jersey. The firm plans to begin business on or about December 1, 1997. Approximately $400,000 will be required. Of this amount, $15,000 will be spent to purchase inventory (approximately 20 caskets @ $750 average cost); $75,000 will be spent on furniture and fixtures and $60,000 on leasehold improvements; another $150,000 will be required for the purchase of vehicles (a limousine, a hearse, and a lead car); and $100,000 will remain for working capital. The firm will be financed as follows:

Bank loan	$150,000
Subordinated debt	$150,000
Common stock	$100,000
	$400,000

Jackson Funeral Home, Inc. seeks to raise $200,000 from an outside investor or venture capitalist. It is proposed that $150,000 of this amount be in the form of a subordinated term credit payable over the next four years, interest only for the first two years, with an interest rate of 10%. The remaining $50,000 will be employed to purchase 50% of the common stock of the company. Mr. Ben Jackson will invest $50,000 of his personal funds to purchase the other 50% of the common stock.

Figure 6.1. An Executive Summary.

6.3 Complete Analysis of the Industry

The next section of the business plan should contain a detailed analysis of the industry in which the proposed venture will operate. The economic, social, demographic, and political characteristics of the industry should be explored in depth.

Data about the industry may be secured from the U.S. Department of Commerce. Almost every business has a standard industrial classification (SIC) code and census data are gathered every five years indicating total industry receipts, number of employees, industry structure, etc. Forecasts and projections are provided for many industries in the Department of Commerce's *U.S. Industrial Outlook* (available at most U.S. Government Bookstores). Industry data may also be secured from trade associations (which exist for practically every industry), from specific studies done by economists and others, and from large firms in the industry. The entrepreneur should do a thorough library research project on the industry which he intends to enter as one of his first steps in starting a new business. An analysis of the funeral home industry is presented below.

Industry Analysis: The Funeral Home Business

Funeral concerns provide two basic services to society: (1) care of the dead, and (2) assistance to survivors. The first of these prevails universally as a necessary function in all societies. The second has rather uniquely developed in North America.

The means of caring for the dead depends on the customs, laws, and physical environment of a given culture. In the United States, most families employ the services of a funeral director to take charge of the details of disposition. It is generally desired that the remains be transferred from the place of death as soon as possible, and funeral establishments are equipped to accomplish this task quickly and efficiently. The historic custom was to maintain the deceased in the family home during the grieving period (usually from one to several days), but the trend toward urban living with smaller houses and increased apartment dwelling has made this impractical. Today, the usual procedure is to have the dead removed to a funeral home where the body is embalmed, prepared, and placed in state for viewing. After one or more days, a funeral service is held (typically at a church or the funeral home) and the remains are made ready for ultimate disposition. Although all of these services (removal, embalming, preparation, funeral service, conveyance, and disposition) are not used by every family, virtually all deaths result in the utilization of at least some of the services offered by a funeral home.

In the process of caring for the dead, the average funeral home will offer a number of merchandise items including caskets, outside grave liners, vaults, and burial clothing. Some locations also maintain florist shops, and those funeral homes that perform a large number of cremation services may offer a selection of cremation urns. Historically, merchandise played a unique role in the development of the funeral industry, and many modern-day funeral homes have their roots in cabinet and carpentry shops which also manufactured coffins. Nevertheless, in terms of both importance and cost, the casket is currently only one of the many services/products offered by the funeral industry.

American funeral practice has evolved over the years to minimize the inconvenience of the living. Thus, in addition to providing the aforementioned products and services, the typical funeral director will also arrange for conveyance of the remains to distant localities, obtain death certificates, provide statistical reports to public health agencies, prepare newspaper notices, aid in the collection of government benefits, secure the services of other professionals (such as clergymen, policemen, organists) and assist in the notification of relatives.

The SIC code for funeral homes and crematoria is 726. The most recent U.S. Department of Commerce census data indicate there are about 25,000 funeral home locations in the United States. The majority of these are owned and operated by families who have been in the funeral business for generations, and although there are over 1,000 multiunit funeral concerns, only 5 of these are publicly held. The largest funeral concern owns just under 4% of the total number of locations and generates slightly more than 10% of aggregate industry revenues. Despite its fragmentation, the funeral service industry is an important economic market, with consumer expenditures on funerals and burials running annually in excess of $8 billion.

Market studies have discovered several significant variables which determine funeral receipts. The more significant ones include: (1) the mortalities in a given market area, (2) median family income in that area, (3) the proportion of inhabitants over age 65, and (4) the proportion of inhabitants of foreign extraction. The first of these is by far the most significant. In fact, demographic factors are of such significance as determinants that a detailed analysis of population trends, life expectancies, and mortality rates must be made in order to appraise the historical performance and future prospects of the industry.

The death rate per thousand population has declined steadily from about 14.7 persons in 1910 to an all-time low of 8.5 in 1992. Nevertheless, in the past the population increased substantially during most periods such that the absolute number of deaths grew from 697,000 in 1910 to 2,300,000 in 1996. During the 1970s and 1980s, however, a sharp drop in the birth rate slowed the growth of the population. The reduction in the rate of growth of the population, together with a continued drop in the death rate, produced and absolute decline in the number of deaths recorded for several years.

As demographers look to the Twenty-First Century, it becomes increasingly obvious that the death rate will increase dramatically as the age distribution of the population shifts in favor of the elderly. There are currently about 34 million Americans age 65 or older (14% of the population). By the year 2020, that figure should approach 53 million (16% of the population).

Although most Americans have a traditional funeral service at death, the preferred means of final disposition of the body varies by geography and the socioeconomic status of the family of the deceased. Ground interment of the remains is still the choice of most people, but garden crypt or mausoleum entombment is also becoming popular. Cremation prior to final disposition is increasingly favored in certain parts of the United States as well, and approximately 20% of all deaths in the United States now result in cremation. Nevertheless, it should be remembered that only a limited number of families elect to have a "direct cremation" without benefit of a funeral ceremony of some type, and the funeral/cemetery industry provides urns, cemetery garden space and solumbarium niches for the ashes of most of those who are cremated.

Most funeral businesses are characterized by the existence of high levels of fixed costs and substantial excess capacity which must be maintained to meet peak-load periods of demand. Salaries, which for all intents and purposes are a fixed cost for a funeral home, average about 40% of the revenues of

American funeral homes. Facilities account for another 15% and vehicles require about 12%. The most important variable cost is merchandise, and this expense item accounts for about 18% of the funeral revenue dollar.

Although the level of fixed costs for the typical funeral operation is high, this does not necessarily imply that funeral homes are subject to substantial business risk. Actually, the contrary is usually true. Cash flows in the industry are stable due to the nature of the business, and bankruptcy is very rare. Funeral homes have a consistent record of suffering the fewest failures of any business in the United States.

Figure 6.2 An Industry Analysis.

6.4 Form and Organizational Structure of the Company

The form and organizational structure of the business venture should be outlined in the next section of the plan. This section is useful to the entrepreneur in evaluating personnel requirements over the planning period, and it is of interest to those financing the business as well. The people in an organization frequently are the most important determinants of its success. For this reason, many bankers and venture capitalists will often provide financing more on the basis of their confidence in the people involved in the deal than on the outlook for the industry or the *pro formas.* Venture ideas are important but they must take specific form and be executed to be worthwhile. Because people play such an important role in the future success of a new (or existing) business, the section of the business plan devoted to organization is also a good place to provide resumes of the principals in the business. A well-written resume frequently will go a long way toward getting the attention of bankers and venture capitalists. Credibility is a key ingredient in getting the confidence of others and a solid resume enhances credibility.

Ben Jackson has determined that he and eight other employees will be able to handle the projected volume of the Jackson Funeral Home during 1998-2000. In the year 2001, another employee will be required to assist in accommodating the expected growth. Ben has prepared an organizaiton chart for the four years in his planning period and has included a resume in his business plan.

Organizational Structure of the Jackson Funeral Home

The Jackson Funeral Home was incorporated under the laws of the State of New Jersey on July 1, 1997. Its organizational structure is shown below:

Jackson Funeral Home
Organizational Chart 1997-2000

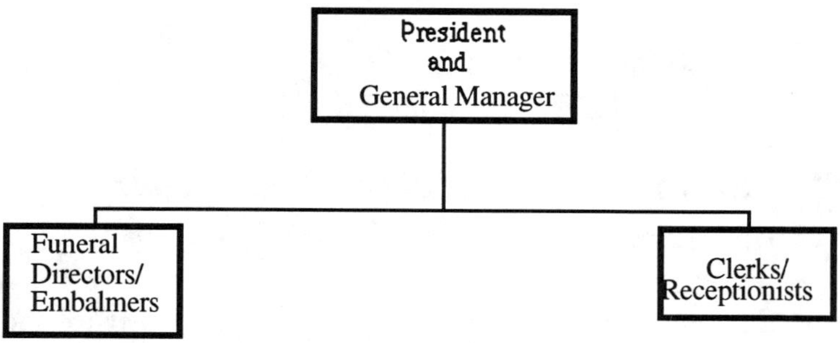

Jackson Funeral Home
Organizational Chart 2001

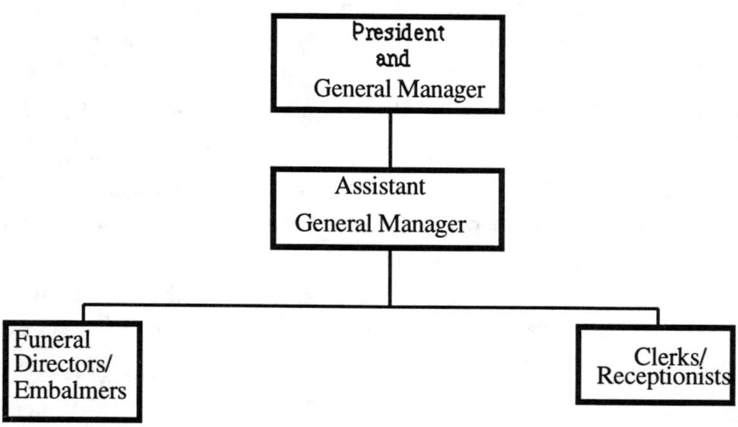

Figure 6.3 Organizational Form and Structure.

Resume

Benjamin R. Jackson, B.S.
Date of Birth: August 21, 1962
Marital Status: Married, one child
Nationality: USA

Present Position
Since 1993: Funeral Director, Shannon Mortuary, Newark, New Jersey
Address: 4875 Gardenia Place
Newark, New Jersey
Previous Positions
Funeral Director and Embalmer, Riverdale Mortuaries, various locations in New York and New Jersey.
Education
1980-1983 New York University, B.S. in Biology
1983-1984 American School of Mortuary Science
Memberships
New York Funeral Directors Association
New Jersey Funeral Directors Association
National Funeral Directors Association
Church Affiliation
St. James Presbyterian Church
References
Available on request.

Figure 6.4. A Resume.

6.5 Pro Forma Financial Statements

Pro Forma financial statements should follow next in the business plan. First, a *pro forma* balance sheet should be prepared to reflect the asset and liability position of the enterprise at the day operations commence (or at the beginning of the planning period if the business is already a going concern). The balance sheet should categorize the funds commitment that the firm contemplates (assets) and where the money will come from to finance the endeavor (liabilities).

A *pro forma* income statement, cash flow analysis, and balance sheet should also be prepared for each year of the planning period. Detailed projections of revenues, expense items, expected profits, debt service, cash flow, assets, and liabilities should be made. Footnotes to the statements should be provided to explain the assumptions behind each figure.

Pro forma data result from the planning process. Each number embodies an initial forecast figure which has subsequently been refined depending upon the objectives of the enterprise. The *pro forma* statements are thus based upon the strategic and operating plans that follow in the business plan (see below). It will probably be necessary for the entrepreneur to involve an accountant in preparing both the *pro forma* balance sheet and the *pro forma* statements of income and cash flow.

After preparing his strategic and operating plans, Mr. Ben Jackson and his accountant were able to construct the *pro forma* balance sheet shown below.

JACKSON FUNERAL HOME, INC.
PRO FORMA BALANCE SHEET
DECEMBER 1, 1997

A *Pro Forma* Balance Sheet			
	Assets	Liabilities	
Cash	$100,000	Note payable (1)	$ 150,000
Inventory	15,000	Subordinated debt (2)	150,000
Furniture, fixtures and equipment	75,000	Stockholders equity (3)	100,000
Leasehold improvements	60,000		
Vehicles	150,000		
	$400,000		$400,000

See accompanying notes.

Figure 6.5. A *Pro Forma* Balance Sheet.

It should be noted in Figure 6.5 that Ben believes bank financing will be available to finance much of his working capital and fixed asset requirements. A loan in the amount of $150,000 secured by $300,000 in inventory, furniture, fixtures, equipment, leasehold improvements and vehicles seems reasonable. (See discussion in Chapter 7 regarding short-term and long-term financing for guidance about realistic terms and structure for such financing.) Ben also believes he should be able to raise $200,000 in subordinated debt and equity financing from a venture capitalist. He is prepared to allow a fifty percent ownership in the business for such financing. (See discussion in Chapter 7 regarding realistic terms and structure for venture capital financing.)

Next, Ben and his accountant have prepared *pro forma* income and cash flow statements for 1998-2001 as indicated below.

JACKSON FUNERAL HOME, INC.
Pro Forma Income and Cash Flow
1998-2001

	1998	1999	2000	2001
Revenues(4)	$570,834	625,838	716,232	854,470
Cost of Services(5)				
Merchandise	102,750	112,651	128,922	154,525
Salaries	228,334	250,335	286,493	343,388
Facilities	85,625	93,876	107,435	128,771
Vehicles	68,500	75,101	85,948	103,016
Administration/ promotion	14,842	16,272	18,622	22,320
Total operating costs	500,051	548,235	627,419	752,020
Operating income	70,783	77,603	88,813	106,450
Interest expense (6)	30,000	30,000	30,000	22,500
Income before taxes	40,783	47,603	58,813	83,950
Income taxes (7)	12,235	14,281	17,644	25,185
Net income	28,548	33,322	41,169	58,765
Add Depreciation (8)	77,000	109,875	48,135	26,662
Deduct: Debt payment	0	0	75,000	75,000
Net cash flow	105,548	143,197	14,304	10,427
Cumulative NCF	105,548	248,745	263,049	273,476

Figure 6.6. ***Pro Forma*** **Income and Cash Flow Statements.**

Next, Ben and his accountant have prepared notes to the previously detailed *pro forma* financial statements. These notes outline the assumptions made in the projections and are indicated below.

JACKSON FUNERAL HOME, INC.
NOTES TO *PRO FORMA* FINANCIAL STATEMENTS

1. The $150,000 Note Payable will be to the Wesson National Bank and will bear interest at a rate of prime plus 2%. It is assumed that prime will be a 8% throughout the life of the Note. The Note will be secured by the inventory, furniture, fixtures, and equipment of the Jackson Funeral Home, Inc. Wesson National Bank has agreed to renew the Note on an annual basis over a four-year period and convert it to a revolving line of credit after two years, assuming the financial condition of Jackson

Funeral Home, Inc. is satisfactory.

2. The $150,000 Subordinated Note will bear interest at a fixed rate of 10%. The Note will require the payment of interest only for the first two years and will be repaid in two equal installments of $75,000 on Dec. 31, 2000 and Dec. 31, 2001.

3. The shareholders of Jackson Funeral Home, Inc. will be:

Outside investor	$50,000	(50%)
Mr. Ben Jackson	50,000	(50%)
	$100,000	(100%)

4. Revenues are projected as follows:

Year	Number of Services Handled	Average Revenue per Service	Total Service Revenue
1998	93	$5,115	$475,695
1999	99	5,268	521,532
2000	110	5,426	596,860
2001	128	5,589	715,392

The projection of the number of services handled was made by Market Analysis, Inc., a leading market research firm. Market Analysis also examined median family income levels, consumer price income data, and per service funeral expenditures for Wesson. They found income levels and prices to be somewhat above the national average. An extrapolation of average revenue per service was made using past experience. Other revenues (clothing, flower sales, grave liner sales, etc.) will equal 20% of adult service revenues.

5. Cost of services are calculated as a percentage of total revenue. Standard cost percentages for the industry, as determined by a principal trade association, are as follows:

Merchandise	18%
Salaries	40
Facilities	15
Vehicles	12
Total	85%

These standard cost percentages will be used. An administrative/promotion budget will be prepared each year according to perceived requirements. Generally, about 2.6 percent of revenues will be set aside for this purpose.

6. Interest on the \$150,000 bank loan will be (10%×\$150,000) = \$15,000 per year. Interest on the subordinated debt will be:

Year	Balance	Rate	Interest
1998	\$150,000	10%	\$15,000
1999	150,000	10	15,000
2000	150,000	10	15,000
2001	75,000	10	7,500

7. Federal and state income taxes are calculated to average 30% of pretax income.

8. The Internal Revenue Code provides for depreciation classes of 3, 5, 10 and 15 years for tangible property. The 3-year class consists of automobiles, light-duty trucks, and certain other equipment. The vehicles purchased by the Jackson Funeral Home, Inc. have been determined to fall into this class. The 5-year class consists of most other machinery and equipment. The furniture, fixtures, equipment, and leasehold improvements of the Jackson Funeral Home, Inc. have been determined to fall into this class. The depreciation allowance for 3-year and 5-year class property is given below:

Ownership Year	3-Year Class	5-Year Class
1	33.33%	20.00%
2	44.45	32.00
3	14.81	19.20
4	7.41	11.52
5	—	11.52
6	—	5.76

Thus, depreciation for the fixed assets of the Jackson Funeral Home, Inc., will be as follows:

Year	Furniture, etc.	Improve-ments	Vehicles	Total
1998	$15,000	$12,000	$50,000	$77,000
1999	24,000	19,200	66,675	109,875
2000	14,400	11,520	22,215	48,135
2001	8,640	6,912	11,110	26,662

Figure 6.7. ***Pro Forma*** **Footnotes.**

The *pro forma* statements appearing in Figure 6.6 and the assumptions in the footnotes in Figure 6.7 can be portrayed in simple equations which can be analyzed on a computer spread sheet. This simplifies the arithmetic of the process and makes it easy to change assumptions and see the impact such changes make on the results. The equations for the Jackson Funeral Home, Inc. *pro forma* income and cash flow statements include the number of services handled (Q) and the price charged per service (P). These are given in footnote number four. To this, another 20% is added (by assumption) so total revenue (R) is given by

$$R = (1.2)PQ \tag{6.1}$$

The cost of services items are assumed in footnote five and include the cost of merchandise (M), the cost of salaries (S), the cost of facilities (F), and the cost of vehicles (V). Administration and promotion costs (A) are also assumed in footnote five such that

$$M = (.18)R \tag{6.2}$$
$$S = (.40)R \tag{6.3}$$
$$F = (.15)R \tag{6.4}$$
$$V = (.12)R \tag{6.5}$$
$$A = (.026)R \tag{6.6}$$

The total operating costs are given by

$$C = M + S + F + V + A \tag{6.7}$$

And operating income (I) is given by

$$I = R - C \tag{6.8}$$

Interest expense (i) is assumed in footnote six. Thus, income before taxes (B) is given by

$$B = I - i \tag{6.9}$$

The tax rate is assumed to be 0.3 in footnote seven so income taxes (T) would be

$$T = (.3)B \tag{6.10}$$

and net income (Y) would be simply

$$Y = B - T \tag{6.11}$$

Depreciation (d) is assumed in footnote eight and the debt repayment schedule (D) is contemplated in footnote two. Thus, net cash flow (N) would be given by

$$N = Y + d - D \tag{6.12}$$

And cumulative net cash flow would be $\sum N$ over each year. These equations allow for a complete specification of all variables in the system. Of course, they could be simplified as follows

$$\begin{aligned} N &= [1 - .3][(1.2)PQ - (.876)(1.2)PQ - i] + d - D \qquad (6.13) \\ N &= (.1042)PQ - .7i + d - D \end{aligned}$$

where values for the variables P,Q, i, d, and D are given by assumption.

6.6 The Strategic Plan

Strategic planning is devoted to determining what products or services the venture is going to offer to which class of customers in which specified geographical areas. The strategic plan is an integral part of the complete business plan but it will rarely be included as part of the summary or financing plan. The strategic plan takes into account the broad goals of the organization and typically deals in horizons of several years. The strategic plan emanates from the steps previously outlined in preparing the business plan (see Chapter 5). It will contain a statement of the enterprise mission, a definition of the business, a listing of the goals of the enterprise, the strategies contemplated to achieve the delineated goals, a statement of the planning premises, and a listing of the specific objectives of the venture over the planning period. The strategic plan for the Jackson Funeral Home is provided below.

JACKSON FUNERAL MOME, INC.
STRATEGIC PLAN, 1998-2001

Statement of the Enterprise Mission: To provide the Wesson area community with the highest quality funeral home facilities and services while permitting the proprietor of the business to achieve personal and financial independence and pride in a sensitive service well performed.

Definition of the Business: The Jackson Funeral Home will be a full-service mortuary providing service and merchandise related to the care and disposition of the dead and assistance to their families in the area surrounding Wesson, New Jersey.

Enterprise Goals:

1. To provide the highest quality funeral home facilities and services.
2. To be recognized as an honorable and ethical firm.
3. To provide the proprietor of the business with personal and financial independence and pride in a sensitive service well performed.
4. To earn a fair rate of return for the investors in the business.

Enterprise Strategies

1. To provide a dignified and meaningful service to the people of Wesson.
2. To price our merchandise and services at a fair and competitive level.
3. To achieve optimum long-term profitable growth in order to establish a leadership position among Wesson's funeral homes.
4. To hire and train the most imaginative and competent people available, of high character, principles and sensitivity.
5. To develop and maintain an organization whose conduct at all levels and at all times justifies the trust of the community.
6. To recognize and reward our employees according to their abilities and contributions while maintaining a working environment which makes it unnecessary for our employees to seek outside representation.

Statement of Planning Premises:

1. We shall be able to lease the location of the old Second Avenue Mortuary and be operating by December 1, 1997.
2. We shall be able to hire eight qualified employees by December 1, 1997.
3. We shall have opening ceremonies and open house at the funeral home during early December, 1997.

4. We shall advertise our presence during December, 1997, and January, and February, 1998. A special budget will be prepared for this purpose.

5. The mortality rate in Wesson will stabilize in 1997, while the absolute number of mortalities will decrease slightly in each subsequent year.

6. We shall achieve a 25% share of the relevant market in 1998 and this will increase to 35% by 2001.

7. We expect to handle the following number of services:

1998	93
1999	99
2000	110
2001	128

8. Income levels will be rising in Wesson throughout the planning period.

9. Overall inflation will average 3% per year, and we shall be able to increase our average revenue per service by this percentage.

10. Average revenue per service is calculated to be:

1998	\$5,115
1999	5,268
2000	5,426
2001	5,589

11. We shall borrow \$150,000 from a bank and pay interest averaging 10% on the loan. The loan will be secured by certain assets of the business and will be convertible to a revolving credit.

12. We shall issue \$150,000 in subordinated notes at 10% interest. Such notes will be redeemed in two equal installments of \$75,000 on December 31, 2000 and December 31, 2001.

13. We shall issue \$100,000 in common stock.

14. Other revenues will equal 20% of adult funeral service revenues.

15. Standard cost percentages shall essentially follow the industry pattern:

Merchandise	18%
Salaries	40
Facilities	15
Vehicles	12
	85%

16. Equipment will be depreciated according to the maximum allowed by the Internal Revenue Code.
17. Income taxes will average 30% of pretax income.

Specific Objectives:

1. Over the planning period 1998-2001, we shall achieve or exceed a compounded annual rate of growth in revenues of 14%.
2. Over the planning period, we shall achieve or exceed a compounded annual rate of growth in operating income of 14%.
3. We shall achieve operating income margins of approximately 12%.
4. Our initial return on total assets (operating income/total assets) will exceed 18% in 1998 and will exceed 25% by 2001.
5. Our return on stockholder equity (net income/stockholder equity) will be approximately 28% annually over the planning period.
6. There will be no major capital additions during the planning period after the remodeling of the old Second Avenue location is completed in November 1997.
7. We shall reinvest in the business the major portions of our earnings and the rest shall be used to reduce indebtedness. No dividends will be paid during the planning period.
8. No additional financing will be sought during the planning period after the initial $400,000 is raised in 1997. Cash flows from operations shall be sufficient to finance the projected growth.
9. Our debt/equity ratio shall not exceed 3:1 during the planning period.
10. Our current ratio shall not be less than .75:1 during the planning period.

11. In 1997, prior to commencing operations, we shall hire four highly competent funeral directors/embalmers and four general-purpose clerks/receptionists. During 2001, another employee will be added and the position of assistant general manager will be created.

Figure 6.8. A Strategic Plan.

6.7 The Operating Plan

The operating plan is an important part of the business plan. It determines how to run the venture effectively in the months (year) immediately ahead while progress is made towards the objectives of the strategic plan. The operating plan consists of a marketing (sales) plan, production plan, various expense plans, an operating income plan, cash flow and cash balance plans, a planned balance sheet, a financial plan, and planned operating and financial ratios. Once the operating plan has been determined, various budgets may be prepared to define the anticipated revenue and expense streams. The budgets will become the quantitative statements against which actual performance in the months (year) ahead will be measured. The operating plan for the Jackson Funeral Home is provided below.

JACKSON FUNERAL HOME, Inc.
OPERATING PLAN, 1998

Marketing (Sales) Budget

93 services @ $5,115 average	$475,695
Other revenue items:	
Grave liner and vault sales (50 @ $1095)	54,750
Clothing (25 @ $500)	12,750
Cemetery lot commissions (50 @ $450)	22,500
Flower sales	5,389
Total	$570,834

Production Budget:

The funeral home has one chapel and four staterooms. Maximum capacity is therefore five per day, but an office can be converted into a stateroom if necessary. With 93 services expected, the average expected number of daily services would be

$$93/365 = .25 \text{ per day}$$

Since Sunday services are rare, a more realistic figure is

$$93/313 = .30 \text{ per day}$$

Assuming the average service requires use of the facilities for two days (one day viewing, one day service), we would expect the facility use to be:

$$2(93)/365 = .50 \text{ per day}$$

These data indicate that at no time should we have to worry about peak-load demand problems. There may be some days when we handle as many as four or even five services per day, and we have the capacity to perform without inconveniencing our client-families.

Merchandise Expense Budget:

93 caskets @$750 avg.	$69,750
50 liners (vaults) @ $500	25,000
Clothing, flowers, supplies	8,000
	$102,750

Personnel Salaries and Fringes Budget:

General Manager	$53,934
Funeral Directors/Embalmers 4 @$25,000	100,000
Clerks/receptionists 4 @ $18,600	74,400
	$228,334

Overhead Expense Budget (Facilities):

Rent including insurance, janitorial and maintenance	$48,000
Depreciation of furniture, fixtures, equipment, and leasehold items	27,000
Utilities	10,625
	$85,625

Overhead Expense Budget (Vehicles):

Depreciation	$50,000
Fuel, repairs, and insurance	18,500
	$68,500

Overhead Expense Budget (Administration and Promotion):

Advertising	$10,000
Office supplies	2,000
Other	2,842
	$14,842

Operating Income Budget:

Revenues	$570,834	100.0
Operating costs		
Merchandise	102,750	18.0
Salaries	228,334	40.0
Facilities	85,625	15.0
Vehicles	68,500	12.0
Administrative/promotion	14,842	2.6
Total Operating Costs	500,051	87.6
Operating Income	$70,783	12.4

Cash Flow Budget:

Operating Income	$70,783
Interest expense	30,000
Income before taxes	40,783
Income taxes	12,235
Net Income	$28,548
Add: Depreciation	77,000
Deduct: Debt payment	0
Net cash flow	$105,548

Cash Balance Budget:

Cash balance (Beginning)	$100,000
Sources of cash:	
Net income	$28,548
Depreciation	77,000
Increase in payables	26,250
Uses of cash:	
Increase in receivables	$90,000
Increase in inventories	0
Debt reduction	0
Cash balance (Ending)	$141,798

Budgeted Balance Sheet:

	Dec. 31, 1997	Dec. 31 1998
Assets		
Cash	$100,000	$141,798
Receivables	0	90,000
Inventory	15,000	15,000
FF&E	75,000	60,000
Leasehold	60,000	48,000
Vehicles	150,000	100,000
	$400,000	$454,798

	Dec. 31, 1997	Dec. 31 1998
Liabilities		
Accounts Payable	$0	$26,250
Note Payable	150,000	150,000
Subordinate Debt	150,000	150,000
Common Stock	100,000	100,000
Retained Earnings	0	28,548
	$400,000	$454,748

Finance Budget:

Assets acquired	
Receivables	$90,000

No financing is required since internally generated funds (operating income and depreciation flows) and the initial cash balance, together with the increase in accounts payable, should be sufficient to finance the assets acquired during 1998.

Budgeted Operating and Financial Ratios:

Net margin	$\frac{\text{Net Income}}{\text{Revenues}}$	$\frac{28{,}548}{570{,}834}$	5.0%
Return on total assets	$\frac{\text{Net Income}}{\text{Total Assets}}$	$\frac{28{,}548}{400{,}000}$	7.1%
Return on equity	$\frac{\text{Net income}}{\text{Stockholder equity}}$	$\frac{28{,}548}{100{,}000}$	28.5%
Debt to equity (1997)	$\frac{\text{Total debt}}{\text{Stockholder equity}}$	$\frac{300{,}000}{100{,}000}$	3.0 times
Debt to equity (1998)	$\frac{\text{Total debt}}{\text{Stockholder equity}}$	$\frac{326{,}250}{128{,}548}$	2.5 times
Current ratio (1997)	$\frac{\text{Current assets}}{\text{Current liabilities}}$	$\frac{115{,}000}{150{,}000}$	0.8 times
Current ratio (1998)	$\frac{\text{Current assets}}{\text{Current liabilities}}$	$\frac{246{,}738}{176{,}250}$	1.4 times
Receivables turnover (1998)	$\frac{\text{Revenues}}{\text{Receivables}}$	$\frac{570{,}834}{90{,}000}$	6.3 times
Average collection Period (1998)	$\frac{\text{Days in year}}{\text{Receivables turnover}}$	$\frac{365}{6.3}$	58 days
Inventory turnover (1998)	$\frac{\text{Cost of merchandise}}{\text{Inventory}}$	$\frac{102{,}750}{15{,}000}$	6.9 times
Average days in inventory (1998)	$\frac{\text{Days in year}}{\text{Inventory turnover}}$	$\frac{365}{6.9}$	53 days

Figure 6.9. An Operating Plan.

6.8 Appendices

The appendices of the business plan should include all pertinent data and documents which add substance to and support the main body of the business plan. Examples of items that may be employed include: contracts, leases, plant or facility layout, major equipment required, other technical information, feasibility studies, market analysis, news stories, etc. Background information on the principals may also be included here instead of in the body of the plan. The appendices for the Jackson Funeral Home Business Plan include the Report of Market Analysis, Inc. (see Figure 6.1), a copy of the proposed lease on the property (omitted), and the building and grounds plan showing layout of the facilities, parking area, and vehicle circulation (omitted).

6.9 Summary and Conclusions

The complete business plan will consist of the following: (1) an Executive Summary,(2) a complete analysis of the industry, (3) a presentation of the form and organizational structure of the company, (4) *pro forma* financial statements, (5) the strategic plan, (6) the operating plan, and (7) appendices including pertinent contracts, technical information, and supporting data. The summary (financing) plan would be comprised of the same material except for the strategic and operating plans and certain of the appendices.

Once the plans have been prepared, consideration must be given to the methods used for presenting them. Since the complete business plan is subject to change as conditions warrant, it should be compiled in a loose-leaf format in an attractive binder. However, the summary plan may often be in bound form with an aesthetically pleasing cover since it will be given to potential financing and investor sources. It must be a professional-looking volume that will create an immediate favorable impression and cause the reader to devote sufficient time its analysis.

References

[1] Collins, O., and Moore, G., *The Organization Makers,* New York: Appleton-Century-Crofts, 1970.

[2] Findlay, M., III, and Williams, E.E., *An Integrated Analysis for Managerial Finance*, Englewood Cliffs: Prentice-Hall, Inc., 1970.

[3] Hoad, W.M. and Rosko, P., *Management Factors Contributing to the Success and Failure of New Small Manufacturers*, Ann Arbor: Bureau of Business Research, University of Michigan, 1964.

[4] Liles, P.R., *New Business Ventures and the Entrepreneur*, Homewood, Illinois: Richard D. Irwin, Inc., First Edition, 1974.

[5] Mayer, K.B., and Goldstein, S., *The First Two Years: Problems of Small Firm Growth and Survival*, Washington, D.C.: Small Business Administration, U.S. Government Printing Office, 1961.

[6] McClelland, D., *The Achieving Society*, Princeton: Van Nostrand, 1961.

[7] McGuire, J.W., *Factors Affecting the Growth of Manufacturing Firms.* Seattle: School of Business, University of Washington, March, 1963.

[8] Schumpeter, J.A. *The Theory of Economic Development*, Cambridge, Massachusetts: Harvard University Press, 1934.

[9] Stevenson, H., Roberts, M.J., and Grosbeck, H.I., *New Business Ventures and the Entrepreneur*, McGraw Irwin, Fourth Edition, 1994.

[10] Williams, E.E. and Manzo, S.E., *Business Planning for the Entrepreneur*, New York: Van Nostrand, 1983.

[11] Williams, E.E. and Thompson, J.R., *The Economics of Production and Productivity: A Modeling Approach*, Austin: Capital Book Company, 1996.

[12] Woodruff, A.M. and Alexander, T.G., *Success and Failure in Small Manufacturing*, Pittsburgh: University of Pittsburgh Press, 1958.

[13] Woodworth, Robert T., et al, *The Entrepreneurial Process and the Role of Accountants, Bankers and Lawyers*, Seattle: School of Business, University of Washington, 1969.

Chapter 7

Planning Enterprise Growth

7.1 Introduction

In the last two chapters, we have outlined the steps that must be taken in preparing a business plan, and we have actually constructed a plan for a prospective new enterprise. In this chapter, we shall delve more deeply into the mechanics of planning for growth during the first and future years of operations of a new company (or the forthcoming and future years for an existing business) and we shall enumerate the means of financing that growth.

Earlier in this book, we discussed the importance of setting the broad goals and specific objectives of the enterprise as key starting points in the planning process. Any number of possible goals and correlated objectives might be established by the firm and the principal reason for formally positing goals and objectives is to preclude the pursuit of strategies designed to achieve mutually exclusive (or conflicting) goals. Thus, it is perfectly acceptable for an entrepreneur to have public service as a principal goal so long as it is recognized that this goal *might* be inconsistent with a second goal of building a highly profitable company. Clearly, noneconomic goals may be quite legitimate and may be incorporated into the business plan. Nevertheless, economic goals normally play an important, if not the most important, role in planning; and virtually every economic goal centers around the concept of growth.

7.2 Growth in the First Year

During the first year of operations of the new enterprise, it is critically important to plan for growth on a timely and controlled basis. If revenues do not come in as rapidly as expected, there may be insufficient cash flow to keep the firm alive past the first few months of operations. Alternatively, if revenues grow more rapidly than expected, the business may also run into difficulties as receivable and inventory levels advance beyond the financial capacities of the enterprise. Thus, planning must be even more specific than was done in preparing the strategic and operating sections of the business plan.

For some entities, it will be necessary to construct detailed revenue, production, expense, and cash flow interim budgets by month, by week or even by day in order to assure the survival of the business. Surprises can kill a fledgling company, and one cannot wait until the end of the first fiscal quarter to find out what is happening. Certain kinds of businesses can get along with monthly budgets and monthly revenue and expense reports. Firms which sell large ticket items infrequently (automobile dealerships, large appliance dealers, builders, etc.) would not get much out of a daily or even a weekly budgeting and control system. A restaurant, on the other hand, might be in deep trouble if management did not plan for and know how many meals were served each day from the very beginning of operations. Businesses which record a number of daily sales where sales may vary rather significantly from one day to the next should prepare daily budgets and daily operating statements. In general, the following budgets should be constructed:

1. A monthly (weekly, daily) marketing (sales) budget.
2. A monthly (weekly, daily) production budget.
3. A monthly (weekly, daily) purchases budget.
4. A monthly (weekly, daily) personnel budget.
5. A monthly (weekly, daily) overhead budget.
6. A monthly (weekly, daily) operating income budget.
7. A monthly (weekly, daily) cash flow budget.

8. A monthly (weekly, daily) cash balance budget.

9. A monthly (weekly, daily) financing budget.

Not all of the above will be needed in every situation, and some businesses will have to have a more detailed breakdown than that outlined. In all instances, of course, the budgets that are prepared within the fiscal year time frame will be based on the operating plan that was included in the complete business plan.

Ben Jackson has determined that monthly budgeting and control will be best suited for the Jackson Funeral Home. As a result, he has prepared appropriate budgets by month for the first year of operations of his new business. These budgets were based on the operating plan that he prepared and will become a part of a monthly budgeting/control system. That is, Ben will do his budgets by month; he will then have his accountant prepare monthly operating statements at the end of each month. These statements will be used to make managerial decisions about how to operate the business (including a possible decision to cease operations) and will be reflected in replanning to the extent that major assumptions about the business prove to be incorrect.

First, Ben has prepared a marketing (sales) budget that describes the number of funeral services he expects to handle each month for the first year he is in business (see Figure 7.1). He has also estimated the average price he will obtain per service, and he has listed the other sources of revenue he anticipates. The monthly projections reflect what Ben considers to be reasonable expectations about the growth of the firm during the year. Thus, services handled are expected to be few in the early months and to advance in number as the Jackson Funeral Home becomes better known in the community. Ben's figures also are consistent with the seasonal pattern which is characteristic of funeral demand. More people die in the unpleasant winter months than during the summer, and the requirement for funeral services is consequently higher during the months of November, December, January, February, and March than at other times of the year.

Jackson Funeral Home, Inc. A Marketing (Sales) Budget Fiscal Year 1998, By Month							
	Jan.	Feb.	Mar.	Apr.	May	June	
Number of services	4	5	7	11	10	10	
Average price	5,115	5,115	5,115	5,115	5,115	5,115	
Funeral revenue	20,460	25,575	35,805	56,265	51,150	51,150	
Other revenue:							
Liners and vaults	2	3	3	6	5	5	
Price	1,095	1,095	1,095	1,095	1,095	1,095	
Revenue	2,190	3,285	3,285	6,570	5,475	5,475	
Clothing	1	1	2	3	2	3	
Price	500	500	500	500	500	500	
Revenue	500	500	1,000	1,500	1,000	1,500	
Lots	2	3	3	6	5	5	
Commission	450	450	450	450	450	450	
Revenue	900	1,350	1,350	2,700	2,250	2,250	
Flower sales	232	290	406	638	580	580	
Total revenue	24,282	31,000	41,846	67,673	60,455	60,955	
	July	Aug.	Sept.	Oct.	Nov.	Dec.	Year
Number of services	7	6	6	7	9	11	93
Average price	5,115	5,115	5,115	5,115	5,115	5,115	5,115
Funeral revenue	35,805	30,690	30,690	35,805	46,035	56,265	475,695
Other revenue:							
Liners and vaults	4	3	4	4	5	6	50
Price	1,095	1,095	1,095	1,095	1,095	1,095	
Revenue	4,380	3,285	4,380	4,380	5,475	6,570	54,750
Clothing	2	2	2	2	2	3	25
Price	500	500	500	500	500	500	500
Revenue	1,000	1,000	1,000	1,000	1,000	1,500	12,500
Lots	4	3	4	4	5	6	50
Commission	450	450	450	450	450	450	450
Revenue	1,800	1,350	1,800	1,800	2,250	2,700	22,500
Flower sales	406	348	348	406	522	638	5,389
Total revenue	43,391	36,673	38,218	43,391	55,282	67,673	570,834

Figure 7.1. A Marketing (Sales) Budget.

Next, Ben has constructed a merchandise purchases budget (see Figure 7.2). To the extent that a firm's inventories are not bought (manufactured) coterminously with its sales, there will be a difference in the purchases and usage of inventory. The inventory purchases budget will be significant in determining the cash flow of the business whereas the inventory actually sold will be employed in determining the operating income of the business. In the case of the Jackson Funeral Home, most of the inventory was bought during December of the previous year (prior to commencing operations) and subsequent purchases coincide exactly with sales. In the event of either inventory build-ups (purchasing more inventory than sales) or inventory liquidations (purchasing less inventory than sales), such changes would be reflected in the merchandise purchases budget.

Jackson Funeral Home, Inc. Merchandise Purchases Budget Fiscal Year 1998, By Month							
	Jan.	Feb.	Mar.	Apr.	May	June	
Unit casket inventory (beginning)	20	20	20	20	20	20	
Caskets purchased	4	5	7	11	10	10	
Caskets sold	4	5	7	11	10	10	
Unit casket inventory (ending)	20	20	20	20	20	20	
Costs in dollars of caskets purchased (@ 750)	3,000	3,750	5,250	8,250	7,500	7,500	
Cost of caskets sold (@750)	3,000	3,750	5,250	8,250	7,500	7,500	
Value of casket inv. (beginning)	15,000	15,000	15,000	15,000	15,000	15,000	
Value of casket inv. (ending)	15,000	15,000	15,000	15,000	15,000	15,000	
	July	Aug.	Sept.	Oct¿	Nov.	Dec.	Year
Unit casket inventory (beginning)	20	20	20	21	21	21	20
Caskets purchased	7	6	7	7	9	11	93
Caskets sold	7	6	7	7	9	11	93
Unit casket inventory (ending)	20	20	20	20	20	20	20
Costs in dollars of caskets purchased (@ 750)	5,250	4,500	5,250	5,250	6,750	8,250	69,750
Cost of caskets sold (@750)	5,250	4,500	5,250	5,250	6,750	8,250	69,750
Value of casket inv. (beginning)	15,000	15,000	15,000	15,000	15,000	15,000	15,000
Value of casket inv. (ending)	15,000	15,000	15,000	15,000	15,000	15,000	15,000

Figure 7.2. A Merchandise Purchases Budget.

The merchandise expense budget is determined directly from the merchandise purchases budget. Units sold become expense items in preparing the operating statement (see Figure 7.3).

Jackson Funeral Home, Inc. Merchandise Expense Budget Fiscal Year 1998, By Month							
	Jan.	Feb.	Mar.	Apr.	May	June	
Cost of caskets sold	3,000	3,750	5,250	8,250	7,500	7,500	
Cost of liners and vaults sold	1,000	1,500	1,500	3,000	2,500	2,500	
Cost of clothing sold	250	250	500	750	500	750	
Clost of flowers sold	76	95	130	205	190	190	
Total	4,326	5,595	7,380	12,205	10,690	10,940	
	Jul.	Aug.	Sept.	Oct.	Nov.	Dec.	Year
Cost of caskets sold	5,250	4,500	5,250	5,250	6,750	8,250	69,750
Cost of liners and vaults sold	2,000	1,500	2,000	2,000	2,500	3,000	25,000
Cost of clothing sold	500	500	500	500	500	500	6,250
Clost of flowers sold	130	114	114	130	171	205	1,750
Total	7,880	6,614	7,114	7,880	9,921	12,205	102,750

Figure 7.3. A Merchandise Expenses Budget.

The next budget prepared by the entrepreneur is the personnel expense budget. For the Jackson Funeral Home this is a rather straightforward matter of listing the employees hired (expected to be hired) and the salaries Ben plans to pay them. Raises, of course, are programmed into the figures. For a more complicated business with hourly workers and other types of incentives than salary, it may be necessary to coordinate a production plan and an inventory plan with the personnel expense plan (see Figure 7.4).

Jackson Funeral Home, Inc.
Personnel Budget
Fiscal Year 1998, By Month

	Jan.	Feb.	Mar.	Apr.	May	June	
General manager	4,495	4,495	4,495	4,495	4,495	4,495	
Funeral directors/ embalmers	8,333	8,333	8,333	8,333	8,333	8,333	
Clerks/receptionists	6,200	6,200	6,200	6,200	6,200	6,200	
Total	19,028	19,028	19,028	19,028	19,028	19,028	
	July	**Aug.**	**Sept.**	**Oct.**	**Nov.**	**Dec.**	**Year**
General manager	4,495	4,495	4,495	4,495	4,495	4,489	53,934
Funeral directors/ embalmers	8,333	8,333	8,333	8,333	8,333	8,337	100,000
Clerks/receptionists	6,200	6,200	6,200	6,200	6,200	6,200	74,400
Total	19,028	19,028	19,028	19,028	19,028	19,026	228,334

Figure 7.4. A Personnel Budget.

The other expense items anticipated for the Jackson Funeral Home are detailed in the overhead expense budget (see Figure 7.5). Many of these expenses are fixed and are simply allocated by month. It is important to distinguish between fixed *cash* expenses and fixed *noncash* charges, however. Fixed cash expenses (such as rent) must be paid each month and affect the cash position of the company. Fixed noncash charges (such as depreciation) represent items that have already been paid for and are simply being expensed over time in order to provide for an accounting matching of income and expenses. Thus, fixed cash expenses have an impact on the statements of cash flow whereas fixed noncash charges do not. Both are determinants of operating income, of course.

The next budget prepared for the Jackson Funeral Home is the operating income budget (see Figure 7.6). The operating income budget summarizes the budgets previously discussed and portrays the expected accounting operating income profit anticipated for the business. Notice that Ben Jackson expects to have operating losses during the first two months of operations but that operating income is projected to become positive by March. The firm is expected to continue to have positive operating income until the summer slow-down reduces revenues in August and September. The firm returns to a profitable condition for the rest of the year and is expected to earn $70,783 in operating income for 1998.

Jackson Funeral Home, Inc. Overhead Expense Budget Fiscal Year 1998, By Month							
	Jan.	Feb.	Mar.	Apr.	May	June	
Facilities expense:							
Rent	4,000	4,000	4,000	4,000	4,000	4,000	
Depreciation	2,250	2,250	2,250	2,250	2,250	2,250	
Utilities	885	885	885	885	885	885	
	7,135	7,135	7,135	7,135	7,135	7,135	
Vehicles expense:							
Depreciation	4,167	4,167	4,167	4,167	4,167	4,167	
Fuel, repairs, insurance	1,542	1,542	1,542	1,542	1,542	1,542	
	5,709	5,709	5,709	5,709	5,709	5,709	
Administrative/ promotion:							
Advertising	833	833	833	833	833	833	
Office supplies	167	167	167	167	167	167	
Other	250	250	250	250	250	250	
	1,250	1,250	1,250	1,250	1,250	1,250	
Total overhead expenses	14,094	14,094	14,094	14,094	14,094	14,094	
	July	Aug.	Sept.	Oct.	Nov.	Dec.	Year
Facilities expense:							
Rent	4,000	4,000	4,000	4,000	4,000	4,000	48,000
Depreciation	2,250	2,250	2,250	2,250	2,250	2,250	27,000
Utilities	885	885	885	885	885	890	10,625
	7,135	7,135	7,135	7,135	7,135	7,140	85,625
Vehicles expense:							
Depreciation	4,167	4,167	4,167	4,167	4,167	4,163	50,000
Fuel, repairs, insurance	1,542	1,542	1,542	1,542	1,542	1,538	18,500
	5,709	5,709	5,709	5,709	5,709	5,701	68,500
Administrative/ promotion:							
Advertising	833	833	833	833	833	837	10,000
Office supplies	167	167	167	167	167	163	2,000
Other	250	250	250	250	250	92	2,842
	1,250	1,250	1,250	1,250	1,250	1,092	14,842
Total overhead expenses	14,094	14,094	14,094	14,094	14,094	13,933	168,967

Figure 7.5. An Overhead Expense Budget.

The next two budgets are the cash flow budget (see Figure 7.7) and the cash balance budget (see Figure 7.8). These budgets will normally be prepared after the operating income budget and describe the movement of cash through the enterprise. The cash flow budget begins with operating income, subtracts interest expense and income taxes, adds back depreciation flows, and then deducts debt payments. It is constructed in such a fashion so as to focus on the ability of the company to service its debt (interest and principal payments). For the Jackson Funeral Home, operating income in 1998 is planned to be sufficient to cover interest expense, which the bank and the venture capitalist wish to have paid monthly. When depreciation flows are added back to income, the firm is expected to have a positive cash flow of $105,548 for the year. No debt repayment is scheduled during 1998.

The cash balances budget begins with the expected opening cash balance from the previous period and then adds in all sources of cash expected. The principal sources include: the operating income for the period, noncash charges that do not affect the cash position but which were subtracted from operating income (the principal noncash charge for most businesses will be depreciation), nonoperating income, increases in liabilities (such as accounts payable and other indebtedness), and the sale of stock. Next, the uses of cash are subtracted. The principal uses are: increases in the assets (besides cash) held by the firm, repayment of debt, redemption of stock, nonoperating expenses (such as interest), income tax payments (assumed to be estimated for the year but paid monthly regardless of estimated monthly income), and dividend payments. In general, the income generated by the firm plus increases in liabilities are uses of cash. Nonoperating expenses, income tax payments, and dividend distributions are also possible uses of cash.

Jackson Funeral Home, Inc.
Operating Income Budget
Fiscal Year 1998, By Month

	Jan.	Feb.	Mar.	Apr.	May	June	
Revenues	24,282	31,000	41,846	67,673	60,455	60,953	
Cost of services:							
Merchandise	4,326	5,595	7,380	12,205	10,690	10,940	
Salaries	19,028	19,028	19,028	19,028	19,028	19,028	
Facilities	7,135	7,135	7,135	7,135	7,135	7,135	
Vehicles	5,709	5,709	5,709	5,709	5,709	5,709	
Adm./prom.	1,250	1,250	1,250	1,250	1,250	1,250	
Total operating costs	37,448	38,717	40,502	45,327	43,812	44,062	
Operating income	(13,166)	(7,717)	1,344	22,346	16,643	16,891	
	July	Aug.	Sept.	Oct.	Nov.	Dec.	Year
Revenues	43,391	36,673	38,218	43,391	55,282	67,673	570,834
Cost of services:							
Merchandise	7,880	6,614	7,114	7,880	9,921	12,205	102,750
Salaries	19,028	19,028	19,028	19,028	19,028	19,026	228,334
Facilities	7,135	7,135	7,135	7,135	7,135	7,140	85,625
Vehicles	5,709	5,709	5,709	5,709	5,709	5,701	68,500
Adm./prom.	1,250	1,250	1,250	1,250	1,250	1,092	14,842
Total operating costs	41,002	39,736	40,236	41,002	43,043	45,164	500,051
Operating income	2,389	(3,063)	(2,018)	2,389	12,239	22,509	70,783

Figure 7.6. An Operating Income Budget.

The cash budgets for the Jackson Funeral Home suggest that no additional financing (besides a budgeted increase in payables) will be necessary for 1998. Hence, a financial plan is omitted. The cash position opens with the $100,000 remaining from the original financing in 1997 (after the purchase of inventories, furniture, fixtures, equipment, leasehold improvements, and vehicles). The position is expected to deteriorate during the first three months of operations due to low volume, the necessity of extending credit to client families, and the requisite interest on outstanding indebtedness. The position is anticipated to improve gradually over the summer, deteriorate from August through October and then grow during November and December as volume improvements more than offset the other cash requirements. The company is projected to end the year with almost half again as much cash as it began with ($141,798 versus $100,000) despite a $90,000 build-up in receivables and the necessity to pay $30,000 in interest. At no time does it appear that the firm might be in danger of running out of cash unless the volume projections fall well short of anticipations.

Jackson Funeral Home, Inc.
Cash Flow Budget
Fiscal Year 1998, By Month

	Jan.	Feb.	Mar.	Apr.	May	June	
Operating income	(13,166)	(7,717)	1,344	22,346	16,643	16,891	
Interest expense	(2,500)	(2,500)	(2,500)	(2,500)	(2,500)	(2,500)	
Income before taxes	(15,666)	(10,217)	(1,159)	19,846	14,143	14,391	
Income taxes	(1,016)	(1,016)	(1,016)	(1,016)	(1,016)	(1,016)	
Net income	(16,682)	(11,233)	(2,175)	18,830	13,127	13,375	
Add: Depreciation	6,417	6,417	6,417	6,417	6,417	6,417	
Less Debt payment	0	0	0	0	0	0	
Net cash flow	(10,265)	(4,816)	4,242	25,247	19,544	19,792	
	July	Aug.	Sept.	Oct.	Nov.	Dec.	Year
Operating income	2,389	(3,063)	(2,018)	2,386	12,239	22,509	70,783
Interest expense	(2,500)	(2,500)	(2,500)	(2,500)	(2,500)	(2,500)	(30,000)
Income before taxes	(114)	(5,563)	(4,518)	(111)	9,739	20,009	40,783
Income taxes	(1,016)	(1,016)	(1,016)	(1,016)	(1,016)	(1,059)	(12,235)
Net income	(1,130)	(6,579)	(5,534)	(1,127)	8,723	18,950	28,548
Add: Depreciation	6,417	6,417	6,417	6,417	6,417	6,413	77,000
Less Debt payment	0	0	0	0	0	0	0
Net cash flow	5,287	(162)	883	5,290	15,140	25,363	105,548

Figure 7.7. A Cash Flow Budget.

Jackson Funeral Home, Inc.
Cash Balance Budget
Fiscal Year 1998, By Month

	Jan.	Feb.	Mar.	Apr.	May	June	July	Aug.	Sept.	Oct.	Nov.	Dec.	Year
Cash balance (beginning)	100,000	84,423	74,295	73,225	93,160	107,392	121,872	121,847	116,373	111,944	111,922	121,750	100,000
Sources of cash:													
Operating income	(13,166)	(7,717)	1,341	22,346	16,643	16,891	2,386	(3,063)	(2,018)	2,389	12,239	22,509	70,783
Depreciation	6,417	6,417	6,417	6,417	6,417	6,417	6,417	6,417	6,417	6,417	6,417	6,413	77,000
Increase in payables	2,188	2,188	2,188	2,188	2,188	2,188	2,188	2,188	2,188	2,188	2,188	2,182	26,250
Debt incurred	0	0	0	0	0	0	0	0	0	0	0	0	0
Stock sold	0	0	0	0	0	0	0	0	0	0	0	0	0
Uses of cash:													
Increase in receivables	(7,500)	(7,500)	(7,500)	(7,500)	(7,500)	(7,500)	(7,500)	(7,500)	(7,500)	(7,500)	(7,500)	(7,500)	(90,000)
Increase in inventories	0	0	0	0	0	0	0	0	0	0	0	0	0
Increase in fixed assets	0	0	0	0	0	0	0	0	0	0	0	0	0
Debt repaid	0	0	0	0	0	0	0	0	0	0	0	0	0
Stock redeemed	0	0	0	0	0	0	0	0	0	0	0	0	0
Interest expense	(2,500)	(2,500)	(2,500)	(2,500)	(2,500)	(2,500)	(2,500)	(2,500)	(2,500)	(2,500)	(2,500)	(2,500)	(30,000)
Income taxes paid	(1,016)	(1,016)	(1,016)	(1,016)	(1,016)	(1,016)	(1,016)	(1,016)	(1,016)	(1,016)	(1,016)	(1,059)	(12,235)
Dividends paid	0	0	0	0	0	0	0	0	0	0	0	0	0
Cash balance (ending)	84,423	74,295	73,225	93,160	107,392	121,872	121,847	116,373	111,944	111,922	121,750	141,798	141,798

Figure 7.8. A Cash Balance Budget.

7.3 Determining a Growth Strategy

Appropriate growth strategies depend upon the goals and objectives that have been established by the enterprise. What may be a realistic growth objective for one firm may be totally inappropriate for another. In order to assess what is feasible, the entrepreneur will have to have examined the external and internal factors that affect the business. Once viable growth objectives have been set, however, the planning and control process again becomes critical to the achievement of those objectives.

To some extent, growth strategies depend upon the relative past success of the enterprise. Thus, it is necessary to measure past objectives against actual accomplishments. This is done by considering the budgets (and long range plans) of the enterprise in light of achieved operating results. Let us suppose that the year 1998 has passed and Ben Jackson has before him the operating statements for that year. As a good manager, he has spent some time comparing the actual results of the year with the budgeted objectives he had prepared the previous year.

Jackson Funeral Home, Inc.
Comparison of Actual vs. Budgeted Revenues
Fiscal Year 1998

	Actual	Budget	Variance
Number of services	87	93	(6)
Average price	5,478	5,115	363
Funeral revenue	476,586	475,695	891
Other revenue:			
Liners	43,800	54,750	(10,950)
Clothing	5,000	12,500	(7,500)
Lots	14,850	22,500	(7,650)
Flower sales	5,741	5,389	352
Total revenues	545,977	570,834	(24,857)

Figure 7.9. Comparison of Actual vs. Budgeted Revenues.

Of course, Ben has been carefully examining his actual operating results each month and has compared them with his budgets. His actual versus budgeted revenues are analyzed in Figure 7.9. For the first two months of operations, the number of services handled was well below expectation (one in January versus four budgeted, and two in february versus five budgeted). His expenses were somewhat higher than expected, and his cash flow was running substantially negative. As a consequence, Ben spent more than he originally anticipated on promotion and he did not replenish his casket inventory as sales were made. By March, he was closer to budget (five services versus a budgeted seven) and by April he was exactly on budget. He continued to watch his cash balances carefully, ordering only part of the inventory that had been sold. He also took the maximum payment terms offered to him by suppliers thereby increasing his accounts payable and reducing the immediate demand on his cash. In May, he was actually over budget by one service, while he was two under in June, three under in July, and on budget in August. Volume picked up unexpectedly in September (three over budget) and continued above budget or on budget for the rest of the year. Ben completed fiscal 1998 having handled 87 services, only six short of his budgeted objective. During the remainder of the year, Ben aggressively collected his accounts receivable, and he was in a positive cash position for the last half of the year.

Upon reflecting on the annual results for 1998, Ben discovered that his shortfall in services handled was more than overcome by the average price he was able to charge per service. Whereas he had expected to attain an average of $5,115 per service, his actual average was $5,478 per service. Thus, he had a favorable variance of actual over budgeted funeral revenue of $891. Unfortunately, he turned out to have been overly optimistic about his other sources of revenue, and negative variances were experienced for liner sales, clothing and lot commissions. His flower sales were somewhat higher than expected, but the overall variance of actual revenues from budget was a negative $24,857. All in all, Ben was not too disappointed by the revenue figures. He had budgeted total revenues at $570,834 and actually had revenues of $545,977.

Ben was not pleased with his ability to keep expenses in line (see Figure 7.10). He was able to sell less expensive merchandise at higher prices than originally anticipated (hence producing a favorable variance in the cost of merchandise), but he was off the mark in facility expenses, vehicle expenses, and administrative and promotion costs. The principal cost categories of error were: utilities (unfavorable variance of $1,735), vehicle fuel (unfavorable variance of $1,895), vehicle repairs (unfavorable variance of $2,840), and promotion (unfavorable variance of $6,305). The latter unfavorable variance was intentionally experienced in order to remedy the volume problem that was suffered early in the year. The total variance of all expense categories was a favorable $26,657, due to the sale of less merchandise at lower cost. Thus, the variance in net operating income of was a favorable $1,800 (see Figure 7.11).

Jackson Funeral Home, Inc. Comparison of Actual vs. Budgeted Expenses Fiscal Year 1998			
	Actual	Budget	Variance
Cost of merchandise	63,075	102,750	39,675
Salaries	228,354	228,334	(20)
Facilities expense	87,410	85,625	(1,785)
Vehicle expense	73,250	68,500	(4,750)
Administrative, promotion	21,305	14,842	(6,463)
Total	473,394	500,051	26,657

Figure 7.10. Comparison of Actual vs. Budget Expenses.

The early months of 1998 were producing substantial losses for the firm and a severe cash drain. As a result of the actions taken by Ben, the cash flow problem was alleviated, and the firm actually ended the year in a stronger cash position than he originally had budgeted (see Figure 7.12). Whereas he had expected to have his cash position go up by $41,798 during the year, it actually improved by $61,758 Stretching his accounts payable (discussed later in this chapter), reducing (rather than increasing) his inventories, and (most dramatically) collecting his accounts in a more expeditious manner than originally expected were the determining factors in causing the cash improvement.

Jackson Funeral Home, Inc. Comparison of Actual vs. Budgeted Net Income Fiscal Year 1998			
	Actual	Budget	Variance
Revenues	545,977	570,834	(24,857)
Expenses	473,394	500,051	26,657
Operating income	72,583	70,783	1,800
Interest expense	30,000	30,000	0
Income before taxes	42,583	40,783	1,800
Income taxes	12,775	12,235	(540)
Net income	29,808	28,548	1,260

Figure 7.11 Comparison of Actual vs. Budget Net Income.

Jackson Funeral Home, Inc. Comparison of Actual vs. Budgeted Cash Balance Fiscal Year 1998			
	Actual	Budget	Variance
Cash balance (beginning year)	100,000	100,000	0
Sources of cash:			
Operating income	72,583	70,783	1,800
Depreciation	77,000	77,000	0
Increase in payables	28,450	26,250	2,200
Debt incurred	0	0	0
Stock sold	0	0	0
Uses of Cash:			
Increase in receivables	(75,000)	(90,000)	15,000
Increases in inventories	1,500	0	1,500
Increase in fixed assests	0	0	
Debt repaid	0	0	
Stock redeemed	0	0	
Interest expense	(30,000)	(30,000)	0
Income taxes paid	(12,775)	(12,235)	(540)
Dividends paid	0	0	0
Cash balance (ending)	161,758	141,798	19,960

Figure 7.12. Comparison of Actual vs. Budget Cash Balances.

Jackson Funeral Home, Inc.
Pro Forma and Actual Results 1998 and 1999

	Pro Forma 1998	Actual 1998	*Pro Forma* 1999
Revenues	$570,834	$545,977	$625,838
Cost of services			
Merchandise	102,750	63,075	112,651
Salaries	228,334	228,354	250,335
Facilities	85,625	87,410	93,876
Vehicles	68,500	73,250	75,101
Administrative/ promotion	14,842	21,305	16,272
Total operating costs	500,051	473,394	548,235
Operating income	70,783	72,583	77,603
Interest expense	30,000	30,000	30,000
Income before taxes	40,783	42,583	47,603
Income taxes	12,235	12,775	14,281
Net Income	$28,548	$29,808	$33,322

Figure 7.13. ***Pro Forma*** **and Actual Results.**

Jackson Funeral Home, Inc. Fiscal Year 1998-2001 Planning Premises and Objectives	
Premises	Objectives
1. The mortality rate and absolute number of mortalities in Wesson will stabilize in 1997 and will increase slightly in each subsequent year. 2. We shall achieve a 25% share of the market in 1998 and this will increase to 35% by 2001. 3. We expect to handle 93 cases in 1998, 99 in 1999, 110 in 2000, and 128 in 2001. 4. Income levels will be rising in Wesson throughout the planning period. 5. Average revenue per service is calculated to be $5,115 in 1998, $5,268 in 1999, $5,426 in 2000, and $5,589 in 2001. 6. Other revenue will equal 20% of funeral service revenues. 7. Standard cost percentages shall follow the industry pattern of: merchandise, 18%; salaries, 40%; facilities, 15%; and vehicles, 12%.	1. Over the planning period, we shall achieve or exceed a compounded annual growth rate of revenues of 14%. 2. Over the planning period, we shall achieve or exceed a compounded annual growth rate of operating income of 14%. 3. We shall achieve operating income margins of approximately 12%. 4. Return on assets (operating income/total assets) will exceed 18% in 1998 and will exceed 25% by 2001. 5. Return on stockholder equity will be approximately 28% over the planning period. 6. There will be no major capital additions during the planning period. 7. No dividends will be paid during the planning period. 8. No additional financing will be sought during the planning period. 9. The firm's debt/equity ratio shall not exceed 3:1 during the planning period. 10. The current ratio shall not be less than .75:1 during the planning period.

Figure 7.14. Planning Premises and Objectives.

After having reviewed the actual results for fiscal 1998, Ben Jackson has gone back to the four-year plan he prepared before entering business. He sees no reason to change the statement of enterprise mission, definition of the business, the broad enterprise goals, or the enterprise strategies for the Jackson Funeral Home, Inc. based on the results of fiscal 1998. He does feel, however, that the planning premises and specific objectives of the firm may have to be altered somewhat. From the four-year plan, he has iterated the 1998 and 1999 *pro forma* and 1998 actual figures as shown in Figure 7.13. He has also listed salient elements of the planning premises and specific objectives of the strategic plan in Figure 7.14.

In reviewing the planning premises, Ben has found that he was essentially correct about the mortality rate and number of mortalities in Wesson for 1997. During the year, there were 3,165 deaths (up from 3,038 in 1996). Preliminary data suggest that the number increased in 1998 to 3,184. Given a population of approximately 308,000 during the year, the death rate was about 10.3 per thousand (up from 9.8 in 1996 and 10.0 in 1997). For the seven census tracts that constitute the relevant market for the Jackson Funeral Home, Inc., there were 380 deaths with a mortality rate of 12.5 per thousand population. Unfortunately, the market share for the Jackson Funeral Home was below expectations for the year. Instead of handling 93 cases, only 87 services were provided. This represented a market share of less than 23%.

On the other hand, income levels did rise in Wesson and average revenue per service exceeded the premised amount ($5,478 versus $5,115). Other revenues fell short of 20% of funeral service revenue ($69,391/$476,586 = 14.6%) and the cost percentages did not follow the industry pattern exactly:

	Industry	Jackson 1998 Actual
Merchandise	18.0	11.6
salaries	40.0	41.8
Facilities	15.0	16.0
Vehicles	12.0	13.4

In considering the achievement of objectives, Ben found it necessary to review the actual and budgeted balance sheets for December 31, 1998. These comparisons are shown in Figure 7.15.

Jackson Funeral Home, Inc. Comparison of Actual vs. Budgeted Balance Sheets, End of Year 1998			
	Actual	Budget	Variance
Assets:			
Cash	$161,758	$141,798	$19,960
Receivables	75,000	90,000	(15,000)
Inventory	13,500	15,000	(1,500)
FF&E	60,000	60,000	0
Leasehold	48,000	48,000	0
Vehicles	100,000	100,000	0
	$458,258	$454,798	$3,460
Liabilities:			
Accounts payable	$28,450	$26,250	$2,200
Note payable	150,000	150,000	0
Subordinated debt	150,000	150,0000	0
Common stock	100,000	100,000	0
Retained earnings	29,808	28,548	1,260
	$458,258	$454,738	$3,460

Figure 7.15. Comparison of Actual vs. Budgeted Balance Sheets.

Thus, Ben failed to achieve many of the objectives he established for 1998. Consequently, he has decided his objectives were unrealistic and that more reasonable objectives will be established for 1999. In light of his original four-year plan and the 1998 operating experience, Ben has assumed the following premises for 1999:

1. The mortality rate and absolute number of mortalities in the seven census tracts Wesson that is the market for the Jackson Funeral Home, Inc. will reflect the 1998 pattern. That is, there will be 380 deaths. Given a slight contraction in the population, the mortality rate will rise to 12.6 per thousand.
2. Income levels will continue to rise in Wesson.
3. No new funeral establishments will open in the city.

Given the above premises, objectives have been set for 1999. Notice that several of the items that were premises for the first year of operations now fall into the objectives category. This is because a number of variables could only be assumed originally and can only become targets to shoot for *after* reasonable parameters have been discerned. The 1999 objectives for the Jackson Funeral Home, Inc. are:

1. We shall achieve a market share of 25%
2. We shall handle 95 services during the year.
3. Average revenue per service will advance by 5% to $5,752.
4. Funeral service revenue will equal $546,4400.
5. Other revenue will equal 15% of funeral service revenue, or $81,966.
6. Revenue will grow by over 15% from 1998 to $628,406.
7. The following cost percentages will be attained:

Merchandise	12.0
Salaries	42.0
Facilities	16.0
Vehicles	13.0

8. An operating margin of 14% will be earned.
9. Return on assets will approach 17%.
10. Return on stockholder equity will exceed 25%.
11. There will be no major capital additions or employees hired during the year.
12. No dividends will be paid during the year.
13. No additional financing will be sought during the year.
14. The firm's debt/equity ratio shall not exceed 2.5 during the year.
15. The current ratio shall not be less than 1.4:1 during the year.

From this set of objectives, a budgeted income statement and balance sheet for fiscal 1999 may be prepared as shown in Figures 7.16 and 7.17. Of course, at this juncture, it would be appropriate to prepare a revised business plan with new projections (perhaps going out to year 2002) in light of the experience of 1998.

Jackson Funeral Home, Inc. Budgeted Net Income Statement Fiscal 1999		
Revenues	$546,440	100.0%
Cost of services		
Merchandise	65,573	12.0
Salaries	229,505	42.0
Facilities	87,430	16.0
Vehicles	71,037	13.0
Administrative/promotion	16,393	3.0
Total operating costs	469,938	86.0
Operating income	76,502	14.0
Interest expense	30,000	5.5
Income before taxes	46,502	8.5
Income taxes	13,951	2.6
Net Income	$32,551	5.9%

Figure 7.16. A Replanned Budgeted Net Income Statement.

Jackson Funeral Home, Inc. **Actual and Budgeted Balance Sheets** **December 31, 1998 and 1999**			
	1998 Actual	1999 Budgeted	Change
Assets:			
Cash	$161,758	$296,184	$134,426
Receivables	75,000	80,000	5,000
Inventory	13,500	16,500	3,000
FF&E	60,000	36,000	(24,000)
Leasehold	48,000	28,800	(19,200)
Vehicles	100,000	33,325	(66,675)
	$458,258	$490,809	$32,551
Liabilities:			
Accounts payable	$28,450	$28,450	$0
Note payable	150,000	150,000	0
Subordinated debt	150,000	150,000	0
Common stock	100,000	100,000	0
Retained earnings	29,808	62,359	32,551
	$458,258	$490,809	$32,551

Figure 7.17. A Replanned Budgeted Balance Sheet.

7.4 Financing a Growth Strategy

Once a growth strategy has been determined for the firm for the forthcoming year, it becomes necessary to decide how to finance that growth. Basically, there are two principal types of finance: funds generated internally and funds raised externally. In the finance literature, the distinction is also often made between *gross* sources of finance and *net* sources. Gross internal sources include all the funds available to the firm to finance its operations such as operating income, depreciation flows and other noncash charges, and asset conversions. Net sources are those that remain after depreciating assets are replenished and all payments are made to suppliers of funds and the government. Retained earnings are the principal net source of internal finance since depreciation flows are typically used to replenish fixed assets. Interest and dividend payments are paid to suppliers of funds, and income taxes are paid to the government out of operating income (or other non-operating sources).

For the new enterprise, concentrating on net internal sources of finance may be misleading. At this stage of development, the firm is usually fluid and the timing of fixed asset replacement may be more critical than the assumption that fixed assets must be replaced eventually to keep the firm operating (an important reason for focusing on net rather than gross sources of finance). Thus, the new firm may have purchased fixed assets at the founding of the enterprise and those assets may not have to be replaced for several years. In the meanwhile, the depreciation charges that are made for income statement purposes are sources of funds that may keep the company in business. To be sure, if the firm loses money for several years (retained earnings do not become positive), the firm may not be able to replace its operating assets and it may be forced out of business.

Asset conversions are another important source of gross internal finance. An asset conversion takes place when one form of asset is liquidated to employ cash elsewhere or when an asset is liquidated to repay a liability. Technically, depreciation is an asset conversion in that depreciation charges reduce fixed assets and the funds made available may be used to purchase other assets or reduce liabilities, but every asset is capable of being converted. Thus, accounts receivable may be collected at a faster rate than new receivables are put on the books. The result is an increase in the cash position of the firm and, hence, the firm has a source of funds that may be used to purchase other assets, pay off liabilities, or even finance an operating loss. Inventories may similarly be worked down at a faster rate than they are replenished. The result is a build-up in cash that may be deployed as necessary. The reader is reminded, of course, that under conditions of growth it is more likely that receivables levels and inventories will be *increasing* rather than declining and will be a *use* of finance rather than a source. Over time, the same may be said of fixed assets. The growing enterprise will probably be adding to its fixed asset base at a more rapid rate than fixed assets are depreciated. Thus, depreciation sources may be insufficient and will not be available to finance other needs.

The firm may also elect to employ externally secured funds. This may be necessary if internal funds are insufficient to finance the growth of the business or simply because funds are available at attractive rates and the entrepreneur elects to substitute external finance for internal. Normally, a distinction is drawn between short-term and long-term means of external finance. Short-term sources include supplier credit, bank finance, and commercial finance and factoring arrangements, among other sources. Long-term finance includes issuance of long-term obligations (bonds), incurring long-term debt (borrowing from intermediaries such as banks and insurance companies), leasing, and selling common and preferred shares. Of course, long-term sources are really long-term in the sense that their repayment takes place more than one year in the future. As a source of cash, however, long-term funds are normally deployed within the year the funds are raised, or, at most, within a couple of years.

7.5 Short-Term Finance

A principal source of short-term funds may be the firm's suppliers, including some that are not often considered to be sources. For example, to the extent that employees provide useful services to the enterprise prior to the time at which they are paid, they supply funds to the firm at no cost. In addition, a firm earns profits (hopefully) continuously but must only pay taxes quarterly. Within each quarter, the government becomes a free source of funds. The major form of supplier finance, however, is trade credit. Trade credit is granted when a firm purchases raw materials, merchandise, or other items and is not required to pay prior to or at the time of delivery. For example, a supplier may sell on terms "net/10, EOM." This means that payment for purchases made this month are due by the tenth day of the following month. Thus, the supplier is essentially providing funds for at least 10 and conceivably as long as 40 days. These funds are made available at no specific cost, although it may be argued that the supplier includes its cost of finance in the selling price for its goods and services.

Trade credit may also be granted with a discount. For example, terms of "2/10, net 30" mean that if payment is made within 10 days, the purchaser may take a 2% discount, but if the discount is not taken, payment is due in 30 days in any case. The shrewd entrepreneur will pay within 10 days if other, less expensive sources of finance are available. If the discount is not taken, he will take the full 30 days to pay. To do otherwise would involve foregoing an essentially free source of funds. The cost of not taking the discount can be calculated as follows:

$$\frac{\text{Percentage Discount}}{\text{100\% - Percentage Discount}} \times \frac{365}{\text{Total Period - Discount Period}}$$

In the case of terms "2/10, net 30," the annualized cost of funds would be:

$$\frac{2\%}{98\%} \times \frac{365}{20} = 37.2\%$$

Thus, if an invoice for \$960 were presented, only (0.98)(\$960)= \$940.80 would be due if the invoice were paid in 10 days; but \$960 would be due in 30 days. The savings, \$19.20, is the cost of using \$940.80 for 20 additional days. This period of time may be annualized by dividing it into 365, or 365/20 = 18.25. The cost of funds would therefore be:

$$\frac{\$19.20}{\$940.80} \times 18.25 = (0.0204)(18.25) = 37.2\%$$

Although it is recommended that payment be made by the end of the assigned 30-day period, some firms will elect not to do so. This policy is know as "stretching" payables and is followed by weak, cash-deficient companies at most times and by many businesses during periods of tight money. The costs of such a policy in terms of the deterioration of the firm's credit rating, the reluctance of suppliers to sell again on credit, etc., are difficult to quantify but are very real nevertheless. Whenever possible, it is best to apprise suppliers of the problems causing the delay and of when they may expect payment.

Another major source of funds for businesses is bank credit. This is usually the cheapest external form of short-term finance, and the entrepreneur is advised to pay particular attention to developing banking relationships. Although many firms will wait until the need for financing is imminent before discussing matters with their bankers, good planning procedures suggest that the availability of funds should be ascertained well in advance of need. A well-run business will normally keep some minimum balances in the bank, and this is an important first step toward obtaining a loan. It is also desirable for the entrepreneur to provide his or her banker with periodic financial statements so that the banker has a continuing record of the condition of the business. If these two prerequisites are satisfied, the firm should be able to eventually obtain a *line of credit* which is merely an informal agreement on the part of the bank that, other things being equal, it would be willing to lend the firm up to some given amount at a prescribed interest rate. This rate is normally tied to the *prime rate* (the minimum rate charged to borrowers of the best credit worthiness), such as "prime plus 1%." The borrower may also be required to be out of debt to the bank (or the banking system) for some period during the year to demonstrate his liquidity (the so called "clean-up" provision). Although a line of credit arrangement is useful for the entrepreneur to have, it is not legally binding upon the bank and can be greatly reduced if credit conditions tighten.

If the entrepreneur cannot afford to gamble on having the volume of his borrowings reduced, a more formal credit "revolver" may be arranged. A *revolving credit guarantee* is a binding commitment on the part of the bank to lend up to a given maximum amount at a specified interest charge (usually stated in terms of prime) over a stated period (often a year). As in the case of the line of credit, the bank can extract itself from this commitment if the financial condition of the borrower deteriorates substantially, but it may not dishonor the obligation merely because credit conditions tighten. In return for undertaking the obligation, the bank will require that a fee (often 0.5% per year but sometimes a higher figure) be paid on the unborrowed balance. For example, suppose that ABC Company had a \$100,000 revolving credit arrangement at prime plus 2%, with 0.5% being paid on the unborrowed balance, and average borrowings of \$70,000 over the year. If prime averaged 12% during the period, the total cost of the revolving credit arrangement would be:

$$(\$70,000)(0.14) + (\$30,000)(0.005) = \$9,950$$

Since the average amount borrowed during the year was \$70,000, the cost of finance would be:

$$\$9,950)/\$70,000 = 14.21\%$$

As we suggested earlier, bankers will examine closely the balances of the entrepreneur who is requesting a loan. There is a greater likelihood that a bank will lend to one of its own depositors than to a nondepositor. A factor in this regard is the feeling of responsibility the bank has toward its depositors, but it should not be ignored that banks make their profits by lending and investing funds deposited with them and therefore wish to reward and encourage the loyalty of their depositors. As a rule of thumb, many bankers feel that their depositors have the right in normal times (assuming the depositor has collateral or is otherwise a good credit) to look to them for loans of four to five times the depositor's normal balance. In return, the banker expects a certain portion of a loan (usually 15-20%) to be left on deposit in the form of a *compensating balance*. The size of this balance will rise during tight money periods when the banker has more bargaining power. The compensating balance requirement will raise the effective cost of the loan to the borrower, but it may be possible to keep the balance in the form of an interest-bearing time deposit (thus cutting the cost of these idle funds) or to arrange for a third party to provide the compensating balance for a fee (a procedure referred to as "link financing"). In the above example, if it were expected that the ABC Company would always have on deposit at least 20% of the outstanding borrowed balance on its revolver, the true cost of finance to the company would be:

$$(\$9,950)/(0.8)(\$70,000) = 17.77\%$$

In essence, the company would have the use of only (0.8)(\$70,000) = \$56,000, and it would pay \$9,950 for the funds.

Bank financing to the new enterprise is frequently not available. Banks are not in the venture capital business, and loans to entrepreneurs are usually made on the basis of the borrowing capacity (personal assets and earning power) of the individual rather than his company. In the case of the incorporated new entity, the entrepreneur will usually have to personally guarantee any loans to his company, and the bank will be looking to the entrepreneur for payment in case the business gets into difficulty.

Banks and commercial finance companies are in the business of making short-term loans on the current assets held by smaller enterprises, and it is frequently possible to borrow from 50 to 80% of the face value of receivables and 30 to 60% of the cost of inventories. If the loan is arranged with a bank, the rate charged may be some 2% to 3% over prime, with an additional fee for handling the receivables of 1% to 2%. If the borrowing is from a commercial finance company, the rate may be appreciably higher. Most entrepreneurs prefer to borrow against their receivables on a "non-notification" basis. Under this procedure, the customer represented by the receivable continues to make his payments to the company, and the company forwards them to the lender. This method is preferred because the customer need not be informed that a third party has been brought into the relationship. It is less favored by lenders, however, because they have less control over the money. On a "notification" basis, the customer makes his payment directly to the lender.

It is also possible to sell (or factor) receivables. This method may have the advantage to the company of shifting the responsibility of credit department costs and bad debt losses to a factoring company if the receivables are sold on a non-recourse basis. Under non-recourse factoring, the factor actually purchases the receivables and has no recourse against the company selling the receivables in the event of non-collection. For this service the factor charges a fee (often around 2% of the receivables purchased) which only covers the credit and collection function. The company selling the receivables must still wait until they are collected before it receives any funds. Should the company want its money sooner, it may obtain and advance from the factor at some stated rate of interest. Should the company keep its money on deposit with the factor after the receivables are collected, it may also receive interest.

Computing the cost of factoring receivables involves taking into account the factor fee, the savings in bad debts generated if the factoring is done without recourse, the savings resulting from not having to maintain a credit department, and the interest paid (or earned) on factored accounts. Suppose the ABC Company had credit sales of \$500,000 per year and had an average receivables turnover of 5 times per year (every 73 days). The average receivable balance maintained by ABC would be \$500,000/5 or \$100,000. If a factor would lend ABC up to 80% and charged a fee of 2% on the total volume of receivables factored, the gross cost of factoring would be:

$$(0.02)(\$500,000) + (0.18)(\$80,000) = \$24,400$$

If the company had a typical bad debt write off of 1/2% of sales and would have to spend \$5,000 on credit evaluations and collections, its savings would be:

$$(0.005)(\$500,000) + \$5,000 = \$7,500$$

Thus, the net cost of factoring would be: \$24,400 - \$7,500 = \$16,900, or:

$$\$16,900/\$80,000 = 21.13\%$$

It should be remembered, of course, that factoring without recourse means the factor has the right to approve the credit worthiness of the firm's customers. The factor will naturally take a more conservative posture than the company's marketing department might wish, and the result may be lost sales to customers to whom the company would have sold but of whom the factor would not approve.

A review of the 1999 operating plan for the Jackson Funeral Home (see previous section) reveals that no external funds are actually needed for 1999. The only sources of finance will be internally generated. The planned net profit of \$32,551 together with depreciation flows of \$109,875 will be sufficient to finance the \$5,000 increase in receivables and the \$3,000 increase in inventory. The planned cash balances budget and projected operating and financial ratios are shown in Figures 7.18 and 7.19 below.

Jackson Funeral Home, Inc. Cash Balance Budget Fiscal Year 1999	
Cash balance (beginning year)	$161,758
Sources of cash:	
Operating income	76,502
Depreciation	109,875
Increase in payables	0
Debt incurred	0
Stock sold	0
Uses of Cash:	
Increase in receivables	(5,000)
Increases in inventories	(3,000)
Increase in fixed assests	0
Debt repaid	0
Stock redeemed	0
Interest expense	(30,000)
Income taxes paid	(13,951)
Dividends paid	0
Cash balance (ending)	$296,184

Figure 7.18. A Replanned Cash Balance Budget.

Jackson Funeral Home, Inc. Operating and Financial Ratios Actual 1998 and Budgeted 1997		
	Actual 1998	Budgeted 1999
Net operating margin	.13	.14
Return on total assets	.18	.17
Return on equity	.30	.25
Debt to equity	2.92	2.02
Current ratio	1.40	2.20
Receivables turnover	—	7.29
Average collection period	—	51 days
Inventory turnover	4.20	4.86
Average days in inventory	87 days	75 days

Figure 7.19. Replanned Operating and Financial Ratios.

7.6 Why Grow?

As the entrepreneur reconsiders long range goals and objective after the first year in business, it is wise to reflect on the role that growth should play in the deliberations. There is no law that requires a business to grow. Its sales do not have to advance each year, profits are not required to expand, and margins do not have to improved year-by-year. Indeed, some entrepreneurs do not wish to have their companies grow beyond a certain size because of the managerial (and other) problems that accompany "big business."

On the other hand, it should be remembered that there is a human desire for progress and change. Most of us get bored from doing the same thing year after year, and growth and change do seem to go together. Often it is the case that our most worthy employees are motivated by the stimulation and rewards (financial and otherwise) that accompany a growth situation, and the "brightest and the best" may move on to new associations if they find their current ones to be moribund. Also, there is some truth to the old adage that it may be necessary to grow in order to survive. Without forward momentum, an organization can become lethargic and stagnate in ways other than financial. Thus, it is wise to weigh ones growth strategy carefully.

Growing can be risky. A mistake in a larger entity is usually more expensive than when one is made by a smaller organization, although a larger company may be better able to absorb a mistake than a smaller one. As a firm becomes larger, it may be necessary to bring other partners into the operation. Creditors, bankers, and even other holders of stock may become integral to financing growth. The entrepreneur may lose control of the business eventually as it grows to a complex entity. The entrepreneurial skills that so masterfully got the business off the ground and allowed it to survive may not be so necessary to the complicated managerial organization. It might, in fact, be true that the entrepreneur at some point becomes absolutely detrimental to his or her own business and has to step aside and appoint "professional managers" to run the firm. For many entrepreneurs, this is a stiff price to pay for growth. Alternatively, it may be more enticing to own 15% of a large, publicly-held corporation with stock worth many millions of dollars than to own all of a small business that is illiquid and can, at best, pay its proprietor a good salary.

As the reader may have discovered, this book is not intended to set goals for the entrepreneur, and now is not the time for the authors to begin to do so. A strategy that has been successful for many entrepreneurs, however, is one that adopts a conservative growth posture. That is, the firm is encouraged to grow as conditions, financing, and opportunities permit. Growth for its own sake is avoided as a strategy.

7.7 Simple Growth Calculations

In their most elementary form, growth calculations are merely ratios of two (or more) numbers expressed over a time horizon. Thus, if a company enjoyed sales of $5 million in 1998 and $6 million in 1999, it could be said that the firm had a growth rate in sales of ($6 million - $5 million)/($1 million) or 20% during that one-year period. A convenient formula may be employed to express the growth relationship:

$$G = \frac{X_1 - X_0}{X_0} \tag{7.1}$$

where

G = the growth rate for the period in question
X_1 = the value of the variable at the end of the period in question
X_0= the value of the variable at the beginning of the period in question

The time periods may be years, months, or even days. Longer periods (two years, five years, etc.) can also be considered, and the growth rate may be calculated for variables that are themselves taking place over time (e.g., sales, profits, etc.) or for variables that are recorded at one point in time. For example, we might compare sales from 1998 to 1999 (as in the above illustration) where sales take place *during* 1998 and 1999; or we might consider the volume of inventory as of December 31, 1999 (say $3.5 million) and compute the growth rate over the year (($3.5 million—$2.5 million)/($2.5 million) = 40%).

Growth rates may be determined over periods that have already taken place, but they are also quite useful for planning purposes. Thus, it is often convenient to establish specific objectives that are stated in terms of growth rates rather than absolute numbers. A company may have earned \$100,000 in profits for 1997 and its operating plan may call for profits to grow by 20% during the next year. The planned growth in dollar profits would be (0.20 × \$100,000)= \$20,000 and the absolute value of dollar profits would be [\$100,000 + (0.20 × \$100,000)] = \$120,000. The convenient growth relationship formula determined above may be rewritten to solve for the value of the variable at the end of the period in question:

$$X_1 = X_0(1 + G) \tag{7.2}$$

Thus, one plus the growth rate may be multiplied by the value of the variable at the beginning of the period to get the value at the end of the period. Restating the example X_1=(\$100,000)(1.20)=\$120,000.

Computations beyond the one-period case are somewhat more complicated and require the use of the simpler equation as a foundation. Computations involving more than one period are done on what is called a *compounded* basis. Thus, if a firm had \$100,000 in profits in 1997 and wished to have profits grow by 20% per year for the next five years, the planned profit for 2002 would be:

$$\begin{aligned}
X_{1998} &= (\$100,000)(1.20) = \$120,000 \\
X_{1999} &= (\$120,000)(1.20) = \$144,000 \\
X_{2000} &= (\$144,000)(1.20) = \$172,800 \\
X_{2001} &= (\$172,000)(1.20) = \$207,360 \\
X_{2002} &= (\$207,360)(1.20) = \$248,832
\end{aligned}$$

Notice that all we have done here is iterate the simple growth relationship:

$$X_1 = X_0(1 + G) \tag{7.3}$$

several times. This can become a nuisance, and, fortunately, a much easier procedure is available. This procedure is based on a rearrangement of the simple formula as follows:

$$X_n = X_0(1 + G)^n \tag{7.4}$$

Thus, in the numerical example given above, we could compute the profit objective after the first year as:

$$X_1 = X_0(1 + G)^1 \tag{7.5}$$

$$X_{1998} = (\$100,000)(1+0.20)^1 = (\$100,000)(1.2) = \$120,000$$

and the objective after the second year as:

$$X_2 = X_0(1+G)^2 \tag{7.6}$$

$$X_{1999} = (\$100,000)(1+0.20)^2 = (\$100,000)(1.44) = \$144,000$$

By analogy, the following may be determined:

$$\begin{aligned} X_3 &= X_0(1+G)^3 \\ X_4 &= X_0(1+G)^4 \\ X_5 &= X_0(1+G)^5 \end{aligned}$$

or, in general

$$X_n = X_0(1+G)^n \tag{7.7}$$

For the example above after 5 years, we would find:

$$X_{2002} = (\$100,000)(1+0.20)^5 = (\$100,000)(2.48832) = \$248,832$$

Before the days of cheap hand-held calculators, (7.7) would have been represented by compound interest tables. In these days, of course, we use a calculator to implement (7.7) directly.

7.8 Determinants of Growth and Return on Investment

Each entrepreneur has his or her own reasons for wanting to grow and his or her own strategy for achieving growth. Similarly, each firm has its own peculiar set of growth determinants. No two companies are exactly alike, and the factors that will enable one firm to thrive are not necessarily the same for another—even one in the same general line of business. Nevertheless, there are broad determinants that will be important for many firms. Many of the external variables that were identified in Chapter 5 will be important in determining revenue growth. Overall economic activity, housing starts, consumer expenditures, business investment, interest rates, the rate of inflation, etc., may all be salient factors. Also, key internal variables (identified in

Chapter 5 as well) may be relevant. The firm's marketing strategy, its promotion policies, how it prices its products, and its methods of distribution may be quite significant determinants of the revenue growth pattern.

Many of the factors that influence sales growth trends will also influence profit growth. Indeed, it is usually the case that the most important reason for higher profits is a larger sales volume. Of course, the other side of the profit equation includes costs, and expense control can also contribute to growth in net income. Even with a constant or declining sales volume, profits can increase if cost of goods sold, selling expenses, administrative expenses, and other costs of doing business can be brought down.

Growth in return on investment (ROI) will depend on revenue and profit growth plus the investment required to generate increased sales. As a rule, a firm must acquire assets in order to produce a product or service. The asset investment may be in fixed assets (property, plant, equipment, etc.) but the dollars tied up in current assets should not be ignored. For many enterprises, the investment in receivables, inventories, and even cash itself may be a very significant ROI determinant. Just as revenue growth is usually the most important explanation for profit growth, profit growth is typically the most significant factor in improving ROI. Nevertheless, it is possible for a firm to increase its return on investment even when profits are declining if it can reduce the volume of assets required to generate sales.

For may years, students of finance have employed a simple equation to analyze ROI. This equation identifies the major determinants of investment return and can be useful in demonstrating why returns are increasing or decreasing. The formula is:

$$\text{ROI} = \frac{\text{Operating income}}{\text{Total assets}} = \frac{\text{Sales}}{\text{Total assets}} \times \frac{\text{Operating income}}{\text{Sales}}$$

Thus, return on investment is defined as the ratio of operating income to the assets tied up in the business; but this ratio is really composed of two other ratios: the asset turnover ratio (sales divided by total assets) and the operating margin ratio (operating income divided by sales). Essentially there are two ways to improve ROI. Either the entrepreneur can generate more sales per dollar of assets invested or increase the profit earned per dollar of sales. A detailed analysis of the elements of this formula should play a major role in the firm's profit planning and control function. Summarizing the determinants of sales, profit, and ROI growth:

- Determinants of Sales Growth
    - Economic (overall economic activity, housing starts, consumer expenditures, business investment, interest rates, inflation, etc.)
    - Marketing (promotion, pricing, distribution, etc.)
- Determinants of Profit Growth
    - Sales
    - Costs (COGS, selling expenses, administrative expenses, etc.)
- Determinants of ROI Growth
    - Sales
    - Profits
    - Asset investment

7.9 Financing Long-Term Growth

In Section 7.4, we discussed the major forms of short-term financing. We shall complete the discussion of financing a growth strategy here with a delineation of the major sources of long-term finance.

Term debt consists of loans with a maturity in excess of one year. Such loans are typically made by banks with maturities in the three- to five-year range, insurance companies with maturities in the five- to fifteen-year range, and other intermediaries (such as pension funds) for longer maturities. Term debt will often be secured with the fixed assets of the enterprise and will generally be made available upon the signing of a *loan agreement* that will have positive and negative covenants about the condition of the firm. A positive covenant is one that represents that the firm *will* do certain things—such as maintain a current ratio of 2:1 or better. A negative covenant is one that represents that the company *will not* do other things—such as pay a dividend while the loan is outstanding. Typical covenants include the following:

- Minimum working capital requirements
- Limits on capital expenditures
- Minimum liquidity requirements
- Limits on dividends, officer salaries, and stock repurchases
- Limits on the sale of assets
- Limits on the amount of additional debt that may be incurred
- Provisions preventing other creditors from obtaining senior status regarding asset or income claims
- Requirements for contracts with noncompete clauses for senior management
- Requirements for key man life insurance made out in favor of the lender

Term loans are usually repaid on an "amortized" basis. That is, a certain percentage of the loan is repaid periodically. Often, it is possible to borrow with a larger "balloon" payment due at the maturity of the loan. A typical 5-year loan might thus call for 15% of the loan to be repaid in each of the first four years of the existence of the loan with a balloon for the remaining 40% of maturity.

Although *leasing* is not commonly recognized by entrepreneurs as a source of financing, the accounting community now recognizes it as such. A lease is merely acquiring the use of an asset without having to purchase it. Thus, an automobile might be purchased by means of taking out a term loan for a three-year period. Alternatively, it might be leased over the same span. Instead of paying interest and having depreciation expense, the firm would make lease payments that would cover the cost of capital, depreciation, and a profit factor for the lessor. Many leasing companies make available "lease purchase" contracts whereby the lessee makes lease payments for a certain period of time and then can purchase the asset for its existing market value or some other specified sum. The accounting fraternity now requires that existing lease arrangements be capitalized under certain conditions. This arrangement "discounts" future lease payments at some appropriate interest rate (called a "capitalization rate"), and the resulting figure is added to the balance sheet as both an asset and an offsetting liability.

Bond issues are similar in many respects to term notes but are more formal in nature. The essential difference between the two results from the fact that a term loan is usually negotiated with one lender whereas a bond issue is generally sold to an investment banker who, in turn, distributes it to the investing public. Because there are numerous lenders, it is necessary for them to have a representative. This representative is designated the "trustee" for the issue and is often the trust department of a bank or trust company. In place of the loan agreement, an "indenture" is drawn which specifies the rights and duties of the lenders and borrower. The indenture is negotiated by the borrower and the trustee as representative of the lenders. In the past, it was believed that the most secure type of bond was the mortgage bond. Mortgage bonds have a specific lien against property owned by the firm. It has come to be recognized, however, that interest and principal payments are made from income, not assets, and companies are increasingly able to sell unsecured bonds (debentures) on acceptable terms. subordinated and junior subordinated debentures have even lower income and asset priority than senior debentures and are frequently sold as part of a package which may include equity "kickers" (see below).

Preferred stock is a curious combination of various features of debt and common stock. It is like common stock in that the instrument is called stock and is included in the equity section of the balance sheet. Also, payments to its holders are called dividends and are not deductible for corporate income tax purposes. The payment of preferred dividends is not legally required, and the issue normally has no fixed maturity. On the other hand, preferred stock is like debt in that the dividends usually have a fixed maximum rate.

Preferred shareholders generally have no vote in the election of directors unless a specified number of dividends have been passed. Also, preferred stockholders are entitled to no more than the amount paid into the firm in case of liquidation. Although some entrepreneurs like to use preferred stock as opposed to "diluting" their equity position, it is an expensive form of finance. For a company in the 50% federal and state income tax bracket, debt finance (term debt, leasing, bond issue, etc.) costs only half of the amount actually paid to creditors (the government picks up the other half as a deduction). The full cost of the preferred dividend is borne by the company, however.

Frequently, when the entrepreneur borrows from a long-term lender, he or she will be asked to allow the lender to participate in the growth of the enterprise. This may be accomplished simply by letting the lender purchase some of the firm's common stock, or it may be done by making the debt "convertible." Convertible securities contain the option of being tendered to the company in exchange for its common stock. For example, an insurance company may have purchased \$200,000 of ABC Corp. 12% bonds due in 2010. The bonds may be converted into 50,000 shares of ABC common stock at \$4 per share. The *conversion ratio* indicates the number of shares that would be obtained from converting the bond (if the ABC bonds were \$1,000 par value, each bond would be convertible into 250 shares). The *conversion price* is the par value of the bond divided by the conversion ratio (for the ABC bonds, this would be \$1,000/250=\$4).

Venture capitalists often like to lend to entrepreneurs and get *warrants* as their "kicker." A warrant is a legal instrument that allows its holder the right to purchase stock at a given price. Thus, a venture capitalist may be willing to lend the ABC Corp. \$200,000 but would also require that warrants be attached to purchase 50,000 shares at \$4 per share. This arrangement is not different from the previous one whereby the holder of the convertible security would give up his bond for 50,000 shares. In the case of the warrant, the venture capitalist would have to have his bond repaid (receiving \$200,000) in order to exercise his warrant. Venture capitalists will often ask for warrants to buy stock at nominal prices. Thus, a venture capitalist might be willing to lend \$200,000 but would want the right to buy 50,000 shares at \$0.10 per share. This would allow the venture capitalist to get back its \$200,000 investment as the bond (or note) is repaid and have an equity position for only 50,000 × \$0.10 = \$5,000. The entrepreneur should be careful about offering equity kickers, since potential additional stockholders are obtained in the bargain.

The sale of *common stock* to raise money is the first source of finance obtained by the fledgling corporation. Typically, these funds will be supplied by the entrepreneur, although it may be necessary to allow others to participate if substantial sums need to be raised.

Selling stock to others is like taking partners into any deal. It may be a good idea, and then again it may not. In the first place, if shares are sold to others, the equity of the entrepreneur is diluted. In the second place, minority shareholders can be a nuisance and can even instigate litigation if their rights are not scrupulously guarded. On the other hand, it may not be possible to raise money any other way. Also, some equity partners can be very useful. Venture capitalists, for example, may be far more than just investors and may supply the firm with much needed managerial and financial expertise. Furthermore, the presence of equity capital makes it easier to borrow and thus substantially more money may be raised if stock is made available to others.

As we suggested earlier, the principal source of finance to the firm that has gotten off the ground and is profitable may be the earnings it retains each year. This is the easiest source of finance to tap (assuming the company is making a profit) and requires no formalities (such as loan agreements, bond indentures, warrant agreements, etc.). All that is required to retain earnings is for the board of directors *not* to declare a dividend. It is that easy and that passive. Unless a dividend is declared (and there are few instances where a privately-held company should ever pay a dividend if it is growing and profitable), earnings are automatically retained.

The decision to "go public" is beyond the scope of this book, but it should be noted that the entrepreneur who really wants his firm to grow may have no other choice. Nevertheless, going public is expensive and time consuming. A filing with the Securities and Exchange Commission may be required, and state "blue-sky" laws must be complied with. It may be necessary for the entrepreneur to give away a major part of the firm in order to sell shares to the public, and it is not uncommon for the accounting, legal, and underwriting costs of taking a firm public to absorb 20 to 30% of the proceeds of the offering.

Alternatively, there are few better ways to allow a company to grow rapidly than by going public. In addition, many entrepreneurs have become very wealthy much quicker by having gone public. A public market for your stock improves the liquidity of your personal holdings, establishes a value for the major asset of most entrepreneurs (the stock in their company), and provides more acceptable collateral for borrowing. Furthermore, the entrepreneur may leave his or her heirs in far better condition by bequeathing them stock in a public company than a private one (which might have to be liquidated to pay estate and inheritance taxes), and the sale of some stock while alive may allow the entrepreneur to purchase other assets and thereby diversify a personal portfolio.

Lastly, as we said earlier in this chapter, it may in fact, be more enticing to own 15% of a public corporation worth $100 million than all of a private one worth $1 million! In any event, the decision to go public should not be made lightly. Once you have done it, it is hard to "go private" again. The best counsel and advice should be sought, and the entrepreneur should spend a lot of time analyzing the consequences of this decision.

After having completed his revised strategic plan through 2002, Ben Jackson has summarized where he expects to be in four years. From beginning his firm from scratch a year ago, Ben anticipates having a business doing nearly $1,000,000 in volume by 2002. He intends to make almost $170,000 in operating profits and be generating an ROI of about 50% on his asset investment. Moreover, during the five years that he will have been in business by 2002, he will have paid off *all* of the $300,000 he borrowed in 1997 and have a firm with a net worth of over $500,000. The outside investor who Ben solicited will have gotten $150,000 in debt capital back and will still own 50% of the stock, while Ben will own 50%

In the process of growing through 2002, the Jackson Funeral Home, Inc. will mainly employ internally generated funds. Accounts payable are expected to grow along with the increase in volume, but other sources of finance will be unnecessary. If Ben's plans work out, the business should have several options available to it in 2002. By having paid down all outstanding debt, the debt capacity of the company should be several hundred thousand dollars. Given the growth of the enterprise, outside stockholders could also be attracted to make possible expansion to additional locations. It is even conceivable that the firm could go public and begin an active acquisition program of other funeral homes. Ben could also exercise the purchase option he has on the mortuary property which continues to increase in value and carries favorable owner financing terms with a below market fixed interest rate for a 30-year mortgage. At the very worst, Ben believes his company will be worth at least $1,000,000 by 2002. This represents a multiple of less than seven times pre-tax 2002 income and just over two times book value—a conservative evaluation in Ben's mind. Thus, if Ben's plans are realized, the worst that could happen to him would be that he earned a reasonable salary for five years, parlayed a $50,000 investment into $500,000, and had a great time in the process. The best that could happen—who knows? Ben has already thought about opening a new location or buying out one of his competitors in Wesson. He has even talked to his venture capitalist partner about putting up some more money if things work out!

7.10 Summary and Conclusions

Many businesses fail because the entrepreneur does not engage in the detailed periodic planning and budgeting required to permit the proper evaluation of progress and identification of danger signals before conditions get out of control.

Throughout this book, the authors have stressed the importance of planning as an anticipatory activity. With careful, realistic, and detailed planning the entrepreneur has greater assurance of success in his venture. The sort of financial planning described in this chapter is a key element in the planning and controlling functions of management. By means of the analysis of actual results and trends as compared with projections, the entrepreneur is in a better position to take advantage of opportunities for increasing profits or to take corrective actions if performance is below standard. This procedure also permits the periodic review and updating of planning goals, objectives, strategies, and premises for the enterprise, thus leading to the development of a continuing growth plan.

The reader should reflect upon the Jackson Funeral Home experience as it unfolded: From the beginning, through its first year of operation, to the revised business plan extending to its fifth year of existence, Ben Jackson has been in control of his business rather than the reverse. He has established goals and objectives and adopted policies to achieve them. His detailed financial planning and intimate knowledge of all factors in his budgets are the key elements in his management control and resulting success.

If the entrepreneur starting a new enterprise (or one managing an ongoing company) follows the principles and techniques discussed and illustrated in this book, the chances of being successful are certain to be enhanced substantially.

References

[1] Collins, O., and Moore, G., *The Organization Makers,* New York: Appleton-Century-Crofts, 1970.

[2] Findlay, M., III, and Williams, E.E., *An Integrated Analysis for Managerial Finance*, Englewood Cliffs: Prentice-Hall, Inc., 1970.

[3] Hoad, W.M. and Rosko, P., *Management Factors Contributing to the Success and Failure of New Small Manufacturers*, Ann Arbor: Bureau of Business Research, University of Michigan, 1964.

[4] Liles, P.R., *New Business Ventures and the Entrepreneur*, Homewood, Illinois: Richard D. Irwin, Inc., First Edition, 1974.

[5] Mayer, K.B., and Goldstein, S., *The First Two Years: Problems of Small Firm Growth and Survival*, Washington, D.C.: Small Business Administration, U.S. Government Printing Office, 1961.

[6] McClelland, D., *The Achieving Society*, Princeton: Van Nostrand, 1961.

[7] McGuire, J.W., *Factors Affecting the Growth of Manufacturing Firms.* Seattle: School of Business, University of Washington, March, 1963.

[8] Schumpeter, J.A. *The Theory of Economic Development*, Cambridge, Massachusetts: Harvard University Press, 1934.

[9] Stevenson, H., Roberts, and Grosbeck, *New Business Ventures and the Entrepreneur*, McGraw Irwin, Fourth Edition, 1994.

[10] Williams, E.E. and Manzo, S.E., *Business Planning for the Entrepreneur*, New York: Van Nostrand, 1983.

[11] Williams, E.E. and Thompson, J.R., *The Economics of Production and Productivity: A Modeling Approach*, Austin: Capital Book Company, 1996.

[12] Woodruff, A.M. and Alexander, T.G., *Success and Failure in Small Manufacturing*, Pittsburgh: University of Pittsburgh Press, 1958.

[13] Woodworth, Robert T., et al, *The Entrepreneurial Process and the Role of Accountants, Bankers and Lawyers*, Seattle: School of Business, University of Washington, 1969.

Problems

7.1 Using the methodology suggested in Chapter 4, determine Ben Jackson's return on his investment (see section 7.9) if his business is sold in the year 2002 for $1,000,000.

7.2 Using the methodology suggested in Chapter 4, determine the venture capitalist's return on its investment (see section 7.9) if the business is sold in the year 2002 for $1,000,000 and all other payouts to the venture capitalist are made in a timely manner.

7.3 Recalculate problems 7.1 and 7.2 on an after-tax return basis assuming Ben Jackson pays a 20% capital gains tax and the venture capitalist is a partnership paying flow-through personal taxes of 40% on ordinary income (interest, dividends, etc.) and 20% on capital gains.

7.4 Suppose the venture capital partners that financed Ben Jackson had an objective of earning a 20% after-tax return on their investment. Using the methodology suggested in Chapter 4, determine what ownership share of the business the venture csapital partner would have to have hdad in the Jackson Funeral Home to achieve their objective.

Chapter 8

An Introduction to Forecasting

8.1 Introduction

Prediction is always fraught with some uncertainty, frequently with surprises of monumental proportions. Yet, an entrepreneur will always be confronted with the necessity of making predictions as a matter of coping. Some years ago, one of us was examining short term forecasts of fat cattle prices for a large feedlot company. The company seemed to have acquired an ideal situation for the raising of fat cattle. They purchased calves cheaply and fattened them on milo raised in the Texas Panhandle. The situation was very profitable indeed, and the enterprise seemed to have a lower cost of production than that anywhere else in the world, not excepting Australia. Unfortunately for the company, in 1973 the United States State Department, as a secret tit for tat, allowed the Soviet Union to purchase some millions of tons of wheat at spot prices. Because of the substitutability of wheat, for some uses, by lesser grains, and these grains by lesser ones still, quickly even the price of milo rose dramatically. In a twinkling, the feedlot company saw its cost of production exceed the selling price of its end product. There was nothing wrong with the forecasting procedures, which were quite stable, absent, what amounted to, an event as unexpected as an invasion from Mars. This sort of thing can happen to any entrepreneur: i.e., an event not on the radar screen.

One of the most important tasks of the entrepreneur is also one of the most difficult, namely the ability to predict relevant bits and pieces of the future. We shall look at some of the situations where forecasting is not particularly difficult, others where forecasting is at best a crap shoot. We note how very different extrapolation is from interpolation. If we know that a stock had an average value of 100 for February, 110 for March, 130 for May, and 140 for June, we probably we not be too far wrong to supply for the "missing value" in April, a value of 120. It will be much more problematical to predict, standing at the end of June, what the stock will average in July. We would probably guess that the stock would average around 150, based on the linear growth which seems typical of the stock in recent history. We would be even less confident at predicting an August average of 160 or a September average of 170. Over the short amount of records available, the stock has grown ten points a month, but it would be insanity to assume this will continue indefinitely absent further supplementary information.

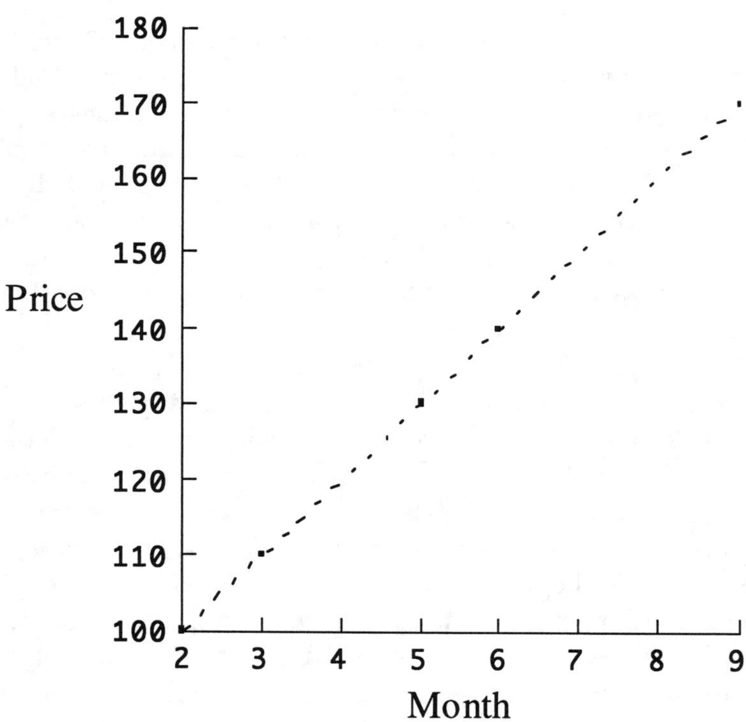

Figure 8.1. Stock Price vs Month.

We have already seen, in Chapter 5, how our case study entrepreneur, Ben Jackson, used some fairly practical devices to do some forecasting of the middle term variety. Anytime we are urged by gurus with computer magic to "bet the store" on something which, after careful analysis, defies common sense, we are generally well advised to pass on the opportunity. One of the best rules that any entrepreneur can follow is that if some prediction cannot be explained in terms of common sense and fundamentals of the market, then we should place no more confidence in it than we would on, say, a long term weather forecast. We can generally expect that daytime temperatures in Houston, Texas, in July will reach into the nineties more days than not. If someone has a clever model to tell us that this year, no temperatures in July will make it past 80 degrees, then we should be very cautious. If we get the supplementary information that a volcano in Mexico has blown up, however, and are told that the circulating ash will depress temperatures in the American south-central and southwestern United States, then, the forecast might be given a bit more weight.

Below, we shall examine a few rather intuitive forecasting procedures in degrees of varying intrinsic uncertainty. Previously in this book, we have examined broad aspects of entrepreneurship and productivity. at the the macro and micro levels. We have observed that there are times when deterministic approaches to problems may be adopted, and there are times when probabilistic or stochastic approaches provide superior insight. One of the most difficult tasks we shall undertake is the prediction of future values of various variables relevant to the production process when prediction is required for the analysis of the problems at hand. There are, of course, situations where a forecast is relatively easy. For example, we can easily determine the value of a fixed rate US Treasury Bill due in 26 weeks. Other variables are much more difficult to determine. For example, the real value of the Treasury Bill will be determined by the rate of inflation over the ensuing 26 weeks; that rate will actually change more or less continuously during the time period; and we do not know how the rate will change. The longer out into the future we try to forecast the inflation rate, the less confidence we will have in our prediction.

When it comes to predicting the future, we shall frequently be driven to empirical models, sometimes models more implied than specific. Below we shall consider a variety of forecasting techniques. It is generally rather clear from the context how much confidence we can place in our forecasts. Those who place their faith in some model for predicting a commodity price two years in the future are generally doomed to disappointment. The nature of business requires us to forecast many variables. Happily, we are seldom required to "bet the store" on our forecasts.

What if we are asked to forecast the value of an index fund (i.e., a mixed bag of stocks chosen to reflect the overall average performance of the market) 20 years into the future? That is a difficult problem indeed and one which no market analyst in the world can undertake with much confidence. On the other hand if a financial analyst is asked to advise an employee whether to invest, over the next 20 years, \$100/week in the index fund or rather invest \$100/week in Treasury Bills, he can be rather confident in advocating the index fund option.

The subject of forecasting is as old as recorded history. We recall how the Patriarch Joseph achieved his important position as Minister of Planning for Pharaoh as a result of predicting that Egypt, and the adjacent territories, would experience seven years of plenty followed by seven years of famine. It is interesting to note that Joseph achieved his promotion, not as a result of the accuracy of his forecast, but rather on the spot, largely as a result of the forecast itself. This is a recurring aspect of forecasting, namely that a forecast is only valuable prospectively. Should Pharaoh have tarried for the full fourteen years to determine the accuracy of the forecast, then it would have been worth relatively little. Happily, Pharaoh accepted the forecast straightaway, to the benefit of Pharaoh, the forecaster, and, most importantly, to the people of the region.

Of course, Joseph had the benefit of divine revelation, an insight which few forecasters can credibly claim. In many other ancient cultures, the mapping of future events was regarded not so much as a special revelation, but as a holistic science. The future was regarded as more or less fixed. If one could only understand the movements of the celestial bodies and their correlations with events on earth, then, since there was an absolutely predictable regularity to the movements of the planets, there was the possibility of reliable predictability of the events which affect the course of human lives. For example, we have abundant evidence that the Mayans spent a large fraction of the product of human industry on the maintenance of a hierarchy of priestly astronomers whose task was simply to predict the inevitable. The Mayans were not alone in this fixation, and we note that even today, billions of dollars are expended annually in some cultures to predict the favorable dates for weddings, new business ventures, etc. So numerous have been the astrologers in some of these societies that the name of astrologer is as common as that of Smith (Schmidt, Kowalski, etc.). For example, "Joshi" (astrologer) is one of the more common Mahratta surnames (and in Bengali "Ghosh" also meaning astrologer). We occasionally see obvious cultural transferals of this tendency into Western societies. The recent cyclical theories of the tenured SMU Professor of Economics, Ravi Batra in his best selling book *The Great Depression of 1990* is one such example. Even absent such cultural transferals, some American investors appear to place mystical faith in this or that financial guru.

A characteristic of the Hellenistic society (which is usually referred to as Western Civilization) is the belief that individuals are not the pawns of some fatalistic kismet but that they can, by human action make a difference in the flow of events. Such a belief in free will should cause a healthy skepticism regarding the predictability of most complex phenomena which involve human beings. It is true that we can predict the position of the moon 2,000 years hence with phenomenal accuracy. However, any prediction as to human exploitation of the resources of the moon is a matter of very unreliable conjecture. Does this mean, then, that no "best guessing" should be attempted? By no means. It simply means that we should carefully assess every attempt at forecasting made by ourselves or others as to how much credence we can reasonably place in the forecast. Our beliefs in the forecast will depend upon many factors. One major factor is the planning horizon of the forecast. For example, we are fairly confident in predicting that the profits of tourism to Mars by the year 2000 will be zero. We should have no great confidence in anyone's prediction as to what this profit will be by the year 2100.

Another factor to be considered in the reliability of a forecast is the process considered. Let us, for example, consider the prediction as to the nominal value of a U.S. Treasury bond paying 5% per year, starting with one unit of capital at time zero. If compounding is carried out annually, then we can easily compute the total principal at the t years as simply

$$P(t) = P(0)[1 + .05]^t \tag{8.1}$$

Should the interest be compounded k times per year, then the principal is given by

$$P(t) = P(0)[1 + \frac{.05}{k}]^{kt} \tag{8.2}$$

Should the interest be continuously compounded, we find in the limit as $k \to \infty$,

$$P(t) = P(0)e^{.05t} , \tag{8.3}$$

If we wish to use an arbitrary interest rate of α , then the principal is given by

$$P(t) = P(0)e^{\alpha t} . \tag{8.4}$$

Forecasts based on compound interest would appear to be completely reliable. Of course, the country might be overthrown or the government could default on its bonds, and it is this fact that still causes so many citizens of other countries to invest a substantial portion of their resources in gold. But, inasmuch as the United States has not defaulted on any of its bonds for well over a hundred years, we might do well to make the assumption that (8.4) will serve our needs. From the standpoint of such well defined systems as compound interest, it might seem that nontrivial forecasting is not required.

This would indeed be the case if there were no inflation. In the Middle Ages, a ruler who denigrated his currency in any way was deemed to have lost his legitimacy. As medieval philosophers reasoned, if currency could arbitrarily lose its value, then money would not be a reliable means of exchange and the country could be driven essentially to a barter system. Furthermore, individuals who had saved money for their families against the eventuality that they would, for reasons of death, sickness or age, lose their ability to earn for them, would have labored in vain. Thus, denigration of currency was tantamount to stealing from widows and orphans, one of the crimes "crying to heaven for vengeance."

This extreme reluctance to inflate the currency is not followed by most modern states. (Interestingly, it is followed by Switzerland and Japan.) Consequently, the value of the principal in constant dollars after a period of time t , assuming an interest rate of α and an inflation rate of i is given by

$$P(t) = P(0)e^{(\alpha - i)t} . \tag{8.5}$$

Now, we see immediately a problem, for although α may be fixed by contract, it is likely that i will vary in time. Consequently, we might more properly write

$$P(t) = P(0)e^{\int_0^t (\alpha - i(\tau))d\tau} . \tag{8.6}$$

But we have simply symbolically assumed away the problem, for the reality is that, in most situations, we will not know $i(t)$. Part of our task in this chapter will be to forecast things like the inflation rate so that we will be able, realistically, to predict the actual value of a fixed interest investment at some time in the future.

8.2 Forecasting in a Monotonically Increasing System

Let us now consider situations in which the system to be forecast is not well understood but has the property of increasing or decreasing in time. In those cases where we have such a series, the use of the human eye can be invaluable in assessing a pattern not understood a priori. The best known exponent of the use of the eye to identify patterns is also the founder of modern time series analysis, John W. Tukey. The technique, named by Tukey, *Exploratory Data Analysis*, is actually a collection of techniques, only a few of which we shall have time to cover in this chapter. (For a more extensive introduction to EDA, see [6, pp. 133-148] or [7].)

Let us attempt to carry out an analysis of the tabulated data below in Table 8.1.

Table 8.1. Increasing Data Set.

t	$Y(t)$
0	3.0000
1	3.6642
2	5.4664
4	6.6766
5	8.1548
6	9.9604
7	12.1656
8	14.8591
9	18.1489
10	22.1672
11	27.0751
12	33.0695

Let us consider the following plot of the data in Table 8.1:

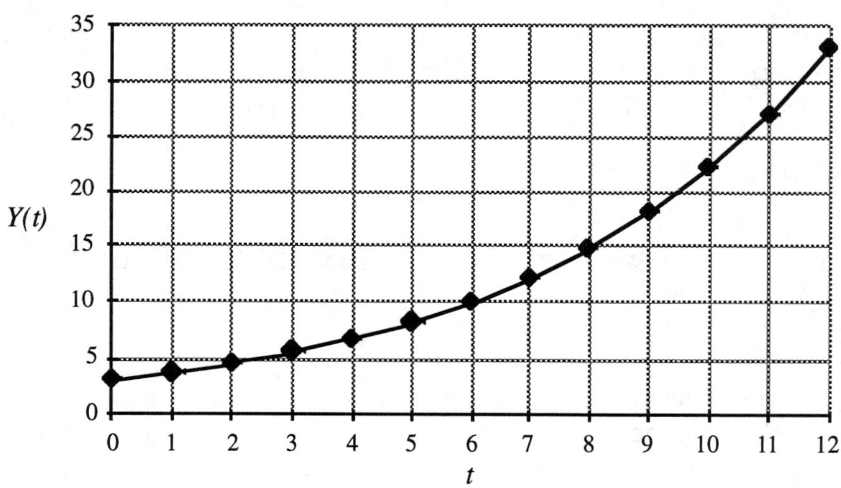

Figure 8.2. Untransformed Data.

We note that there seems to be practically no noise in the system. But the relationship between time t and $Y(t)$ is not immediately apparent. The fact is that the only functional relationship which can be perceived by the human eye is the straight line. Let us address a means of utilizing the ability of the human eye to recognize a straight line. We might suppose that since linear relationships are not all that ubiquitous, the fact that we can recognize straight lines is not particularly useful. Happily, one can frequently reduce monotone relationships to straight lines through transformations. We note that $Y(t)$ appears to be growing very fast. Let us see what happens when we plot $\ln(Y(t))$ versus t as in Figure 8.4.

We note here that we have been fortunate in that our first attempt to transform the data to linearity worked. Since $\ln(Y(t))$ is linear in t, the following must hold

$$\ln(Y(t)) = a + bt\ . \tag{8.7}$$

Exponentiating both sides, we have:

$$Y(t) = e^{a+bt} = e^a e^{bt} = ke^{bt}\ . \tag{8.8}$$

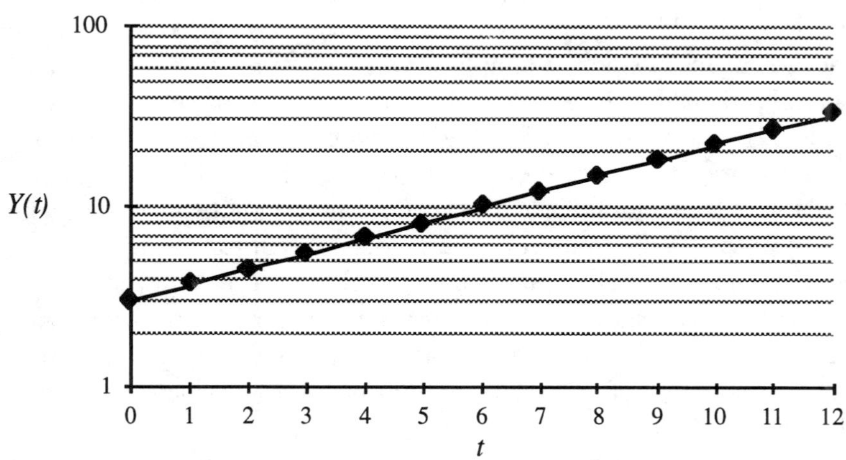

Figure 8.3. Semilogarithmic Plot.

From Table 8.1, it is now a fairly easy matter to solve for k and b. Since the $\ln(Y(t))$ line reveals little in the way of "jiggle" we can use virtually any two points to give the values of these parameters. Generally speaking, when fitting a straight line in this fashion, it is best to pick points near the extremes of the data set. So, using $t =$ 0 and t=12, we have the following two equations in two unknowns

$$\ln(3) = a = \ln(k) \tag{8.9}$$

$$\ln(33.07) = \ln(k) + 12b \tag{8.10}$$

Solving, we obtain immediately the relationship

$$Y = 3e^{.2t} \,. \tag{8.11}$$

How comfortable should we feel in using (8.11) for forecasting purposes? The answer, as with answers to most important questions, is ambiguous. We should feel very much encouraged that the empirical model is so faithful to the data base. We have used a two parameter model to fit a curve through 13 points, and the fitted curve passes virtually through the points. If the fit had been very close with a 10 parameter model, our confidence should be lessened somewhat, when we remember that we can always find an $n+1$ parameter curve which will pass precisely through n points.

In general, we should not feel very confident about any model unless we can understand it theoretically as well as empirically. For example, should we, upon further investigation, discover that the mechanism in question is simply an annuity starting with 3 million dollars and paying interest at the rate of 20% per year, then that would give us a different level of confidence than would Table 8.1. Furthermore, any merely empirical relationship is likely to be believed with more confidence for shorter forecast lead times than with longer ones. We would feel pretty good about leasing equity in a security which had the track record exhibited in Table 8.1 for a period, say, of one year. Unless we understood the security better, our confidence would be much less for a lead, say, of twenty years. Unfortunately, we shall of necessity, more often than we would wish, deal with very empirically perceived models. Now we have transformed the relationship between t and $Y(t)$ to a linear one. By recalling how we transformed the data, we can complete our task of identifying the functional relationship between t and $Y(t)$. So, then, we recall that we started with an unknown functional relationship

$$Y(t) = f(t). \tag{8.12}$$

We will not usually get our transformation to linearity after trying simply a semilog plot (though, as we saw in the case of Ben Jackson's forecast in Chapter 5, one does get lucky, frequently, when dealing with phenomena related to compound growth). Consider another possible functional relationship between Y and t:

$$Y(t) = 3t^{.4} \,. \tag{8.13}$$

Here, simply taking the logarithm of $Y(t)$ will not give a linear plot, since

$$\ln(Y) = \ln(3) + .4\ln(t) \tag{8.14}$$

is not linear in t . But, as we see immediately from (8.22), we would get a straight line if we plotted $\ln(Y)$, not versus t, but versus $\ln(t)$. And, again, as soon as the transformation to linearity has been achieved, we can immediately infer the functional relationship between t and Y and compute the parameters from the linear relationship between $\ln(Y)$ and $\ln(t)$.

From the above we see that simply using semilog and log-log plots will enable us to infer functional relationships of the forms

$$Y = ae^{bt} \tag{8.15}$$

and

$$Y = at^b \ , \tag{8.16}$$

respectively.

The transformation to essential linearity has been in use for over a century in the empirical modeling of complex systems in mechanics and thermodynamics. We shall consider a more general family of transformations than simply the logarithmic. Let us first consider the curves in Figure 8.4.

We note that curve A is growing faster than linearly for t large. Thus, if we wish to investigate transformations which will bring its rate of growth to that of a straight line, we need to use transformations which will reduce its rate of growth.

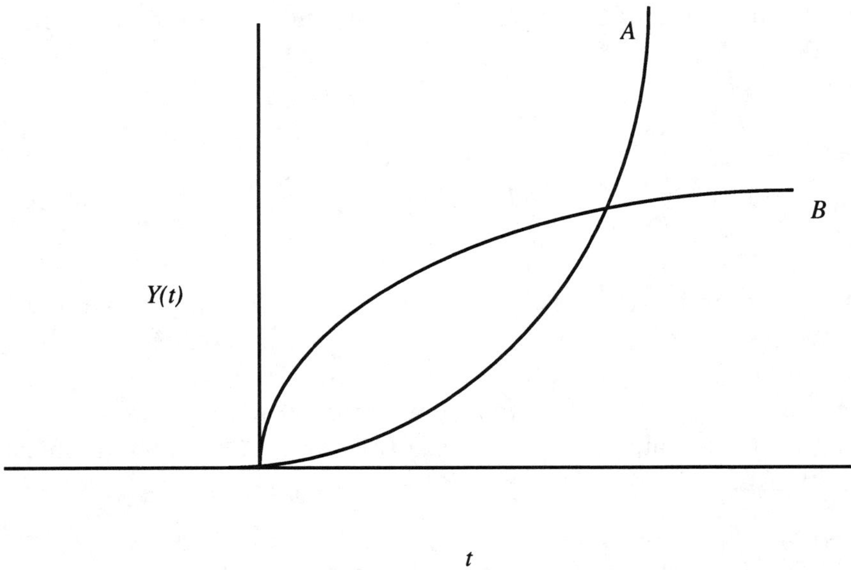

Figure 8.4. Concavities Up and Down.

For example, let us consider the following transformations in increasing order of tendency to reduce the apparent rate of growth:

- $Y^{\frac{1}{2}}$
- $Y^{\frac{1}{4}}$
- $\ln(Y)$
- $\ln(\ln(Y))$.

Considering the curve B which is growing more slowly than linearly, we could try, in decreasing order of severity:

- $\exp(e^Y)$
- $\exp(Y)$
- Y^4
- Y^2 .

The two groups of transformations, pooled together, give us Tukey's [7] *transformational ladder*

- $\exp(e^Y)$
- $\exp(Y)$
- Y^4
- Y^2
- Y
- $Y^{\frac{1}{2}}$
- $Y^{\frac{1}{4}}$
- $\ln(Y)$
- $\ln(\ln(Y))$.

The shape of the original Y curve points us up or down the transformational ladder. Using the transformational ladder to find more complicated functional relationships between Y and t becomes much more difficult. For example, it would require a fair amount of trial and error to infer a relationship such as

$$Y = 10 + 2.13t^{1.5} + 17.3t^2 . \qquad (8.17)$$

Moreover, in practice our data will be contaminated by noise. Nevertheless, for a great many situations, such as that of the forecast of Ben Jackson in Chapter 5, the use of the transformational ladder will bring us quickly to an quick understanding of what is going on.

For more complicated problems, such as, say, the output of (8.25) contaminated by noise, we can still be try to use least squares to go through a complex hierarchy of possible models, fitting the parameters as we go.

$$\text{S}(\text{Model}(\text{in } t)) = \sum (Y(t) - \text{Model})^2 . \qquad (8.18)$$

Such an approach has not, to date, proved very effective. Generally speaking, if the transformational ladder approach works, it does so based on a simple graphing via semi-log and log-log plotting.

We now turn to another of the perception based notions of John Tukey [7]: namely the fact that the eye expects continuity, that adjacent points should be similar. This notion was used by NASA starting with the early Mariner pictures of the surface of the moon. For example, let us suppose we have a noisy monochromatic two dimensional photograph with light intensities measured on a Cartesian grid as shown in Figure 8.5.

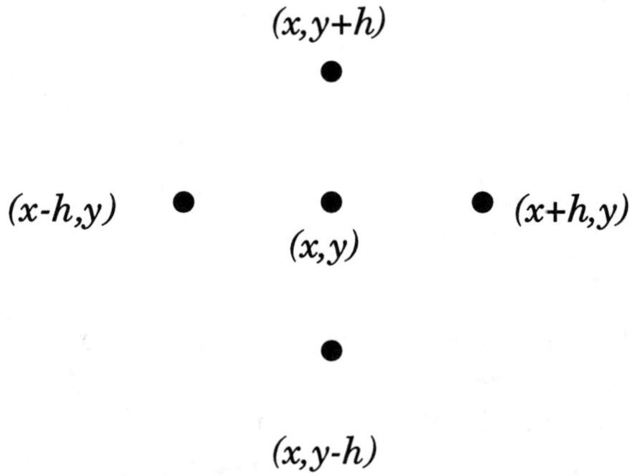

Figure 8.5. Digital Filter.

One procedure, which is both intuitive, and simple is to replace the intensity of reflective light at a point by an average of that intensity with an average of intensities about the point of interest:

$$I(x,y) \leftarrow \frac{4I(x,y) + I(x-h,y) + I(x,y-h) + I(x,y+h) + I(x+h,y)}{8}, \tag{8.19}$$

where $I(x,y)$ is the light intensity at grid point (x,y).

For a one dimensional data set, we have that used by Tukey many years before the Mariner voyages in connection with time series data, namely the Hanning rule

$$I(x) \leftarrow \frac{2I(x) + I(x-h) + I(x+h)}{4}. \tag{8.20}$$

This rule is frustrated whenever one of the points is miswritten or seriously contaminated by "noise". Let us consider below a data set where all of the values really should be "10", but one of the values has been miswritten as "1,000" We show below the data set followed by successive Hanning smooths:

Table 8.2. Repeated Hanning Smooths.		
Data	H	HH
10	10	10
10	10	10
10	10	71.88
10	257.50	257.75
1,000	505.00	381.25
10	257.50	257.75
10	10	71.88
10	10	10
10	10	10

We see that the *outlier* value of 1,000 has effectively contaminated the entire data set. This problem plagued analysts in many areas from space photography to stock market forecasting for many years. Tukey has proposed a smooth based on medians of groups of three down the data set, i.e., we use the rule

$$I(x) \leftarrow Med(I(x-h), I(x), I(x+h)) \ . \qquad (8.21)$$

In our discussion, the endpoints will simply be left unsmoothed. However, somewhat better rules are readily devised. In the data set above, the smoothing by threes approach gives us what one would presumably wish, namely a column of ones.

Happily, Tukey's median filter is readily used by the computer. Unlike the older smoothing devices, such as Hanning, it can be "turned loose" on the data without fear that it will oversmooth. It is a very localized filter, so that typically if we apply it until no further changes occur (this is called the 3R smoother), we will not spread values of points throughout the data set. We note that repeated applications of the Hanning filter will continue to change the values throughout the set until a straight line results. On the other hand, the 3R smoother does tend to move from plateau to plateu, giving artificial flat spots in the smooth. Consequently, it is frequently appropriate to use the 3R filter followed by one application of the Hanning filter (H). The combined use of the 3RH filter generally gets rid of the wild points (3R), and the unnatural plateaus of the 3R are smoothed by the H. Still more elaborate algorithms are, of course, possible. We could, if we believed that two wild points could occur in the same block of three points, simply use a 5R (median of five values) filter. Or, we could use a 7R smooth, etc.

Table 8.3. Various Smooths.

Month	Production	3	3R	3RH
1	50.00	50.00	50.00	50.00
2	52.00	52.00	52.00	52.25
3	56.00	55.00	55.00	54.50
4	55.00	56.00	56.00	56.25
5	58.00	58.00	58.00	58.00
6	60.00	60.00	60.00	61.50
7	65.00	63.00	63.00	62.75
8	63.00	65.00	65.00	64.75
9	66.00	66.00	66.00	66.25
10	68.00	68.00	68.00	68.50
11	73.00	72.00	72.00	70.75
12	72.00	73.00	73.00	74.00
13	78.00	78.00	78.00	76.75
14	81.00	78.00	78.00	78.00
15	76.00	80.00	78.00	77.50
16	80.00	76.00	76.00	76.25
17	75.00	75.00	75.00	75.25
18	73.00	75.00	75.00	74.50
19	75.00	73.00	73.00	73.50
20	73.00	73.00	73.00	72.25
21	70.00	70.00	70.00	71.50

In Table 8.3 we perform a 3RH smooth on a data set of number of monthly burials formed by a funeral home .A graph quickly shows how the 3RH smooth approximates closely what we would do if we smoothed the raw data by eye. At this point, we should mention that all the smooths of EDA are curve fits (and hence purely empirical), not derived models. We clearly find the 3RH smooth a more visually appealing graph than the raw data. But the data was measured precisely; the fluctuations really were there. So, in a sense, we have distorted reality by applying the 3RH smooth. Why have we applied it nevertheless? The human visual system tends to view and store in memory such a record holistically. Whether we smoothed the data or not, our eye would attempt to carry out more or less equivalent operations to those of 3RH. The human eye expects continuity and we do not readily perceive data digitally. The smooth gives us a benchmark (the forest) around which we can attempt to place the trees.

Another advantage of an empirical smooth like the 3RH is that, in a situation where there is a fair amount of noise in a time series, it is better to forecast along a smooth than along the wiggly data. In the funeral data set examined in Figure 8.6, it would probably not be unreasonable simply to draw the arrowed forecast line freehand through the last epoch of the 3RH smooth as shown in Figure 8.7 below.

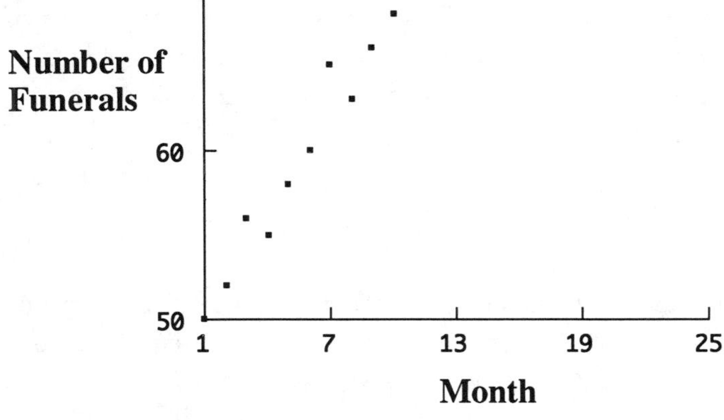

Figure 8.6. Raw Data (number of funerals per month).

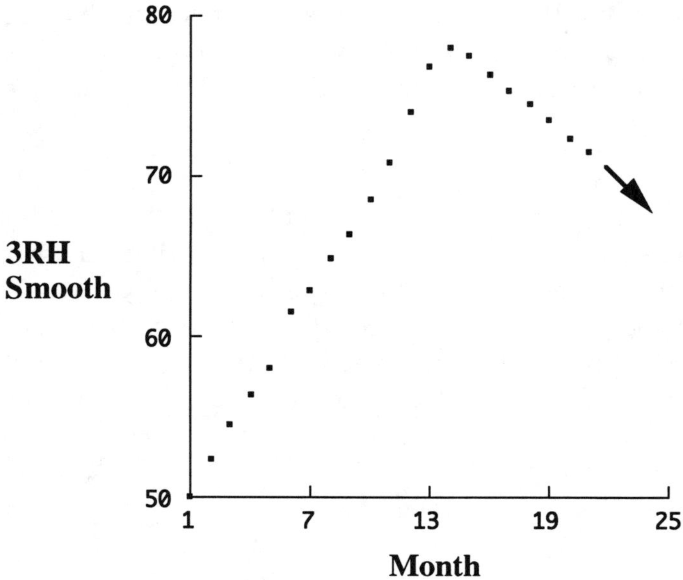

Figure 8.7. Freehand Forecast Based on a 3RH Smooth.

To put much credence in such a forecast past a few days would be ill-advised. Note that we have chosen to make our forecast along a straight line. (In most empirical analyses, it will be preferred to carry out extrapolation forecasts by the use of a straight line.) Now we have admittedly engaged in a very simple tool for obtaining forecasts. We shall shortly examine much more complex techniques for forecasting. However, the reader should be warned that, absent insights into the generation of the process at hand, there is no advantage to using a complex methodology rather than a simple one for the purposes of forecasting. Many an investor has lost his entire investment because he assumed that a bit of forecasting software was reliable simply because it was complex.

8.3 Forecasting as Regression

The subject of linear regression has been one of the most popular techniques for dealing with empirical models. In a forecasting context, the argument can be advanced as follows. Suppose that we believe that Y is a function which is dependent upon time. Then we may write this fact down as shown in equation (8.22) below.

$$Y(t) = f(t). \tag{8.22}$$

Now, assuming that $f(t)$ has derivatives of all orders, we may expand $f(t)$ as a Taylor's series expansion about $t = t_0$ where t_0 is any time origin we select:

$$Y(t) = f(t_0) + (t - t_0)f'(t_0) + \frac{(t - t_0)^2}{2!}f''(t_0) + \dots . \tag{8.23}$$

Now, if we knew $f(t)$ explicitly in functional form, we could carry out the evaluation of each of the derivatives at t_0 . Then, we would have

$$Y(t) = a_0 + a_1 t + a_2 t^2 + \dots . \tag{8.24}$$

This form is called "linear" because it is linear in the coefficients. Now we note the effect of the factorials in the denominators of the terms in (8.24) to give diminishing effects to the higher order terms in $(t - t_0)$ for time series which are not growing at a very fast rate. So we might be tempted to disregard some of the higher order terms in t. Consequently, we might try something like

$$Y(t) = a_0 + a_1 t + \epsilon \tag{8.25}$$

where ϵ represents the error due to truncation of the series.

Now since we typically will not know $f(t)$ or its derivatives, we will have to estimate them from the data. There is no unique method for carrying this out. However, one of the simplest, developed by Karl Friedrich Gauss is that of least squares. According to this procedure, if we have a set of n data points $\{t_i, f(t_i)\}_{i=1}^n$, we select a_0 and a_1 so as to minimize the sum of squares of deviations of $a_0 + a_1 t$ from $Y(t)$. That is, we find the parameters which minimize the sum of squares

$$S(a_0, a_1) = \sum_{i=1}^{n} [Y(t_i) - (a_0 + a_1 t)]^2 . \tag{8.26}$$

To find estimates of the parameters can be accomplished by differentiating S with respect to each and setting the derivatives equal to zero.

$$\frac{\partial S}{\partial a_0} = \sum_{i=1}^{n} [Y(t_i) - \hat{a}_0 - \hat{a}_1 t_i] = 0 \tag{8.27}$$

$$\frac{\partial S}{\partial a_1} = \sum_{i=1}^{n}[t_i(Y(t_i) - \hat{a}_0 - \hat{a}_1 t_i)] = 0 \ . \tag{8.28}$$

This gives the estimates

$$\hat{a}_1 = \frac{\sum_{i=1}^{n} t_i Y(t_i) - \frac{\sum_{i=1}^{n} t_i \sum_{i=1}^{n} Y(t_i)}{n}}{\sum_{i=1}^{n} t_i^2 - \frac{(\sum_{i=1}^{n} t_i)^2}{n}} \tag{8.29}$$

$$\hat{a}_0 = \frac{\sum_{i=1}^{n} Y(t_i)}{n} - \frac{\hat{a}_1 \sum_{i=1}^{n} t_i}{n} \ . \tag{8.30}$$

Here, as elsewhere in our discussion, a"hat" over a parameter indicates an estimate rather than the true value of the parameter. Another popular linear regression model is one which looks upon a stock price, say, as having a linear trend on top of a sinusoidal cycle as in

$$Y(t) = a + bt + c\cos[\frac{2\pi t}{p}] \tag{8.31}$$

where the period p is known.

The coefficients here are computed as above. If p is unknown and must be estimated as part of the least squares algorithm, however, then no simple closed form for a,b,c, and p is available, and we must resort to a nonlinear optimization technique, such the Nelder-Mead algorithm given in the Appendix to the next chapter.

It would be nice if the linear regression approach worked well, for there is no difficulty in finding, in the polynomial model, say, the least squares estimators of the coefficients for all powers of t, up to the n + 1st power (there is no unique solution if we use more coefficients than we have data points). Unfortunately, this is not the case. Linear regression seldom works, although the less scientists understand about the system in question, the more likely they seem to try linear regression. In the case of the forecasting problem, let us examine some possible inadequacies of linear regression. Fitting a straight line through the data of Figure 8.2 would give something like the situation shown in Figure 8.8 below

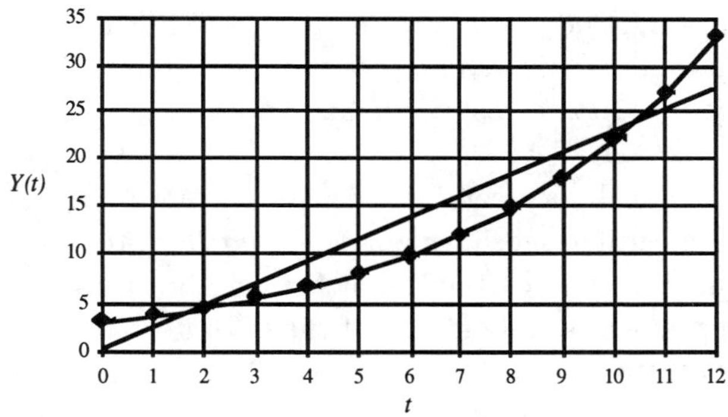

Figure 8.8. Linear Fit.

The fit here, in a smoothly monotonic situation, is not good at all. It would be dangerous to extrapolate along the indicated line. Naturally, in this case, we have been dealing with the growth of an instrument according to the laws of compound interest. If we plotted $\ln(Y(t))$ rather than $Y(t)$ versus t we would obtain an excellent fit, as in Figure 8.3. In econometric situations, growth and decay is more generally expected, at least over short epochs, to be exponential rather than linear in time. So if we insist on using linear regression, we should try it, not only on $Y(t)$, but on $\ln(Y(t))$ as well.

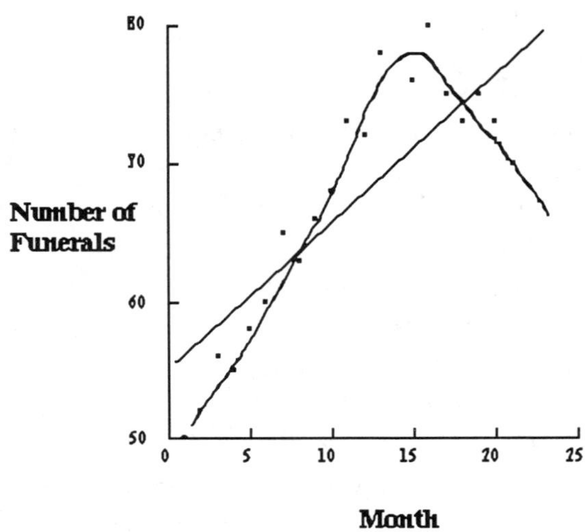

Figure 8.9. Quartic Fit.

A more fundamental objection to regressing the response variable against powers of t is given by observing Figure 8.9. Here we show the result of a fitting a straight line and a polynomial of the fourth degree to the data.

Would we feel very comfortable about forecasting along the continuation of either the linear or the quartic fits? Possibly for very short time horizons, certainly not for long horizons. Well, we could go further and fit a polynomial of the 20th degree which would pass precisely through the data points. Would this give us increased confidence about forecasting into the future? By no means. It is to be remembered that almost every forecasting analysis we pursue should be buttressed by some considerations of stability. At the most basic level, we can investigate stability by perturbing a few of the data points. If the resulting forecast is widely divergent from the forecast using the unperturbed points, then generally speaking, the forecasting strategy is unstable. For high order polynomial strategies in the above example, the results are very unstable. Is there, then, no philosopher's stone which allows us to use mathematical power to give precise predictions of the future? Alas, there is not. But we can do much better than linear regression. A major problem with forecasting is that, properly viewed, the coefficients in equation (8.24) are themselves varying in time, so perhaps we should rewrite (8.32) as

$$Y(t) = a_0(t) + a_1(t)t + a_2(t)t^2 + \ldots . \tag{8.32}$$

Note that in the case of compound interest, the important aspect is that the generating mechanism is not changing in time. Were it not for the time varying aspect of an empirical process, we could indeed try something like polynomial fitting. Once we had figured out what was going on formally, even if we did not understand the process, we could use our polynomial fit to predict the future. As we pointed out early on in this chapter, such *stationarity* in time does not appear to be in the nature of most processes dealt with in business.

In such a world of nondeterminism, what should we do? One very practical attitude might be that we should place more weight on data in the near past than on data in the remote past. Barring catastrophes, i.e., abrupt rather than gradual changes in the generating mechanism, we should expect the market value of a stock tomorrow to be very near to the value today, less so to the value last month, still less so to the value three months ago. It is this notion of smooth rather than abrupt decay in the quality of a time series model which we shall exploit in the next chapter to give us procedures preferred to approaches based on linear regression.

8.4 Forecasts Based on a Brownian Process

Following Hull [5], we introduce the notion of a Brownian Process by giving a construction which might be used to simulate one. First, we divide $[0, T]$ into the k intervals $[0, \frac{T}{k}]$, $[\frac{T}{k}, \frac{2T}{k}]$, ..., $[\frac{(k-1)T}{k}, T]$. Then, let $\{\epsilon_j\}$, be a collection of independent normal random variates with mean 0 and variance 1. We let

$$\begin{aligned} x_1 &= \sqrt{\frac{T}{k}}\epsilon_1 \\ x_2 &= \sqrt{\frac{T}{k}}\epsilon_2 + x_1 \\ \cdots & \quad \cdots \\ x_k &= \sqrt{\frac{T}{k}}\epsilon_k + x_{k-1} \end{aligned} \tag{8.33}$$

A Brownian process is one which gives realizations as constructed above, taking the limit as the number of intervals grows without limit, i.e., as $k \to \infty$.

Starting again from $t = 0$, we generate another random sample of size k:

$$\begin{aligned} x_{k+1} &= \sqrt{\frac{T}{k}}\epsilon_{k+1} \\ x_{k+2} &= \sqrt{\frac{T}{k}}\epsilon_{k+2} + x_{k+1} \\ \cdots & \quad \cdots \\ x_{2k} &= \sqrt{\frac{T}{k}}\epsilon_{2k} + x_{2k-1} \end{aligned} \tag{8.34}$$

A Brownian Process is the collection of all such realizations.

Next, let us consider the difference equation

$$\frac{\Delta X}{X} = r\Delta t \tag{8.35}$$

Letting the time spacing go to zero, gives us simply the law of continuous compound interest

$$X(t) = X(0)e^{rt} . \tag{8.36}$$

Such a model is appropriate for a bank account at fixed rate of interest r.

In the case of a stock, one might suppose that the compounding might work if appropriate modifications were made to account of the variability expected in a free market situation. So, let us consider

$$\frac{\Delta X}{X} = \alpha \Delta t + \sigma \epsilon \sqrt{\Delta t} . \tag{8.37}$$

Here, σ is a measure of the variability of the process as time increases. α is the underlying rate of growth realized if σ were 0. ϵ is a normal variate with mean zero and variance one. In the limit, as Δt goes to zero, such a process is uniquely defined and is commonly referred to as a geometric Brownian process. (Generally speaking, one would expect that α would be greater than r the interest of a "riskless security" such as a bank account).

$$d(\ln X) = \alpha dt + \sigma dz . \tag{8.38}$$

Next, let us suppose we have a continuously differentiable function of two variables $G(x,t)$. Then, taking a Taylor's expansion through terms of the second order, we have

$$\begin{aligned} \Delta G &\approx \frac{\partial G}{\partial x}\Delta x + \frac{\partial G}{\partial t}\Delta t \\ &+ \frac{1}{2}\frac{\partial^2 G}{\partial x^2}(\Delta x)^2 + \frac{1}{2}\frac{\partial^2 G}{\partial t^2}(\Delta t)^2 + \frac{\partial^2 G}{\partial x \partial t}\Delta x \Delta t \end{aligned} \tag{8.39}$$

Next let us consider the **general Ito process**

$$dx = a(x,t)dt + b(x,t)dz \tag{8.40}$$

with discrete version

$$\Delta x = a(x,t)\Delta t + b(x,t)\epsilon\sqrt{\Delta t} \tag{8.41}$$

where z denotes a Brownian process, a and b are deterministic functions of x and t. We note that

$$(\Delta x)^2 = b^2 \epsilon^2 \Delta t + \text{ terms of higher order in } \Delta t . \tag{8.42}$$

Now,

$$Var(\epsilon) = E(\epsilon^2) - [E(\epsilon)]^2 = 1 \ .$$

So, since by assumption $E(\epsilon) = 0$,

$$E(\epsilon^2) = 1 \ .$$

Furthermore, since ϵ is $\mathcal{N}(0,1)$, after a little algebra, we have that $Var(\epsilon^2) = 2$, and $Var(\Delta t\epsilon^2) = 2(\Delta t)^2$. So that, $E(\Delta t\epsilon^2) = (\Delta t)^2$. Thus, if Δt is very small, through terms of order $(\Delta t)^2$, we have that it is equal to its expected value, namely,

$$(\Delta x)^2 = b^2\Delta t \tag{8.43}$$

Substituting (8.49) and (8.51) into (8.47), we have **Ito's Lemma**

$$\Delta G = (\frac{\partial G}{\partial x}a(x,t) + \frac{\partial G}{\partial t} + \frac{1}{2}\frac{\partial^2 G}{\partial x^2}b^2)\Delta t + \frac{\partial G}{\partial x}b\epsilon\sqrt{\Delta t} \tag{8.44}$$

or

$$dG = (\frac{\partial G}{\partial x}a(x,t) + \frac{\partial G}{\partial t} + \frac{1}{2}\frac{\partial^2 G}{\partial x^2}b^2)dt + \frac{\partial G}{\partial x}bdz \tag{8.45}$$

Let us now consider the situation where a stock price follows geometric Brownian motion

$$dS = \mu Sdt + \sigma Sdz \ . \tag{8.46}$$

Now, in Ito's lemma we define $G = \ln S$. Then, we have

$$\frac{\partial G}{\partial S} = \frac{1}{S} \ ; \ \frac{\partial^2 G}{\partial S^2} = -\frac{1}{S^2} \ ; \ \frac{\partial G}{\partial t} = 0 \ .$$

Thus G follows a Wiener process:

$$dG = (\mu - \frac{\sigma^2}{2})dt + \sigma dz \ . \tag{8.47}$$

This tells us simply that if the price of the stock at present is given by $S(0)$, then the value t units in the future will be given by

$$S(t) = S(0)\exp(\mathcal{N}((\mu - \frac{\sigma^2}{2})t, t\sigma^2)) \tag{8.48}$$

where $\mathcal{N}((\mu - \frac{\sigma^2}{2})t, t\sigma^2)$ is a normal random variable with mean $(\mu - \frac{\sigma^2}{2})t$ and variance $t\sigma^2$.

Now, in (8.46), $a = \mu S$ and $b = \sigma S$. Let f be a derivative security,i.e., one which is contingent on S. Then, from Ito's Lemma, we have:

$$df = (\frac{\partial f}{\partial S}\mu S + \frac{\partial f}{\partial t} + \frac{1}{2}\frac{\partial^2 f}{\partial S^2}(\sigma S)^2)dt + \frac{\partial f}{\partial S}\sigma S dz \; . \tag{8.49}$$

Multiplying (8.46) by $\frac{\partial f}{\partial S}$, and isolating $\frac{\partial f}{\partial S}\sigma S dz$ on the left side in both (8.46) and (8.44), we have:

$$\begin{aligned}\frac{\partial f}{\partial S}\sigma S dz &= \frac{\partial f}{\partial S}dS - \frac{\partial f}{\partial S}\mu S dt \\ \frac{\partial f}{\partial S}\sigma S dz &= df - (\frac{\partial f}{\partial S}\mu S + \frac{\partial f}{\partial t} + \frac{1}{2}\frac{\partial^2 f}{\partial S^2}(\sigma S)^2)dt \; .\end{aligned}$$

Setting the two right hand sides equal, we have:

$$df - \frac{\partial f}{\partial S}dS = (\frac{\partial f}{\partial t} + \frac{1}{2}\frac{\partial^2 f}{\partial S^2}(\sigma S)^2)dt \tag{8.50}$$

Let us consider a portfolio which consists of one unit of the derivative security and $-\frac{\partial f}{\partial S}$ units of the stock. The instantaneous value of the portfolio is then

$$\mathcal{P} = f - \frac{\partial f}{\partial S}S \; . \tag{8.51}$$

Over a short interval of time, the change in the value of the portfolio is given by

$$d\mathcal{P} = df - \frac{\partial f}{\partial S}dS = (\frac{\partial f}{\partial t} + \frac{1}{2}\frac{\partial^2 f}{\partial S^2}(\sigma S)^2)dt \tag{8.52}$$

Now since (8.60) has no dz term, the portfolio is riskless during the time interval dt. Thus, the portfolio should pay at the rate r of a risk free security, such as a Treasury short term bill. That means,

$$d\mathcal{P} = r\mathcal{P}dt = r[f - \frac{\partial f}{\partial S}S]dt = (\frac{\partial f}{\partial t} + \frac{1}{2}\frac{\partial^2 f}{\partial S^2}(\sigma S)^2)dt \; . \tag{8.53}$$

Finally, that gives us the Black-Scholes differential equation

$$rf = (rS\frac{\partial f}{\partial S} + \frac{\partial f}{\partial t} + \frac{1}{2}\frac{\partial^2 f}{\partial S^2}(\sigma S)^2) \; . \tag{8.54}$$

It is rather amazing that the Black-Scholes formulation has eliminated both the Wiener term and the stochastic growth factor μ.

Interestingly, however, the *volatility* term σ^2 remains. We note that μ has been replaced by the growth rate r of a riskless security.

Now, a *European call option* is an instrument which gives the owner the right to purchase a share of stock at the *strike price* X t time units from the date of purchase. Naturally, should the stock actually be priced less than X at time T, the bearer will not exercise the option to buy at rate X. Although we get to exercise the option only at time T, we must pay for it today. Hence, we must discount the value of an option by the factor $\exp[-rt]$. Since we have seen that the Black-Scholes equation involves no noise term, it is tempting to conjecture that the fair evaluation of an option to purchase a share of stock at strike price X is given by

$$\begin{aligned} c &= e^{-rt}E[\text{Max}(S(t)-X,0)] \qquad (8.55) \\ &= e^{-rt}\frac{1}{\sqrt{2\pi\sigma^2 t}}\int_{\ln[\frac{X}{S(0)}]}^{\infty}(S(0)e^z - X)\exp[-\frac{1}{2\sigma^2 t}(z-(r-\frac{\sigma^2}{2})t)^2]dz \end{aligned}$$

Many have attacked the Black-Scholes model as overly simplistic. We agree. Models are almost always oversimplifications of reality. The question remains: How should a rational investor determine the real value of an option? Clearly, some forecasting will be required. A retrospective of the options market before the introduction of the Black-Scholes model some twenty years ago, shows that the use of Black-Scholes gave generally better results in evaluating stock options than whatever evaluation procedures were in use at the time. The use of the Black-Scholes model is now rather general as an assist in price evaluations.

We began this chapter by noting that forecasting was a dodgey activity in which we must, willy-nilly, be willing to engage. In the next chapter, we shall explicate one of the most standard empirical forecasting algorithms: the ARIMA technique of Box and Jenkins.

References

[1]Batra, R., *The Great Depression of 1990*, New York: Simon and Schuster, 1987.

[2]Box, G. E.P. and G.M Jenkins, *Time Series Analysis: Forecasting and Control*, San Francisco: Holden-Day, 1976.

[3] Cobb, C.W. and P.H. Douglass, "A Theory of Production," *American Economic Review*, March, 1928, pp. 135-69.

[4] Findlay, M.C. and Williams, E.E., "Financial Theory and political Reality under Fundamental Uncertainty," *Journal of Post Keynesian Economics*, Summer, 1981, pp. 528-44.

[5]Hull, J. C., *Options, Futures, and Other Derivative Securities*, Englewood Cliffs, N.J. : Prentice Hall, 1993

[6] Thompson, J. R., *Empirical Model Building*, New York: John Wiley & Sons, 1989.

[7] Tukey, J. W., *Exploratory Data Analysis*, Reading: Addison- Wesley, 1977.

[8] Williams, E.E. and Thompson, J.R., *The Economics of Production and Productivity: A Modeling Approach*, Austin: Capital Book Company, 1996.

Problems

Problem 8.1 In 1790, Benjamin Franklin invested \$100,000 in a 200 year annuity for the benefit of the University of Pennsylvania. The annuity paid 2.5% interest compounded annually.
(a) Assuming inflation has averaged 1.5% over the total period, find the value of the annuity (in 1790 dollars) when the annuity fell due in 1990.
(b) Compare the value of Franklin's annuity to an alternative strategy he might have used by buying gold in 1790 at the going rate (then) of \$10/ounce to be sold in 1990, assuming gold sold in 1990 for \$400/ounce.

Problem 8.2 Given the following table, infer the functional relationship between X and Y. How sure can you be that you are right? In particular, how comfortable would you be in using your empirical inference to predict the value of Y when $X = 10$? Would you feel more comfortable about inferring what Y is when $X = 5$?

X	Y
.40	.032
1.10	.666
1.91	3.484
4.22	37.576
5.90	102.690
8.10	265.72

Problem 8.3 (a) By means of a sketch supported by an argument, show an hypothetical data plot for which a hanning smooth carried out until the smooth looks satisfactory will be disastrous, but a 3R smooth will work well.
(b) By means of a sketch and an argument show an hypothetical data plot for which a 3R smooth is unsatisfactory but a hanning smooth is satisfactory.
(c) In recording a series of observations–all having magnitude between 1 and 10–a value of 20 is inadvertently and mistakenly added to each of two adjacent values. Neither hanning nor 3R works here. Suggest something which does.
(d) After completing–say–a 3RH3 smooth of stock prices versus time, a market analyst obtains a satisfactorily smoothed graph. However,

before presenting the graph to his boss, he should carry out an additional step to help guard against a false sense of security. Describe this step.

Problem 8.4 In Figures 8.10 we show population figures for the United States.

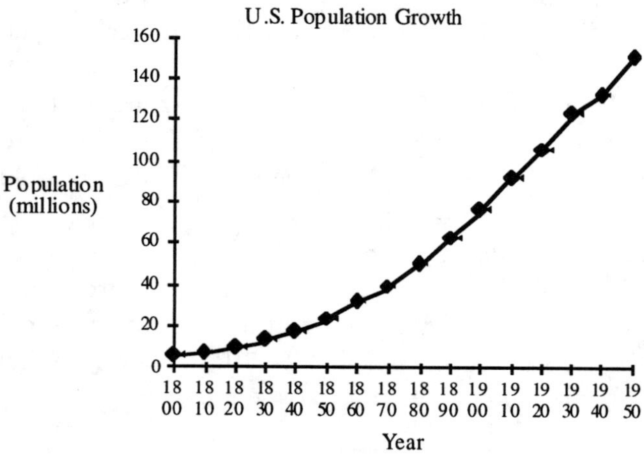

Figure 8.10. USA Population Growth.

Use the data to predict the population of the United States in 1990 (actual value was 248,710,000). Give reasons for the discrepancy of the prediction from reality.

Problem 8.5 The sales division of a mutual fund puts out an advert claiming the average annual return has been 16%. Explain why this may be a misleading figure.

Problem 8.6 Find the Black-Scholes price of a European call option on a non-dividend-paying stock the current price is \$100, the strike price is \$130, the risk-free interest rate is 6% per annum, the volatility is 30% per annum, and the time to maturity is six months.

Chapter 9

Empirical Time Series Modeling

9.1 Introduction

When the **A**uto**R**egressive **I**ntegrated **M**oving **A**verage technique of Box and Jenkins appeared 30 years ago, many received it as a mystical, computer intensive, revelation from Mount Sinai. Some market analysts thought it could be used as an infallible guide for predicting stocks, commodities, whatever. Such illusions were quickly dispelled as some practitioners who "bet the store" on some ARIMA forecast or another managed to lose the store.

As mentioned repeatedly in Chapter 8, forecasting is a task which we approach because it must be addressed, not because we have confidence in any time series modeling strategy yet derived. It is one thing to predict that a mixed bag of American common stocks purchased in regular time intervals will, over some decades, yield over a 7% (above inflation) return. It is quite another to forecast the price of IBM one year from today.

It is no easy task to forecast an aggregate economy one year in the future. Generally, forecasts at the level of a firm, particularly a new firm, are subject to even more uncertainty. Nevertheless, it makes sense in such situations to use reasonable models. The Box-Jenkins ARIMA approach has the advantage of being fairly general with very widely available software for its implementation.

9.2 Simple Exponential Smoothing

A practical option for forecasting in a changing environment is to place heavy reliance on the recent past, less on the remote past. The use of more or less mystical formulas which tend to disregard this rule is by no means a recent innovation. Nearly 100 years ago, the French pioneer in time series analysis, Louis Bachelier, noted that some of his friends from university days had formed a large fund for investing on the Paris stock exchange using such a rule. Bachelier noted that these rules periodically gave sell signals when a stock was on a steady upward climb, and buy signals during a steady decline, as shown in Figure 9.1. No market fundamentals were used to justify this counterintuitive strategy; it was an artifact of mystical and arbitrary formulae.

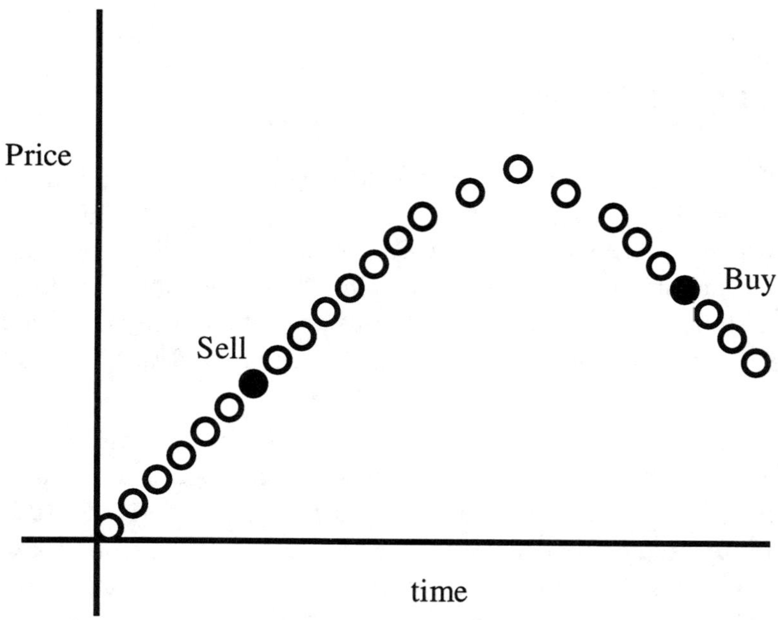

Figure 9.1. Buy-Sell.

When the users of such a mystical formula represent a significant share of the trading in a stock or commodity, then significant market opportunities for the less mystical are made available.

The simple rule suggested by Bachelier was

$$\hat{Y}(t+1) = Y(t) \; . \tag{9.1}$$

This rule says, simply, that tomorrow's market price is best predicted as today's price. Though this rule is not very inspiring, it frequently does better than predictions made by market analysts, econometricians, weather men, and other successors to the shamanistic tradition.

Naturally, we could raise the point that today's market in a particular stock might be somewhat unrepresentative of the overall picture. It would be appropriate to use information going back some days. But we might wish to discount the effect as we go further and further back in time. One such strategy is that of simple *exponential smoothing*. We indicate its use in equation (9.2) (where $0 < \alpha < 1$. Note that we assume that we are standing at time t and trying to forecast forward in time.

$$\begin{aligned}\hat{Y}(t+1) &= \alpha Y(t) + \frac{\alpha}{(1-\alpha)}Y(t-1) + \frac{\alpha}{(1-\alpha)^2}Y(t-2) + \ldots \\ &+ \frac{\alpha}{(1-\alpha)^{t-1}}Y(1) . \end{aligned} \tag{9.2}$$

Now we recall that the sum of a geometric progression

$$1 + r + r^2 + \ldots = \frac{1}{1-r} \text{ , if } 0 \leq r \leq 1 . \tag{9.3}$$

Hence, for t reasonably large, we note that the coefficients in (9.2), very nearly sum to 1. Let us next write down the one step ahead forecast which we would use tomorrow, when we knew $Y(t+1)$.

$$\begin{aligned}\hat{Y}(t+2) &= \alpha Y(t+1) + \frac{\alpha}{(1-\alpha)}Y(t) + \ldots + \frac{\alpha}{(1-\alpha)^{t-1}}Y(2) \\ &= \alpha Y(t+1) + (1-\alpha)\hat{Y}(t) . \end{aligned} \tag{9.4}$$

Thus, one of the advantages of simple exponential smoothing is that as we move forward in time it is very easy to update our forecasts.

One disadvantage of such an approach is that, as presented in unmodified format, exponential smoothing will not be able to predict a constant trend upward or downward in a variable. A series which does not have the same expectation for all values in time is called nonstationary. Practically all of the customary techniques for time series analysis assume that the series is stationary. For example, suppose that the past time records are 5,10, 15, 20, 25, 30, 35, ?. There is no value of α which will give us a predicted value greater than 35, since we are taking a linear combination of values no greater than 35 and the coefficients sum approximately to 1. What can we do to deal with this clear deficiency in the paradigm? At this point, we introduce the difference operator

$$\nabla Y(t) = (1 - B)Y(t) = Y(t) - Y(t-1) . \tag{9.5}$$

Suppose we create the X(t) series defined by

$$X(t) = \nabla Y(t) = Y(t) - Y(t-1) . \tag{9.6}$$

This gives us the $\{X(t)\}$ series 5,5,5,5,5,5,?. Using (9.1), we have

$$\hat{X}(t+1) = 5 . \tag{9.7}$$

But then, our estimate for $Y(t+1)$ becomes

$$\hat{Y}(t+1) = Y(t) + \hat{X}(t+1) = 35 + 5 = 40 . \tag{9.8}$$

In a situation where we believe that the series does not simply fluctuate about a constant average, first differencing may, as in the above case bring us back to a situation where the differenced series does. Notice that if we differenced the differenced series one more time, we would have a sequence of zeroes 0,0,0,0,0,?. Moreover, if the growth were quadratic rather than linear, we could still use exponential smoothing by creating a series based on the second difference

$$\begin{aligned}\hat{X}(t) = \nabla^2 Y(t) = \nabla(\nabla Y(t)) = \nabla(Y(t) - Y(t-1)) \\ = \nabla Y(t) - \nabla Y(t-1) = Y(t) - Y(t-1) - [Y(t-1) - Y(t-2)] \\ = Y(t) - 2Y(t-1) + Y(t-2) = (1-B)^2 Y(t) .\end{aligned} \tag{9.9}$$

In general, little harm, and much good can be done by differencing a time series once or twice. Notice, however, that over the very long haul, if the series fluctuates exponentially, no amount of differencing will reduce the series to one with more or less constant average. All too frequently, we deal with a time series, when we really should be dealing with the logarithm of the series. However, for short forecast leads, failure to take logarithms will not cause much harm.

One issue yet to be addressed is the selection of the weighting coefficient α . This can easily be done, by using the value which minimizes

$$S(\alpha) = \sum_{i=2}^{n}(X(i) - \sum_{j=1}^{i-1} \alpha(1-\alpha)^{j-1}X(i-j))^2 . \qquad (9.10)$$

Since the minimization involves only one scalar parameter, even random search can be used. Or the secant approach can be used. But we should not develop a false sense of confidence simply because we can find α . Remember that exponential smoothing, just as with all the forecasting techniques we shall consider, is simply an empirical device, not reality.

9.3 Autoregressive (AR) Modeling

In the case of exponential smoothing, we had (after we had differenced the series to something approaching local stationarity) only one design parameter to pick, α . Each of the coefficients in (9.2) is determined once α is fixed. Clearly we can gain more generality by allowing more flexibility for these coefficients. One natural way of carrying this out is to use an autoregressive model. The form that we use resembles very closely the regression equation in (8.24), but has the important difference that instead of regressing $X(t)$ on time, we shall regress it on past values. In writing down the autoregressive model, we shall incorporate a useful fiction: the "reduction to white noise." We shall assume that the $\{X(t)\}$ series is the result of an original series having been differenced to approximate stationarity and roughly zero averages.

$$X(t) + \alpha_1 X(t-1) + \alpha_2 X(t-2) + \ldots + \alpha_p X(t-p) = \epsilon(t) \quad (9.11)$$

where $E(\epsilon(t)) = 0$ for all t and $E(\epsilon(t)\epsilon(s)) = \sigma^2$ if $t = s$, 0 otherwise. The autoregressive model, then, can be constructively generated according to the following procedure if we know the p coefficients and the variance σ^2. Let us generate $\epsilon(1)$ from a normal distribution with mean 0 and variance σ^2. Then let

$$X(1) = \epsilon(1) . \qquad (9.12)$$

Next, we generate $\epsilon(2)$ from $N(0, \sigma^2)$ and form

$$X(2) = -\alpha_1 X(1) + \epsilon(2) \ . \tag{9.13}$$

Then we generate $\epsilon(3)$ and form

$$X(3) = -\alpha_1 X(2) - \alpha_1 X(1) + \epsilon(3) \ . \tag{9.14}$$

We continue until we can generate the $X(t)$ with the full p lags. Then we generate many more to allow the start-up transients to die out.

The generation of an AR(p) process, then, is quite easy. But we are going to advocate such models for the description of economic time series. Do we believe that such a generation process actually describes the way the real world series was formed? Certainly not. However, the autoregressive framework is very frequently useful for forecasting purposes. Let us first of all suppose that we really had an AR(p) process and that we knew the p coefficients $\{\alpha_i\}$. If we have a record of $X(t), X(t-1), ..., X(1)$ and wish to forecast $X(t+k)$, how shall we proceed? First, we obtain the estimate for $X(t+1)$ via:

$$\begin{aligned}
\hat{X}(t+1) &= E[X(t+1)] \\
&= -[\alpha_1 X(t) + \alpha_2 X(t-1) + \ldots + \alpha_p X(t-p)] + E(\epsilon_p) \\
&= -[\alpha_1 X(t) + \alpha_2 X(t-1) + \ldots + \alpha_p X(t-p)] \ . \quad (9.15)
\end{aligned}$$

Then, we proceed to the prediction of $X(t+2)$, using in (9.11), our predictor for $X(t+1)$ from (9.15):

$$\begin{aligned}
\hat{X}(t+2) &= E[X(t+2)] \quad (9.16) \\
&= -[\alpha_1 \hat{X}(t+1) + \alpha_2 X(t) + \ldots + \alpha_p X(t+1-p)] \ .
\end{aligned}$$

We continue in this fashion, using (9.11), recalling that the expectations of the white noise $\{\epsilon(t)\}$ terms is zero, and replacing values of $X(t+j)$ by their expectations, obtained in earlier applications of (9.11).

Now that we know how to obtain forecasts, if we know the $\{\alpha_i\}$, it is time to discuss data based procedures for estimating the $\{\alpha_i\}$. The algorithm we discuss below has the advantage of simplicity. (As with other algorithms discussed in this chapter, the reader need never actually have to carry out the computations, since quality software is readily available.)

Let us take (9.11) and multiply by $X(t-j)$, where $1 \le j \le p$. This gives:

$$X(t-j)X(t)+\alpha_1 X(t-j)X(t-1)+\ldots+\alpha_p X(t-j)X(t-p) = X(t-j)\epsilon(t) \; , \tag{9.17}$$

where $0 \le j \le p$. Taking expectations, since $\epsilon(t)$ is independent of $X(t-j)$ for $j > 0$, we have:

$$R(j) + \alpha_1 R(j-1) + \ldots + \alpha_k R(j-p) = 0 \; , \tag{9.18}$$

where $R(j) = E[X(s)X(s+j)]$, for all s.

Writing down (9.18) in extenso for $j = 1, 2, \ldots, p$, we have the Yule-Walker equations:

$$\begin{aligned} R(1) + \alpha_1 R(0) + \alpha_2 R(1) + \ldots + \alpha_k R(p-1) &= 0 \\ R(2) + \alpha_1 R(1) + \alpha_2 R(0) + \ldots + \alpha_k R(p-2) &= 0 \\ \ldots\ldots\ldots\ldots\ldots\ldots\ldots\ldots\ldots &= 0 \quad (9.19) \\ R(p) + \alpha_1 R(p-1) + \alpha_2 R(p-2) + \ldots + \alpha_k R(0) &= 0 \; . \end{aligned}$$

The values of $R(j)$ can be estimated from the data via

$$\hat{R}(j) = \frac{1}{n-j} \sum_{i=1}^{n-j} X(i)X(i+j) \; , \tag{9.20}$$

where $n >> p$ is the length of the time series.

The $R(j)$ is called the autocovariance function of the time series. It can be shown that if the roots of the equation

$$1 - \alpha_1 B - \alpha_2 B^2 - \ldots - \alpha_p B^p = 0 \; , \tag{9.21}$$

lie outside the unit circle, then the series is *first order stationary*, i.e., $E(X(t)) = \mu$, a constant for all t. Again such involved complex variable arithmetic need not be done by hand. Such packages as *TIMESLAB* automatically check for first order stationarity. It can also be shown that in the case of an AR(p) process, the series is *second order stationary*, i.e.,

$$E[(X(t)-\mu)(X(t+j)-\mu)] = E[(X(t-j)-\mu)(X(t)-\mu)] = R(j) \; , \tag{9.22}$$

for all t and j.

9.4 Moving Average (MA) Modeling

Although the autoregressive format for modeling economic time series is generally more intuitive, we need briefly to consider an alternative format. We can write (9.11) as

$$(1 + B\alpha_1 + B^2\alpha_2 + \ldots + B^p\alpha_p)X(t) = \epsilon(t) \; , \tag{9.23}$$

where $B^j X(t) = X(t-j)$. Now, assuming, as always, that the coefficients satisfy the conditions for stationarity, we will be able to treat the operator B as an algebraic quantity and carry out long division as indicated below

$$\begin{array}{r|l} & 1-\alpha_1 B - (\alpha_2+\alpha_1^2)B^2 - \ldots \\ \hline 1+\alpha_1 B+\alpha_2 B^2 + \ldots + \alpha_p B^p & 1 \\ & 1+\alpha_1 B+\alpha_2 B^2 + \ldots + \alpha_p B^p \\ & \text{-------------------} \\ & -\alpha_1 B - \alpha_2 B^2 - \ldots - \alpha_p B^p \\ & -\alpha_1 B - \alpha_1^2 B^2 - \ldots - \alpha_1\alpha_p B^p \end{array}$$

Thus, we could express (9.21) as

$$X(t) = \epsilon(t) - \alpha_1\epsilon(t-1) - (\alpha_2+\alpha_1^2)\epsilon(t-2) - (\alpha_3+2\alpha_1\alpha_2+\alpha_1^3)\epsilon(t-3) + \ldots \; . \tag{9.24}$$

One might well ask why one would ever choose to do any such thing, for we note that even if there is only one autoregressive coefficient, the representation in (9.24) would require an infinite number of terms. The infinite series in (9.24) is called the "transfer function" or "random shock" or "infinite moving average" form and is frequently written as

$$X(t) = (1 + \sum_{i=1}^{\infty} \psi_i B^i)\epsilon(t) \; . \tag{9.25}$$

Let us ask the question what would happen if we had a model where, in fact all but the first few ψ values were zero. Then we would have a model like

$$X(t) = (1 + \beta_1 B + \beta_2 B^2 + \ldots + \beta_q B^q)\epsilon(t) \; . \tag{9.26}$$

Then, if we insisted on expressing the model in autoregressive form, we note that by symmetry, the same sort of argument used in (9.24) would require us to write down a series with an infinite number of terms:

$$(1-\beta_1 B-(\beta_2+\beta_1^2)B^2-(\beta_3+2\beta_2\beta_1+\beta_1^3)B^3-\ldots)X(t) = \epsilon(t)\ . \quad (9.27)$$

It can be shown that the condition that the series be "inverted" to infinite autoregressive stationary (and hence not "blow up") is that the roots of the equation

$$1 + \beta_1 B + \beta_2 B^2 + \ldots + \beta_q B^q = 0 \quad (9.28)$$

lie outside the unit circle. The infinite autoregressive model is frequently referred to as the "inverted form" and is written as

$$(1 + \pi_1 B + \pi_2 B^2 + \ldots)X(t) = \epsilon(t)\ . \quad (9.29)$$

Because of the relatively more intuitive form of the autoregressive model, many workers who are dealing with a pure moving average model as in (9.26), use the inverted form in (9.29) for forecasting purposes. For estimation purposes, however, since (9.29) involves an infinite number of coefficients, it is easier to estimate from the form (9.26) and then use the estimated coefficients in (9.27) for forecasting. As we shall see, shortly, there are times when we will find it convenient to use the transfer function form and others when we will use the inverted form.

9.5 Autoregressive Moving Average ARMA Modeling

In some cases, the autoregressive (AR) model is clearly more natural. In others, the moving average (MA) is preferred. It was the suggestion of George Box and Gwilym Jenkins that much could be gained by creating a model which was a combination of the two types of models as in (9.30).

$$\begin{aligned}(1 + \alpha_1 B + \alpha_2 B^2 + \ldots + \alpha_p B^p)X(t) &= \\ (1 + \beta_1 B + \beta_2 B^2 + \ldots + \beta_q B^q)\epsilon(t)\ . & \quad (9.30)\end{aligned}$$

Such an approach would appear to guard both against those situations where the AR approach is natural and those where the MA is natural. Inasmuch as the $X(t)$ process must frequently be differenced once or twice to obtain stationarity, we might go still further to the autoregressive integrated (i.e., differenced) moving average model, the so-called ARIMA(p, d, q) where we have taken a $Y(t)$ process and reduced it to a stationary $X(t) = (1 - B)^d Y(t)$ process via as shown in (7.2).

$$\begin{aligned}(1 + \alpha_1 B + \alpha_2 B^2 + \ldots + \alpha_p B^p)(1 - B)^d X(t) &= \\ (1 + \beta_1 B + \beta_2 B^2 + \ldots + \beta_q B^q)\epsilon(t)\,. & \qquad (9.31)\end{aligned}$$

Unfortunately, all too many enthusiasts for ARIMA modeling labor under the impression that a model of such generality covers all possibilities. This is simply not the case. Very few time series fit precisely the ARIMA framework. Practically everything reasonable people do in time series analysis is strongly based on heuristics. The ARIMA framework has the advantage of being relatively simple. But we must approach any conclusions reached by its use, as with any other time series methodology, with a healthy skepticism.

We will find it useful to use the flexibility of the ARMA mechanism to use the formulation most profitable for the particular application at hand. For example, suppose we wish to look at the optimal weights for a forecast l units in the future using the random shock (or transfer function) form of the model.

$$\hat{X}(t) = \psi_l^* \epsilon(t) + \psi_{l+1}^* \epsilon(t-1) + \psi_{l+2}^* \epsilon(t-2) + \ldots \qquad (9.32)$$

One reasonable way of picking the ψ^* weights is to minimize the average (expected) squared deviation of predicted values from the actual values via

$$E[X(t+l) - \hat{X}_t(l)]^2 = \qquad (9.33)$$

$$\begin{aligned}E[\epsilon(t+l) + \psi_1\epsilon(t+l-1) + \ldots + \psi_{l-1}\epsilon(t+1) \\ + \sum_{j=0}^{\infty}(\psi_{l+j} - \psi_{l+j}^*)\epsilon(t-j)]^2 \\ = (1 + \psi_1^2 + \ldots + \psi_{l-1}^2)\sigma^2 \\ + \sum_{j=0}^{\infty}(\psi_{l+j} - \psi_{l+j}^*)^2\sigma^2\,.\end{aligned}$$

Thus, the best we can do in our selection of the ψ^*_{l+j} is to let them be equal to the ψ_{l+j} . We have then

$$\begin{aligned} X(t+l) &= (\epsilon(t+l) + \psi_1\epsilon(t+l-1) + \ldots + \psi_{l-1}\epsilon(t+l) + \\ &\quad (\psi_l\epsilon(t) + \psi_{l+1}\epsilon(t-1) + \ldots) \\ &= e_t(l) + \hat{X}(l) \ . \end{aligned} \tag{9.34}$$

where $e_t(l)$ is the error of the forecast at lead time l. Naturally, since we have assumed the ϵ terms are white noise, their expectation, standing at t is 0. So then, standing at time t, the conditional expectation of $X(t+l)$ is the forecast, i.e.,

$$\hat{X}(l) = E_t[X(t+l)] = \psi_1\epsilon(t) + \psi_1\epsilon(t) + \psi_{1+1}\epsilon(t-1) + \ldots \ . \tag{9.35}$$

Now the random shocks form is very convenient means for obtaining the variability of the forecast, since

$$\begin{aligned} Var[e_t(l)] &= E[\epsilon(t+l) + \psi_1\epsilon(t+l-1) + \ldots + \psi_{l-1}\epsilon(t+1)]^2 \\ &= (1 + \psi_1^2 + \ldots + \psi_{l-1}^2)\sigma^2 \ . \end{aligned} \tag{9.36}$$

Thus, standing at time t, we can obtain an approximate 95% confidence interval for the actual value of $X(t+l)$ via

$$\hat{X}_t(l) - 2\sqrt{Var(e_t(l))} \leq X(t+1) \leq \hat{X}_t(l) + 2\sqrt{Var(e_t(l))} \ . \tag{9.37}$$

And we note from (7.7) a ready means for estimating the variance σ^2 of the underlying white noise process, via

$$\hat{\sigma}^2 = \frac{1}{n}\sum_{j=0}^{n}(\hat{X}_t(1) - X(t+1))^2 \ . \tag{9.38}$$

The random shocks form of the ARMA model, as we have seen, provides a very convenient for looking at theoretical considerations of variability. When it comes to the actual forecasting process, however, many will prefer the inverted (infinite autoregressive) form of the model. Looking back to (9.16), we see that the l step ahead forecast standing at time t is given by

$$\begin{aligned} \hat{X}_t(l) &= -\pi_1\hat{X}_t(l-1) - \pi_2\hat{X}_t(l-2) - \ldots - -\pi_{l-1}\hat{X}_t(1) \\ &\quad -\pi_l X(t) - \pi_{l+1}X(t-1) - \pi_{l+2}X(t-2) - \ldots \end{aligned} \tag{9.39}$$

It is clear that the computational details in ARMA modelling would be painful if carried out by hand. Happily, this is not necessary. The time series routines discussed in this chapter have all been available in the IMSL library for 20 years, and this library is available in UNIX, DOS, and MacIntosh formats. ARIMA modeling is fully supported by such software packages as Minitab, SAS, SPSS, SYSTAT.

9.6 Seasonal Effects

We have already observed the fact that many time series have trends and cannot be considered to be stationary (i.e., have constant average) until they have been appropriately differenced. Another phenomenon which is of very practical interest is that of seasonality (i.e., cyclicity). Let us consider the following data set:

Table 9.1. Reduction to Stationarity.

t	$Y(t)$	$(1-B^4)Y(t)$	$(1-B)(1-B^4)Y(t)$
1	1		
2	4		
3	7		
4	6		
5	5	4	
6	8	4	0
7	11	4	0
8	10	4	0
9	9	4	0
10	12	4	0
11	15	4	0
12	14	4	0
13	13	4	0
14	16	4	0
15	19	4	0
16	18	4	0
17	17	4	0
18	20	4	0
19	23	4	0
20	22	4	0
21	21	4	0
22	24	4	0
23	27	4	0
24	26	4	0
25	25	4	0

As is frequently the case, the plotting of the data will give us insights not readily available in the table. We show such a plot in Figure 9.2.

From the graph, it would appear that a cyclical pattern of period 4 is occurring. We can try to capture this fact by taking the difference between every five points in Table 9.2 as indicated. We note immediately the linear trend remaining in the series so differenced. One difference of adjacent points reduces the series to stationarity, i.e., one with constant average. One more differencing reduces the series to zero averages.

It is not difficult at all to note that the above series is deterministic and is simply t added to the repeating sequence: 0,2,4,2,0,2,4,2,0.

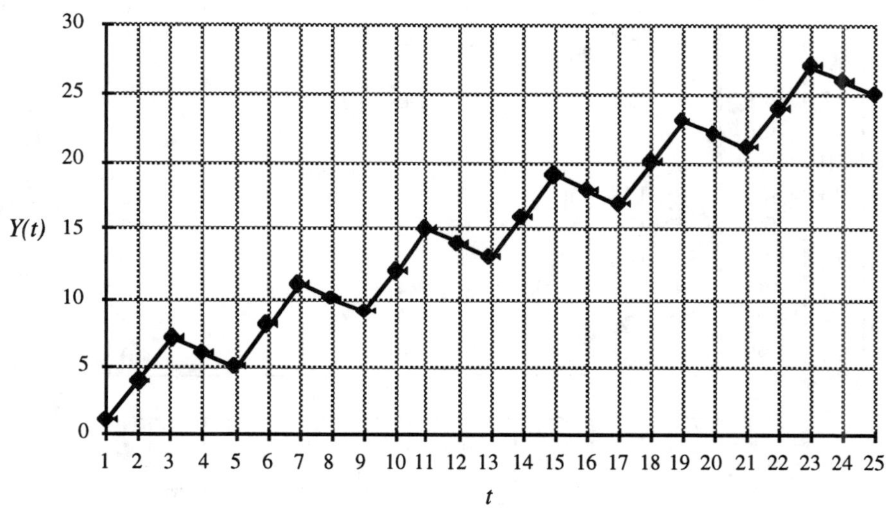

Figure 9.2. Cyclical Series with Linear Trend.

There is more difficulty when the series, as is almost always the case, has a component of noise. One reasonable procedure to try in such a case might be to try difference values at lag 2,3,4,..., until we had eliminated anything appearing like a cycle. There is a problem doing this with the naked eye, since it may be difficult to pick the cycle out of the noise or out of the trend. Consider the data in Table 9.2 below.

Table 9.2. Complex Reduction to Stationarity.				
t	$Y(t)$	$(1-B^5)Y(t)$	$(1-B)(1-B^5)Y(t)$	$(1-B)^2(1-B^5)Y(t)$
1	1			
2	6			
3	13			
4	18			
5	25	24	8	0
6	38	32	8	0
7	53	40	8	0
8	66	48	8	0
9	81	56	8	0
10	102	64	8	0
11	125	72	8	0
12	146	80	8	0
13	169	88	8	0
14	198	96	8	0
15	229	104	8	0
16	258	112	8	0
17	289	120	8	0
18	326	128	8	0
19	365	136	8	0
20	402	144	8	0
21	441	152	8	0
22	486	160	8	0
23	531	168	8	0
24	578	176	8	0
25	627	184	8	0

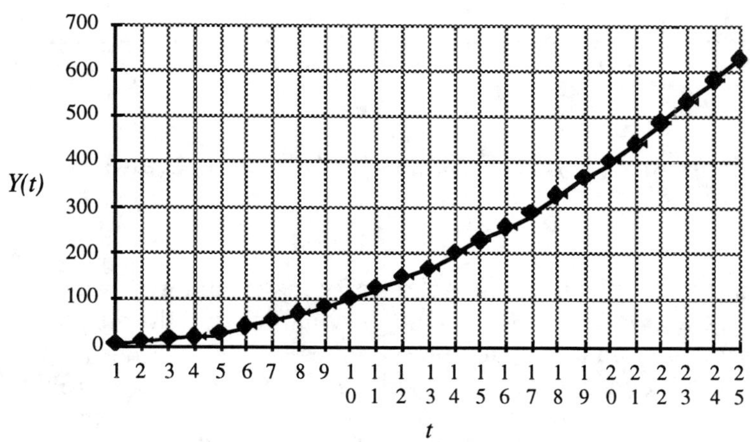

Figure 9.3.Seasonal Series with Quadratic Trend.

A simple graphing of the raw data gives us little insight as we note in Figure 9.3. By making the appropriate differencing transformations to the data, we note that the series is simply t^2 added to the 0,2,4,2,0,... sequence. Even though the series here has no noise, the periodic component is difficult to see with the naked eye, being overwhelmed by the quadratic trend. We would be able better to see what is going on by carrying out the $(1 - B)$ difference first.

Happily, there is a procedure which gives us a plot from which cycles are generally easy to pick up by inspection, from the raw data. Let us suppose we have a time series X(t) given at $t = 0, 1, 2, ..., N = 2q + 1$. We shall evaluate

$$a_0 = \frac{1}{N}\sum_{t=1}^{N} X(t) \tag{9.40}$$

$$a_i = \frac{2}{N}\sum_{t=1}^{N} X(t)\cos(\frac{2\pi i t}{N})$$

$$b_i = \frac{2}{N}\sum_{t=1}^{N} X(t)\sin(\frac{2\pi i t}{N}) .$$

The periodogram consists of the q values

$$I(\frac{i}{N}) = \frac{N}{2}(a_i^2 + b_i^2); i = 1, 2, \ldots, q . \tag{9.41}$$

For a period of, say 4, a plot of I versus i will give high I values at $i = 4$.

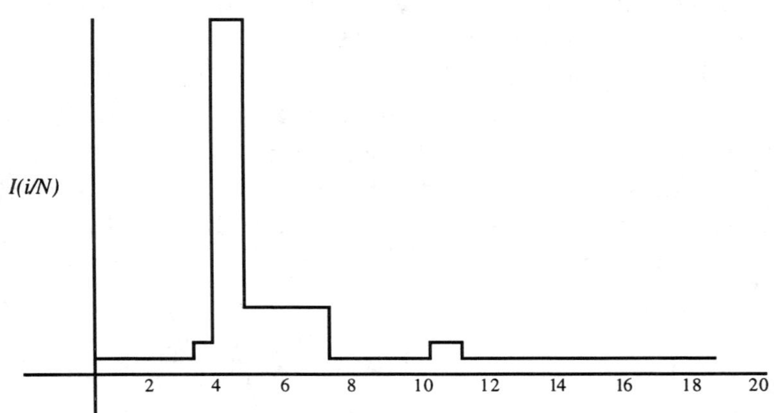

Figure 9.4. Periodogram.

Such a procedure tends to work well, not only on the series in Figure 9.3, but also on series with a high component of noise.

9.7 A Simple Test for White Noise

A recurring trend in economics is the notion that this or that is repeating at a regular cycle. There is, for example, the notion that the economy tends to repetitive patterns every 50 years. This theory goes back, usually to the Mosaic law of forgiveness of debts every 50 years (the Year of Jubilee). Naturally, the Mosaic Law would itself produce a 50 year cycle, with interest rates for long term bonds rising as we departed from year 0. However, 50 is rather an unusual number for the *Torah*, which tends to lean toward primes and binarily elegant numbers, of which 50 is not one. So the theory is that the *Torah* was picking up on some natural economic cycle. Inasmuch as there is no institutionalized Year of Jubilee, it is perhaps interesting that many economists, e.g., Kondratieff, claim to find the 50 year cycle. More recently, Ravi Batra [1] claims to note other periods for the economy.

Another kind of claim is something like "after gold rises past its average over the last 150 days by 10%, it is a good time to buy gold." This would imply a kind of long term autoregressive model described the "equilibrium" or "decline" periods, and that the model was violated at the early term of times of expansion.

It is good to have some means of testing these claims against performance of the historical record. If we can find some simpler formulation tends to give us a white noise process, then we can claim, with some a priori justification, that the "deep" phenomenon may simply be not present but due to purely rational randomness explanations.

An example of such a test is the portmanteau test of Box and Pierce. If we have a series $X(t)$, which we suspect of being simply white noise, then we compute first the estimates of the autocovariances and autocorrelations via

$$\hat{\mu} = \frac{1}{N}\sum_{i=1}^{N} X(t) \tag{9.42}$$

$$\hat{R}(j) = \frac{1}{N-j}\sum_{t=1}^{N-j}(X(t)-\hat{\mu})(X(t+j)-\hat{\mu})$$

$$\hat{\rho}(j) = \frac{\hat{R}(j)}{\hat{R}(0)} \, .$$

We then compute the sum

$$Q = n(n+2) \sum_{j=1}^{m} \frac{1}{n-j} \hat{\rho}^2(j) \approx \chi_m^2 \, . \tag{9.43}$$

If the series does not exceed the Chi-Square statistic for the given value of m, then we cannot reject the assumption that the series has indeed been reduced to white noise.

9.8 Bivariate Autoregressive Modeling

There are many situations in which we will wish to develop forecasts which depend not only on the past values of one variable, but also on past values of another variable. For example, we know that inflation X_1 is related to the increase in the money supply X_2 . Thus, it may be appropriate to model the processes jointly via

$$\begin{aligned} X_1(t) &= -a_{11}^{(1)} X_1(t-1) - a_{21}^{(1)} X_2(t-1) + \epsilon_1(t) \\ X_2(t) &= -a_{12}^{(1)} X_1(t-1) - a_{22}^{(1)} X_2(t-1) + \epsilon_2(t) \, . \end{aligned} \tag{9.44}$$

Here, we are assuming the two dimensional white noise process has the property

$$\begin{aligned} E[\epsilon_1(t)] = E[\epsilon_2(t)] &= 0 \text{ for all } t \; ; \\ E[\epsilon_1^2(t)] = \sigma_1^2; E[\epsilon_2^2(t)] &= \sigma_2^2; \\ E[\epsilon_1(t)\epsilon_2(t)] &= \sigma_{12}; \\ E[\epsilon_1(t)\epsilon_2(t)] &= 0 \text{ if } t \neq s \, . \end{aligned} \tag{9.45}$$

Thus,

$$Cov[\epsilon_1(t), \epsilon_2(t)] = \delta_{t-s} \begin{bmatrix} \sigma_1^2 & \sigma_{12} \\ \sigma_{12} & \sigma_2^2 \end{bmatrix} = \delta_{t-s}\Sigma, \tag{9.46}$$

where $\delta_{t-s} = 1$ if $t = s$ and 0, otherwise.

We assume the process is cross covariance (as well as first order) stationary, i.e., that $Cov[X_1(t)X_2(t+k)] = R_{ij}(k)$, for all t and k.

Multiplying in (9.44) by $X_1(t-1)$, $X_2(t-1)$, and taking expectations, we obtain the Yule-Walker equations for a first order bivariate autoregressive process:

$$\begin{aligned} R_{11}(1) &= -a_{11}^{(1)}R_{11}(0) - a_{21}^{(1)}R_{12}(0) \\ R_{12}(-1) &= -a_{11}^{(1)}R_{12}(0) - a_{21}^{(1)}R_{22}(0) \ . \end{aligned} \tag{9.47}$$

$$\begin{aligned} R_{12}(1) &= -\alpha_{12}^{(1)}R_{11}(0) - \alpha_{22}^{(1)}R_{22}(0) \\ R_{22}(1) &= -\alpha_{12}^{(1)}R_{12}(0) - \alpha_{22}^{(1)}R_{22}(0) \ . \end{aligned} \tag{9.48}$$

We can express (9.47) and (9.48) in matrix form:

$$-\begin{bmatrix} a_{11}^{(1)} & a_{21}^{(1)} \\ a_{12}^{(1)} & a_{22}^{(1)} \end{bmatrix} \begin{bmatrix} R_{11}(0) & R_{12}(0) \\ R_{12}(0) & R_{22}(0) \end{bmatrix} = \begin{bmatrix} R_{11}(1) & R_{12}(-1) \\ R_{12}(1) & R_{22}(1) \end{bmatrix} . \tag{9.49}$$

If we have a data set of total time length n, then we have ready estimates of the $R_{ij}(k)$ via

$$R_{ij}(k) = \frac{1}{n-k}\sum_{l=1}^{n-k} X_i(l)X_j(l+k) \ . \tag{9.50}$$

Clearly, for a second order autoregressive process, we would have:

$$\begin{aligned} \begin{bmatrix} X_1(t) \\ X_2(t) \end{bmatrix} &= -\begin{bmatrix} a_{11}^{(1)} & a_{21}^{(1)} \\ a_{12}^{(1)} & a_{22}^{(1)} \end{bmatrix} \begin{bmatrix} X_1(t-1) \\ X_2(t-1) \end{bmatrix} - \\ & \begin{bmatrix} a_{11}^{(2)} & a_{21}^{(2)} \\ a_{12}^{(2)} & a_{22}^{(2)} \end{bmatrix} \begin{bmatrix} X_1(t-2) \\ X_2(t-2) \end{bmatrix} + \begin{bmatrix} \epsilon_1(t) \\ \epsilon_2(t) \end{bmatrix} \end{aligned} \tag{9.51}$$

For a pth order autoregressive process, we have

$$\begin{aligned} \begin{bmatrix} X_1(t) \\ X_2(t) \end{bmatrix} &= -\sum_{j=1}^{p} \begin{bmatrix} a_{11}^{(j)} & a_{21}^{(j)} \\ a_{12}^{(j)} & a_{22}^{(j)} \end{bmatrix} \begin{bmatrix} X_1(t-j) \\ X_2(t-j) \end{bmatrix} + \begin{bmatrix} \epsilon_1(t) \\ \epsilon_2(t) \end{bmatrix} \\ &= -\sum_{j=1}^{p} \mathbf{A}^{(j)}\mathbf{X}(t-j) + \epsilon(t) \ . \end{aligned} \tag{9.52}$$

Rearranging (9.52) slightly, we have

$$\sum_{j=0}^{p} \mathbf{A}^{(j)}\mathbf{X}(t-j) = \epsilon(t) \;, \tag{9.53}$$

$$\text{where } \mathbf{A}^{(0)} = \begin{bmatrix} 1 & 0 \\ 0 & 1 \end{bmatrix} .$$

This yields the generalized bivariate Yule-Walker equations

$$\sum_{j=1}^{p} \mathbf{A}^{(j)}\mathbf{R}(j-\nu) = \delta_\nu \mathbf{\Sigma} \;. \tag{9.54}$$

It can be shown that a necessary and sufficient condition for a bivariate autoregressive process have a stationary solution is that the zeroes of

$$|\sum_{j=0}^{p} \mathbf{A}(j) z^j| \tag{9.55}$$

lie outside the unit circle.

Although we have only considered bivariate autoregressive processes here, it is a straightforward matter to extend the discussion to a k-variate autoregressive processes.

Appendix. Nelder-Mead Optimization

The reader is encouraged to use standardized software packages for forecasting analysis whenever practical. However, for cases where the appropriate routine is not available, it may be necessary to resort to minimizing a sum of squares, or some other reasonable criterion function. There exist literally hundreds of optimization algorithms. Unfortunately, most of these are not of much use to the applied worker, who is confronted with data contaminated by noise. Below, we consider the polytope algorithm of Nelder and Mead (1965). Let us suppose that we are confronted with the task of minimizing a function F which depends upon k variables—say $(X_1, X_2, \ldots, X_k)$. We wish to find the value which approximately minimizes F. To accomplish this task we start out with $k+1$ trial values of $(X_1, X_2, \ldots, X_k)$, of rank k. We evaluate F at each of these values, and identify the three values where F is the minimum (B), the maximum (W) and the second largest ($2W$). We average all the X points except W to give us the centrum C. We show a pictorial representation for the case where $k = 2$. Note, however, that the flowchart below works for any $k \geq 2$. This is due to the fact that our moves are oriented around the best, the worst, and the second worst points. Note that the algorithm first moves by a succession of expansion steps to a region where F is small. Once this has been achieved, the procedure essentially works by the simplex of vertices surrounding and collapsing in on the optimum (slow in high dimensions). Clearly, the procedure does not make the great leaps characteristic of Newton procedures. It is slow, particularly if k is large. Even, during the expansion steps, the algorithm moves in a zig-zag, rather than in straight thrusts to the target. But the zig-zag and envelopment strategies help avoid charging off on false trails. This algorithm has been presented because of its robustness to noise in the objective function (of particular importance when dealing with such approaches as that delineated in Section 9.4), the ease with which it can be programmed for the microprocessor, and the very practical fact that once learned, it is easy to remember.

Nelder-Mead Algorithm

Expansion

$P = C + \gamma_R(C - W)$(where typically $\gamma_R = \gamma_E = 1$)
If$F(P) < F(B)$, then

- $PP = C + \gamma_E(C - W)$ [a]
- If$F(PP) < F(P)$, then
- Replace W with PP as new vertex [c]
- Else
- Accept P as new vertex [b]
- End If

Else
If$F(P) < F(2W)$, Then

- Accept P as new vertex [b]
- Else

Contraction

If $F(W) < F(P)$, then

- $PP = C + \gamma_C(W - B)$ (typically $\gamma_C = 1/2$) [$a*$]
- If $F(PP) < F(W)$, Then Replace W with PP as new vertex [$b*$]
- Else Replace W with $(W + B)/2$ and $2W$ with $(2W + B)/2$ (total contraction) [$c*$]
- End If

Else

Contraction

If$F(2W) < F(P)$, Then

- $PP = C + \gamma_C(P - B)$ [*aa*]

- If $F(PP) < F(P)$, Then Replace W with PP as new vertex [*bb*]

- Else Replace W with $(W + B)/2$ and $2W$ with $(2W + B)/2$ (total contraction) [*cc*]

Else

- Replace W with P

- End If

End If

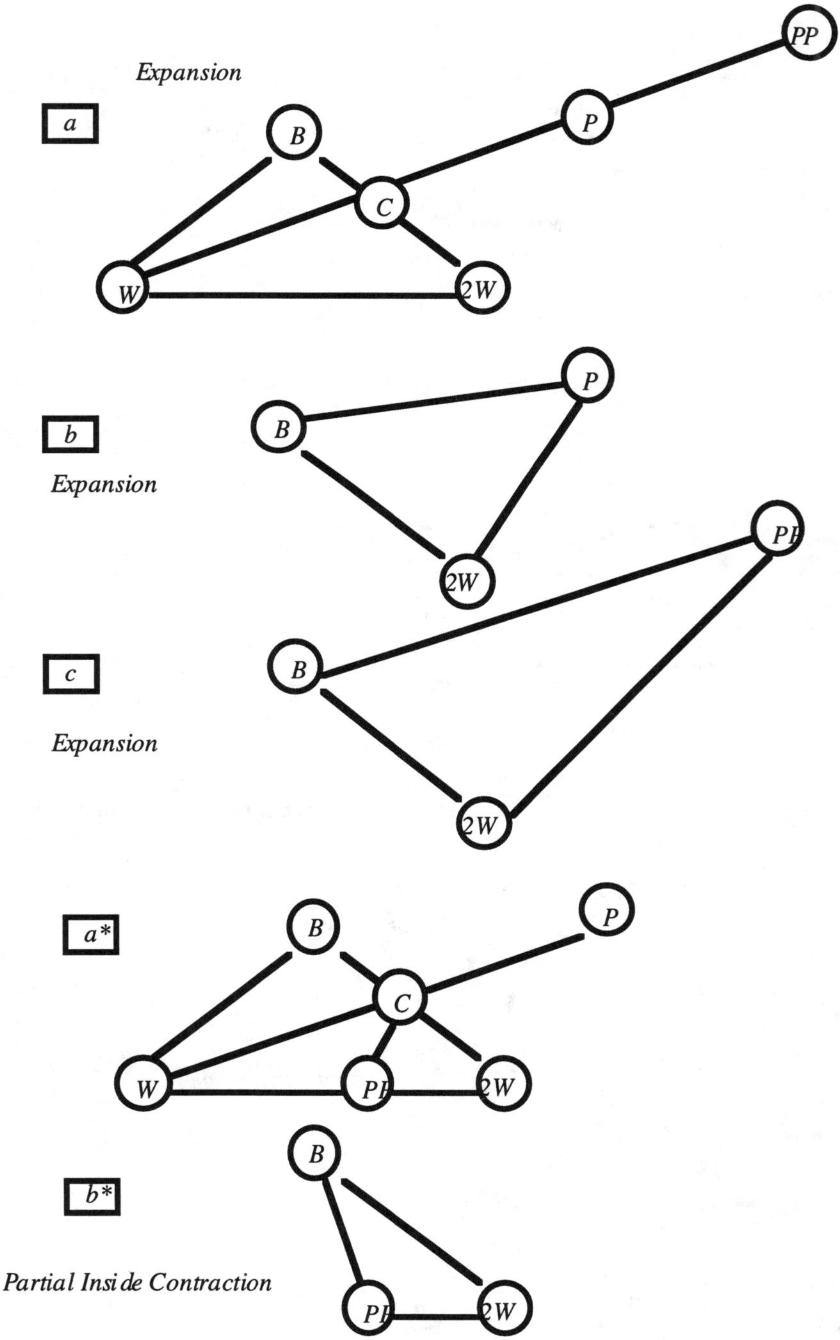

Figure 9.5a. Nelder-Mead Polytope Algorithm.

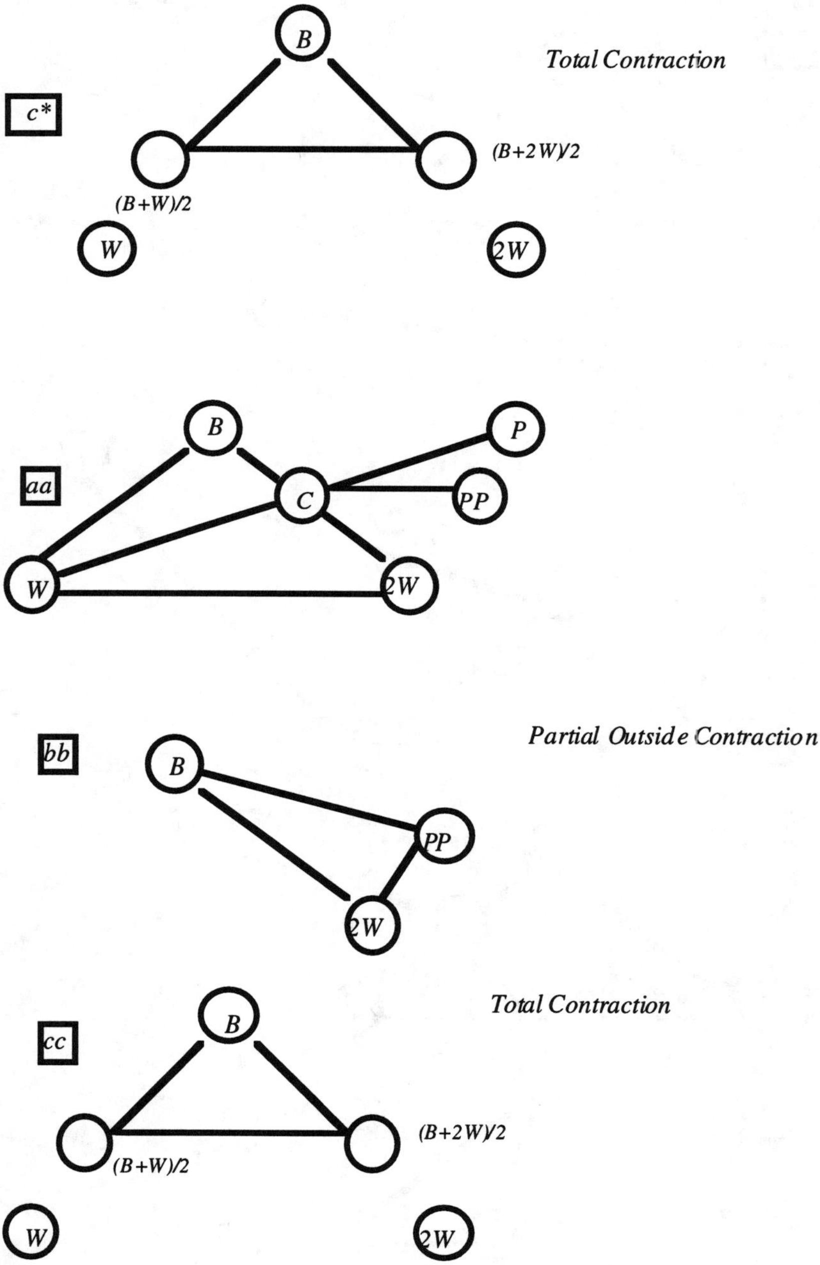

Figure 9.5b.Nelder-Mead Polytope Algorithm.

References

[1]Batra, R., *The Great Depression of 1990*, New York: Simon and Schuster, 1987.

[2]Box, G.E.P. and Jenkins, G. M., *Time Series Analysis: Forecasting and Control*, San Francisco: Holden-Day, 1976.

[3]Cobb, C.W. and P.H. Douglass, "A Theory of Production," *American Economic Review*, March, 1928, pp. 135-69.

[4] Findlay, M.C. and Williams, E.E., "Financial Theory and political Reality under Fundamental Uncertainty," *Journal of Post Keynesian Economics*, Summer, 1981, pp. 528-44.

[5]Nelder, J.A. and Mead, R., "A simplex method for function minimization." *Computational Journal*, 1965, 7, pp. 308-313.

[6]Thompson, J.R. and R.A. Tapia, *Nonparametric Function Estimation, Modeling, and Simulation*, Philadelphia: Society for Industrial and Applied Mathematics, 1990.

[7]Tukey, J.W., *Exploratory Data Analysis*, Reading: Addison- Wesley, 1977.

[8] Williams, E.E. and Thompson, J.R., *The Economics of Production and Productivity: A Modeling Approach*, Austin: Capital Book Company, 1996.

[9]Woods, D.J., *An Interactive Approach for Solving Multi- Objective Optimization Problems*, Rice Tech. Rep. 85-5, 1985.

Problems

Problem 9.1 As a practical matter, relatively short term forecasts in the stock market are frequently done using rather simple models. Consider the following daily price closings of stock of the Widget Corporation.

Stock Prices			
t	$X(t)$	t	$X(t)$
1	19.68	21	22.13
2	19.94	22	21.78
3	20.41	23	22.48
4	20.69	24	22.35
5	21.15	25	23.63
6	20.30	26	21.88
7	21.00	27	22.82
8	20.16	28	22.63
9	21.14	29	23.52
10	21.32	30	23.27
11	21.65	31	23.25
12	21.18	32	23.87
13	21.03	33	23.75
14	21.05	34	23.94
15	21.58	35	23.21
16	21.62	36	23.65
17	22.48	37	24.38
18	21.21	38	24.20
19	20.97	39	23.70
20	21.31	40	24.40

As a first step (in order not to miss trends), take the first differences to obtain $W(t) = X(t)$ - $X(t-1)$. Using the first 20 days of returns, obtain forecasts of $X(t)$ for days 21 through 40 using
(a) Simple exponential smoothing with $\alpha = 0.25$.
(b) An autoregressive model of order 2 (use the Yule-Walker equations to obtain estimates of α_1 and α_2.)

Problem 9.2 Use the difference between the one step ahead forecasts and the actual values in 9.1(a) and 9.1(b). Then perform a white noise test to see whether the models have "reduced the residuals to white noise."

Problem 9.3 Many people prefer to forecast using the simple model

$$X(t) = a + bt$$

Estimate a and b using the data from the first twenty days and use the model to predict the next twenty values.

Problem 9.4 It turns out there is some reason to suppose a relationship between the values of stock of the Widget Corporation (X) and those from the Whatsit Corporation Y.

Stock Prices					
t	$X(t)$	$Y(t)$	t	$X(t)$	$Y(t)$
1	19.68	12.01	21	22.13	12.09
2	19.94	9.99	22	21.78	12.03
3	20.41	11.91	23	22.48	12.02
4	20.69	11.99	24	22.35	12.15
5	21.15	1 2.11	25	23.63	11.96
6	20.30	12.06	26	21.88	12.21
7	21.00	12.20	27	22.82	12.02
8	20.16	12.19	28	22.63	12.09
9	21.14	11.95	29	23.52	12.17
10	21.32	12.15	30	23.27	12.00
11	21.65	12.02	31	23.25	12.23
12	21.18	12.11	32	23.87	12.28
13	21.03	11.84	33	23.75	12.30
14	21.05	12.01	34	23.94	12.28
15	21.58	12.08	35	23.21	12.29
16	21.62	12.22	36	23.65	12.29
17	22.48	12.06	37	24.38	12.15
18	21.21	12.21	38	24.20	12.01
19	20.97	12.05	39	23.70	12.02
20	21.31	11.96	40	24.40	12.16

Using the data from the prior days, obtain one step ahead forecasts for X and Y.

Problem 9.5 One of the easiest functions to minimize is a quadratic like

$$Q = 15 + (X - 3)^2 + (Y - 10)^2$$

Naturally, we know that the minimum is $Q = 15$ when $X = 3$ and $Y = 10$. But, as a test to make sure that your program is correct, use the Nelder-Mead algorithm to find the optimum, using as starting points

Stock Prices		
X	Y	Q
5	5	44
7	1	112
8	9	41

Problem 9.6 The variance, σ^2, of a chemical process follows the formula

$$\sigma^2 = exp[-.001\{(P + T - 210)^2 + 1.3(P - 50)^2\}] + 10T + P^2$$

where P and T are pressure and temperature, respectively. Find the values of P and T which minimize the variance.

Chapter 10

The Deming Paradigm for System Optimization

10.1 Introduction

No discussion of entrepreneurship and productivity would be complete without attention to the management paradigm of the late W. Edwards Deming. At the end of the Second World War, Japan was renowned for shoddy goods produced by automatons living in standards of wretchedness and resignation. The formalism of the Zen culture of Japan appeared to be at the opposite pole of Aristotelian realism which characterized the nations of the First World. If there were ever a society apparently impervious to rapid industrial progress, amongst the civilized nations of the world, Japan would appear to have been the most impervious.

Deming began preaching his paradigm of Statistical Process Control in Japan in the early 1950s. By the mid 1960s, Japan was a serious player in electronics and automobiles. By the 1980s, Japan had taken a dominant position in consumer electronics and, absent tariffs, automobiles. Even in the most sophisticated areas of production, for example, computing, the Japanese had achieved a leadership role. The current situation of the Japanese workers is among the best in the world. A miracle, to be sure, and one far beyond that of, say postwar Germany, which was a serious contender in all levels of production before World War II.

It would seem impossible that the Deming paradigm, which involves no new hardware and which, culturally, seems poles apart from Zen formalism and notions of group tranquility could have made the difference. The fact is that Deming had made several incredibly important observations:

- The key to optimizing the output of a system is the optimization of the system itself.
- Although the problem of modifying the output of a system is frequently one of linear feedback (easy), the problem of optimizing the system itself is one of nonlinear feedback (hard).
- The suboptimalities of a system are frequently caused by a few assignable causes. These manifest themselves by intermittent departures of the output from the overall output averages.
- Hence, it is appropriate to despense with complex methods of system optimization and replace these by human intervention whenever one of these departures is noted.
- Once an assignable cause of suboptimality has been removed, it seldom recurrs.
- Thus, we have the indication of an apparently unsophisticated but, in fact, incredibly effective, paradigm of system optimization.

10.2 Deming's Fourteen Points

We shall see that statistical process control is a rather specific paradigm for optimizing a system in step by step fashion. This is the essence of the Deming philosophy. Those wishing a more extensive discussion of the paradigm have a wealth of books to consider, e.g., [7]. It would be a mistake to treat SPC as some "touchie-feelie" Chamber of Commerce boosterism. In the context of the subsequent discussion, it will be clear to the reader how the Fourteen Points [1] of Deming relate to his paradigm of improvement.

1. Create constancy of purpose toward improvement of product and service, with a plan to become competitive and to stay in business. Decide whom top management is responsible to.

2. Adopt the new philosophy. We are in a new economic age. We can no longer live with commonly accepted levels of delays, mistakes, defective materials, and defective workmanship.

3. Cease dependence on mass inspection. Require instead statistical evidence that quality is built in, to eliminate need for inspection on a mass basis. Purchasing managers have a new job and they must learn it.

4. End the practice of awarding business on the basis of price tag. Instead, depend on meaningful measures of quality, along with price. Eliminate suppliers that can not qualify with statistical evidence of good quality.

5. Find problems. It is management's job to work continually on the system (design, incoming materials, composition of material, maintenance, improvement of machine, training, supervision, and retraining).

6. Institute modern methods of on the job training.

7. Institute modern methods of supervision of production workers. The responsibility of foremen must be changed from sheer numbers to quality. Improvement of quality will automatically improve productivity. Management must prepare to take immediate action on reports from foremen concerning barriers such as inherited defects, machines not maintained, poor tools, fuzzy operational definitions.

8. Drive out fear, so that everyone may work effectively for the company.

9. Break down barriers between departments. People in research, design, sales, and production must work as a team, to foresee problems of production that may be encountered with various materials and specifications.

10. Eliminate numerical goals, posters and slogans for the work force, asking for new levels of productivity without providing methods for improvement.

11. Eliminate work standards that prescribe numerical quotas.

12. Remove barriers that stand between the hourly worker and his right to pride of workmanship.

13. Institute a vigorous program of education and training.

14. Create a structure in top management which will push every day on the above 13 points.

Let us analyze these points one at a time.

1. Management is urged to plan for the long haul. We cannot simply lurch from crisis to crisis. We need to consider what we believe the company really is about. What do we plan to be doing next quarter, next year, five years, ten years from now. It goes without saying that our plans will require constant modification. But we need to ask what our direction is. What new technologies will likely affect us. We need to plan a strategy that will make the firm unique. We need to be pointed on a course which will make us the best in the world in what we do. If we have no such course plotted, it is unlikely that we will simply stumble upon it.

2. A common assumption in some American industries is that a significant proportion of the things they do will simply be defective. Once again, we return to the misconception that machines function as people do. They do not. If we move methodically toward improved production, we need not fear that our improved excellence will be fleeting. A human juggling balls is very different from a production schedule optimally designed. Our goal must be systematic improvement. Once we achieve a certain level of excellence, it is locked in forever. If, on the other hand, we assume that prospective clients will always be satisfied to return defective items or have us repair them, we are due, down the road, to an unpleasant surprise. Sooner or later, a competitor will discover how to produce a product like ours but without the defects.

3. Once we have achieved the middle level of excellence, we will not require extensive inspection. Again, this fact points to the fact that work done by machines will generally be satisfactory once we have determined how to make them operate properly.

One of the major benefits of a well designed system of statistical process control is that it will rather quickly liberate us from carrying out exhaustive (or nearly exhaustive inspection). Similarly, we should be able to demand from those companies who supply us a steady stream of products of excellent quality.

4. Companies which constantly change their suppliers on the basis of marginally lower prices are playing a lottery with quality. We have the right to expect that those companies to whom we sell will think long and hard before replacing us with a competitor. This is not being polite but simply rational. "If it ain't broke, don't fix it," is a good rule. If our supplier is delivering high quality products to us at a reasonable price, then, on the offer by another supplier to deliver us the same products for less, we would probably be wise, as a first step to meet with our original supplier to see whether there might be some adjustment downward in the price of his product. Even if no such adjustment is offered, we probably will be well advised to stick with the original supplier, particularly if the saving involved in the switch is modest and/or if we have no firm evidence that the product being offered is of quality comparable to that from the current supplier.

5. Once a production process has been brought to the middle level of excellence, where day-to-day crisis management is not the norm, we will have arrived at the region where we can increase our understanding of the process and attempt to improve it. Many American firms always operate in crisis mode. In such a mode, it is not easy to effect even the simplest of improvements, such as rearranging the production line to minimize the necessity of transporting intermediate products from building to building.

6. In a modern industrial setting, a worker is a manager, perhaps of other workers, perhaps of machines. The worth of a worker to the company is based on the cumulative knowledge and experience of that worker. If the company is beyond the crisis mode of operation, then there is time to enhance worker knowledge by a well thought out system of on the job training. There are few more profitable investments which the company

might make than those spent in expanding the ability of the worker to deal effectively with the challenges of his current job and of those further down his career path.

7. A foreman should not be a taskmaster, looking to improve production by stressing the workers. This is simply not the way to achieve improved performance, as the failure of economic systems based on such a paradigm indicates. A foreman is a manager of other managers, and his job is to coordinate the goals of the section and to entertain suggestions as to how these might best be achieved.

8. So far from increasing productivity, arguments from management along the lines, "You have to increase your output by 10%, or you are likely to lose your job," are very counterproductive. It is not hard to figure out why. In addition to the natural frustrations associated with any job, management has just added another frustration: a demand that the worker increase his output without being shown how to do so. An upbeat environment in which management provides concrete help for the increase of productivity, without threats, has proved the best way to achieve maximum quality and productivity.

9. Every organization requires some form of structure. Over time, however, changes in products and technology tend to render the boundaries between departments less and less relevant. One solution is to have reorganization of the firm every six months or so. Another, much more appropriate one, is to permit free flow of information and cooperation between departments. Once again, experience shows that such an approach does not impair organizational discipline and does enhance the total quality and productivity of the company.

10. No society has been bigger on goals than that of the Soviet Bloc. No society has been bigger on posters, slogans and the like. The result has been disastrous. A principal duty of management is to show how productivity can been improved. It is unnecessary to emphasize the fact that productivity enhancements are crucial to the life of a firm and to those of the workers. Everyone knows that.

11. Workers need to be shown how to perform better. Simple demands that they do so are generally counterproductive.

12. No human being wishes to be a cog in a machine. Every worker in an effectively managed firm is important. This is reality, not just a slogan. A major source of improvement in the production process is discoveries by workers as to how things might be done better. Such discoveries will be encouraged if those who make the discoveries are given full credit.

13. Beyond on the job training, a firm is well advised to enhance the ability of workers to improve their skills by in house courses.

14. A quality control program which is treated by top management as a pro forma activity is not likely to be effective. Top management needs to be convinced as to the importance of the program and needs to take as much a lead in it as they do in marketing and administration.

10.3 Pareto's Maxim

Many have the impression that quality control is the result of positive thinking and a basically healthy industrial psychology. In other words, many believe that quality control is some sort of "touchie-feelie" attitude adjustment. As such, the science of quality control has obtained a very bad reputation as just another trendy waste of time. Wherever one starts in on trying to implement the Deming paradigm of statistical process control, he is always confronted by a pre-existing Department of Quality Assurance or Department of Total Quality Management or a Zero Defects Team. Like early Christian missionaries being met by Gnostics who used much of the same language of Christianity while meaning something completely different, the statistical process control professional is confronted by something worse than total ignorance. He has to disassociate what he is preaching from that which seems to be the same, but is very much not. Statistical process control is not positive thinking or team spirit or any other sort of sociological silliness. It is a hard engineering approach, a definite paradigm.

A major basis of the paradigm of statistical process control is the empirical observation of Vilfredo Pareto that *the failures in a system are usually the consequence of a few assignable causes rather than the consequence of a general malaise across the system.* This insight is generally known as *Pareto's Maxim.* It is, of course, easy to state "laws" and "maxims". There is little reason, *a priori*, to give Pareto's Maxim any more credence than Pyramid Power or Transcendental Meditation. Perhaps the greatest of the considerable accomplishments of W. Edwards Deming is the demonstration of nearly half a century as to the practical implication of the Maxim of Pareto.

To give an example of Pareto's Maxim, let us imagine a room filled with blindfolded people which we would wish to be quiet but is not because of the presence of a number of noise sources. Most of the people in the room are sitting quietly, and contribute only the sounds of their breathing to the noisiness of the room. One individual, however, is firing a machine gun filled with blanks, another is playing a portable radio at full blast, still another is shouting across the room, and, finally, one individual is whispering to the person next to him. Assume that the "director of noise diminution" is blindfolded also. Any attempt to arrange for a quiet room by asking everyone in the room to cut down his noise level 20% would, of course, be ridiculous. The vast majority of the people in the room, who are not engaged in any of the four noise making activities listed, will be annoyed to hear that their breathing noises must be cut 20%. They rightly and intuitively perceive that such a step is unlikely to do any measurable good. Each of the noise sources listed is so much louder than the next down the list that we could not hope to hear, for example, the person shouting until the firing of blanks had stopped and the radio had been turned off.

The prudent noise diminution course is to attack the problems sequentially. We first get the person firing blanks to cease. Then, we will be able to hear the loud radio, which we arrange to have cut off. Next, we can hear the shouter, request that he be quiet. Finally, we can hear the whisperer and request that he also stop making noise.

If we further have some extraordinary demands for silence, we could begin to seek the breather with the most clogged nasal passages, and so on. But generally speaking, we would arrive, sooner or later, at some level of silence which would be acceptable for our purposes. This intuitively obvious analogy is a simple example of the key notion of quality control. By standards of human psychology, the example is also rather bizarre. Of the noise making individuals, at least two would be deemed sociopathic. We are familiar with the fact that in most gatherings, there will be a kind of uniform buzz. If there is a desire of a master of ceremonies to quiet the audience, it is perfectly reasonable for him to ask everyone please to be quiet. The fact is that machines and other systems tend to function like the (by human standards) bizarre example and seldom behave like a crowd of civilized human beings. It is our tendency to anthropomorphize systems that makes the effectiveness of statistical process control appear so magical.

10.4 False Goals, Shattered Dreams

Let us consider an excerpt from a somewhat definitive publication of the American Management Association Zero Defects: Doing It Right the First Time [8]:

> North American's PRIDE Program is a positive approach to quality that carries beyond the usual system of inspection. It places the responsibility for perfection on the employee concerned with the correctness of his work. Its success depends on the attitude of the individual and his ability to change it. This program calls for a positive approach to employee thinking ... . A good promotional campaign will help stimulate interest in the program and will maintain interest as the program progresses. North American began with a "teaser" campaign which was thoughtfully conceived and carried out to whet the interest of employees prior to the kick-off day ... . Various things will be needed for that daybanners, posters, speeches, and so forth... . Many of the 1,000 companies having Zero Defects programs give employees small badges or pins for signing the pledge cards and returning them to the program administrator. Usually these badges are well received and worn with pride by employees at all times on the job ... . In addition, it is good to plan a series of reminders and interest-joggers and to use promotional techniques such as issuing gummed stickers for tool boxes, packages and briefcases. Coffee cup coasters with printed slogans or slogans printed on vending

> machine cups are good. Some companies have their letterhead inscribed with slogans or logos which can also be printed on packing cases.

There is little doubt that an intelligent worker confronted with the Zero Defects program could think of additional places where management could stick their badges, pins and posters. A worker, particularly an American worker, does not need to be tricked into doing his best. In a decently managed company, employee motivation can be taken as a given. It is the business of management to know precisely what it to be achieved and to put their employees in the picture. If management cannot flowchart what it is their system is (and seldom can American management do so), then simply giving their workers pep talks about "getting with the system" is simply a red herring. Now, for those above to try to obscure their own incompetence by shifting the responsibility to lower levels in the management hierarchy, hoping against hope that somewhere down the line somebody may know what is going on, is not an idea that originated in the United States.

As Pareto himself observed, hierarchies tend to preserve the perks for those at the top without over much concern for betterment of the system itself. One of the principal tasks of the science of management should be to ameliorate the nasty tendencies of hierarchical structures to better the lot of those at the top without concern for the enterprise as a whole.

Perhaps we can better appreciate the very destructive rhetoric from the Zero Defects program by giving its Soviet near equivalent in juxtaposition. We note the following quotation from the Soviet quality control expert Ya. Sorin [5]:

> Socialist competition is a powerful means of improving the quality of production. Labour unions should see to it that among the tasks voluntarily assumed by brigades and factories ... are included those having to do with improving quality control .... In the course of socialist competition new forms of collective fight for quality control are invented. One such form is a "complex" brigade created in the Gorky car factory and having as its task the removal of shortcomings in the design and

> production of cars. Such "complex brigades" consist of professionals and qualified workers dealing with various stages of production. The workers who are members of such brigades are not released from their basic quotas. All problems are discussed after work. Often members of such brigades stay in factories after work hours to decide collectively about pressing problems.

The American version is much more carrot than stick, but allowing for differences in style, it is very similar to that of the Soviets. We see nothing about implementation of a well defined production system presented to the workers by management. Rather, we see pressure from management on the workers to "do something."

The mention of the Gorky car factory is interesting. This was actually introduced into the Soviet Union with help from the Ford Motor Company in the late 1920s. The entire production philosophy of Henry Ford was based on precise design and flowcharting. In the Soviet Union, however, the system of production was based on political reliability. Consequently, management tended to be recruited, not from competent and experienced engineers, but from the politically correct and reliable. It is interesting to note that by the time that the Todt and Sorin articles were written (mid 1960s) the appearance of accountant or lawyer or MBA as manager in American industry had brought forth a kind of notion of how productivity and quality are to be achieved which is all too like that of the Soviet paradigm. It has been argued [6] that there was an apparent infusion of Soviet style management into the American system which occurred during the Roosevelt Administration.

In a management system where nobody has any very good idea of what the goals are, there really is a problem in finding an appropriate criterion for measuring just how well we are doing. For example, as part of the "zero defects" program, employees may be asked to sign cards pledging themselves to the goal of zero defects. When a certain proportion of workers have signed the cards, a day of celebration is decreed to mark this "important event." Note that it is not the achievement of zero defects which is being celebrated, but rather the somewhat less significant pledging of a commitment to zero defects (whatever that means).

A more graphic example of misplaced energy is given in the following example. Some years ago, a young, gung-ho manager of a newly built wood products factory in the Soviet Union set out to have the best run wood products factory in the Empire. He spurred the workers on with promises of bonuses for their enthusiastic cooperation. His plans for efficiency went so far as using the sawdust produced as fuel to power the factory.

At the end of his first year, fully expecting to find the government evaluation of the plant to be very high, he was crushed to find his factory ranked dead last among wood products plants in the Soviet Union.

The next year, he redoubled his efforts. He apologized to the workers, explaining that while their plant was moving forward, no doubt others were as well. He made new plans for accelerated improvement. At the end of the second year, justifiably pleased with the factory's progress, he was informed by Moscow that his plant was still last in the Soviet Union and that his productivity had fallen behind that of the first year. No bonuses for the workers and the danger of demotion of the plant manager.

Distraught to desperation, the young manager boarded the next train to Moscow. Perhaps his plant was at the bottom of the list, but there was no way the productivity of his plant the second year was less than that of the first.

Upon meeting with his bosses in Moscow, he presented graphs and tables to demonstrate how productivity had improved from the first to the second year. Unimpressed, his superiors noted they had also double checked their computations and productivity had indeed declined.

Desperately, the manager asked what criteria were being used for productivity measurement. He discovered that the criterion was a rather simple one, namely the pounds of waste sawdust per worker taken from the plant each year.

The happy ending to the story is that the third year, the bright, but now somewhat cynical, manager achieved his goal of seeing his wood products factory ranked among the highest in the Soviet Union.

10.5 Pareto and Ishikawa Diagrams

In free market economies, we are in a different situation than managers in command economies, for there generally is a "bottom line" in terms of profits. The CEO of an automobile company, for example, will need to explain the dividends paid per dollar value of stock. If it turns out that these dividends are not satisfactory, then he can take "dramatic action" such as having his teams of lobbyists demand higher tariffs on foreign automobiles and instructing his advertising department to launch intimidating "buy American" campaigns. Sometimes, he might take even more dramatic action by trying to build better automobiles (but that is unusual). We note that if the decision is made to improve the quality of his product then there is the question of defining what it means for one car to be better than another. It is all very well to say that if profits are good, then we probably are doing OK, but a reasonable manager should look to the reasons why his sales should or should not be expected to rise. Uniformity of product is the measure which we will be using to a very large degree in the development of the statistical process control paradigm. But clearly, this is not the whole story. For example, if a manufacturer was turning out automobiles which had the property that they all ran splendidly for 10,000 miles and then the brake system failed, that really would not be satisfactory as an ultimate end result, even though the uniformity was high. But, as we shall see, such a car design might be very close to good if we were able simply to make appropriate modification of the braking system. A fleet of cars which had an average time to major problems of 10,000 miles but with a wide variety of failure reasons and a large variability of time til failure would usually be more difficult to put right.

The modern automobile is a complex system with tens of thousands of basic parts. As with most real world problems, a good product is distinguished from a bad one according to an implicit criterion function of high dimensionality. A good car has a reasonable price, "looks good," has good fuel efficiency, provides safety for riders in the event of an accident, has comfortable seating in both front and rear seats, has low noise levels, reliably starts without mishap, etc., etc.

Yet, somehow, consumers manage to distill all this information into a decision as to which car to purchase. Certain criteria seem to be more important than others. For example, market analysts for years have noted that Japanese automobiles seem to owe their edge in large measure to the long periods between major repair. One hears statements such as, "I just changed the oil and filter every five thousand miles, and the thing drove without any problems for 150,000 miles."

Long time intervals between major repairs make up one very important criterion with American car buyers. Fine. So then, an automotive CEO might simply decide that he will increase his market share by making his cars have long times til major repairs. How to accomplish this? First of all, it should be noted that broad spectrum pep talks are of negative utility. Few things are more discouraging to workers than being told that the company has a problem and it is up to them to solve it without any clue as to how this is to be achieved.

A reasonable first step for the CEO would be to examine the relative frequencies of causes of first major repair during a period of, say, three months. The taxonomy of possible causes must first be broken down into the fifty or so groups. We show in Figure 10.1 only the top five. It is fairly clear that management needs to direct a good deal of its attention to improving transmissions. Clearly, in this case, as is generally true, a few causes of difficulty are dominant. The diagram in Figure 10.1 is sometimes referred to as a *Pareto diagram*, inasmuch as it is based on *Pareto's Maxim* to the effect that *the failures in a system are usually the consequence of a few assignable causes rather than the consequence of a general malaise across the system.*

What is the appropriate action of a manager who has seen Figure 10.1? At this point, he could call a meeting of the managers in the Transmission Section and tell them to fix the problem. This would not be inappropriate. Certainly, it is much preferable to a general harangue of the entire factory. At least he will not have assigned equal blame to the Engine Section with 203 failures (or the Undercoating Section with no failures) as to the Transmission Section with 27,955 failures. The use of hierarchies is almost inevitable in management. The Pareto diagram tells top management where it is most appropriate to spend resources in finding (and solving) problems. To a large extent, the ball really is in the court of the Transmission Section (though top management would be well advised to pass through the failure information to the Suspension Section and indeed to all the sections).

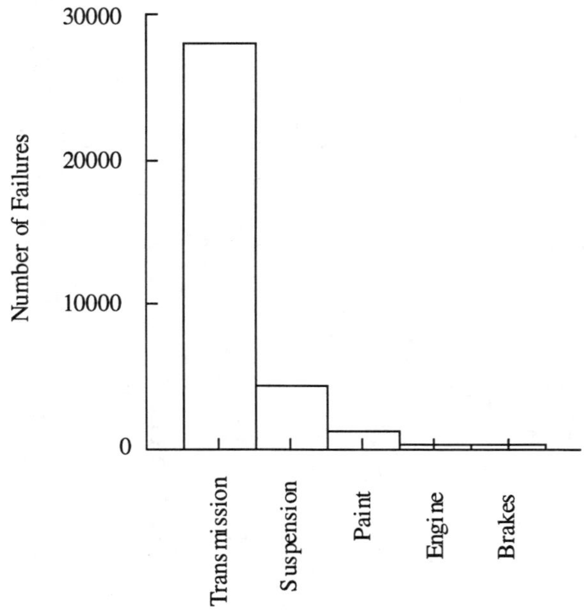

Figure 10.1. Failure Pareto Diagram.

What should be the approach of management in the Transmission Section? The obvious answer is a Pareto diagram on the 27,955 faulty transmissions. That may not be realistic. It is easier to know that a transmission has failed than what was the proximate cause of that failure. We might hope that the on site mechanics will have correctly diagnosed the problem. Generally speaking, in order to save time, repair diagnostics will be modularized; i.e., there will be a number of subsections of the transmission which will be tested as to whether they are satisfactory or not. Naturally some of the transmissions will have more than one failed module.

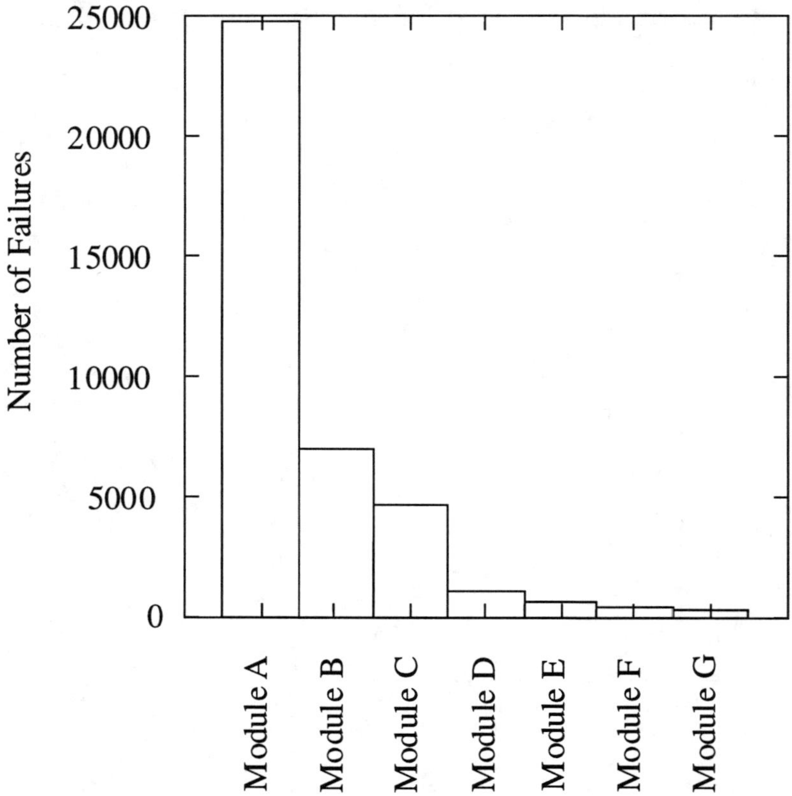

Figure 10.2. Transmission Failure Pareto Diagram.

Clearly, Module A is causing a great deal of the trouble. It is possible to carry the hierarchy down still another level to find the main difficulty with that module. The problem may be one of poor design, or poor quality of manufacture. Statistical process control generally addresses itself to the second problem.

The "cause and effect" or "fishbone" diagram of Ishikawa is favored by some as a tool for finding the ultimate cause of a system failure. Let us demonstrate what such a diagram might look like for the present problem.

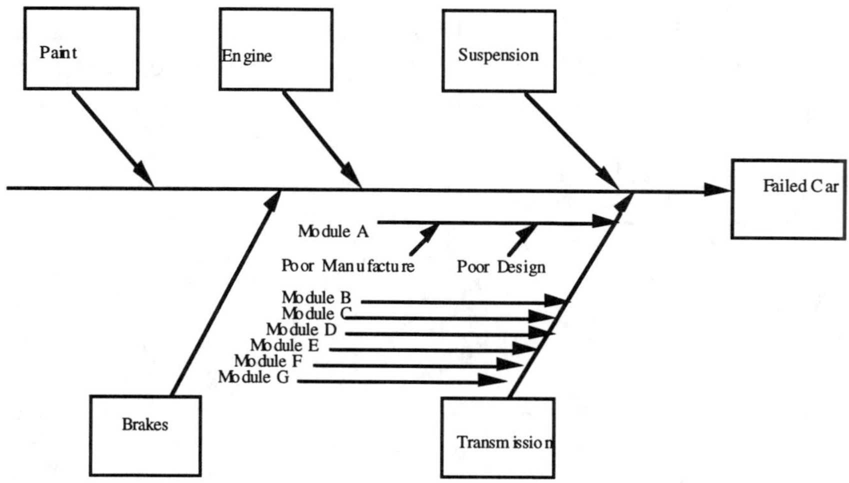

Figure 10.3. Fishbone Diagram.

The fishbone diagram should not be thought of as a precise flowchart of production. The chart as shown might lead one to suppose that the transmission is the last major component installed in the car. That is not the case. We note that Figure 10.3 allows for free form expression such as might come about in a discussion where a number of people are making inputs as to an appropriate representation on the blackboard. Each of the paths starting from a box is really a stand-alone entity. We have here developed only one of the paths in detail. We note that in the case of Transmissions, we go down the next level of hierarchy to the modules and then still one more level to the design and quality of manufacturing. In practice, the fishbone diagram will have a number of such paths developed to a high level of hierarchy. Note that each one of the major branches can simply be stuck onto the main stem of the diagram. This enables people in "brainstorming" sessions to submit their candidates for what the problem seems to be by simply sticking a new hierarchy onto the major stem.

10.6 Quality Assurance By End Inspection

It seems self-evident that the management of every business, certainly the management of every business concerned with production, should be able to write down a chart showing precisely how we get from the inputs to the outputs. Unfortunately, in the United States, even for rather involved production processes, the existence of such a *flow chart* is the exception rather than the rule.

Figure 10.4. Noninformative Flow Chart.

When Henry Ford developed the forever moving assembly line in 1914, he naturally flowcharted his process. But times have changed. And now, there is evidence of a tendency to "wing it," even in involved processes. The production plan frequently exists, however vaguely, only in the heads of a few seasoned operators, and production information is disseminated according to the "oral tradition." In such a situation, disaster is almost guaranteed upon the simultaneous departure of a few key persons. It is probably not coincidental that the Challenger disaster occurred at NASA not long after top management had retired. Realistically speaking, the flowchart most relevant to American business is something like that in Figure 10.4.

For such a poorly catalogued process, there are few tools open to us for the determination as to how well we are doing other than the proportion of the output which is satisfactory for use. Companies basing their quality control on such noninformative charts frequently are driven to inspect 100% of their output. Since such noninformative flow charts are the rule rather than the exception in the United States, anyone starting to implement statistical process control in such a system had better have something which works even in this rather disappointing situation. Happily, as we shall shortly show, there are ways of utilizing data from the noninformative flow chart if these data are indexed by time.

At a major tractor factory in Poland in the early nineties, the engines produced were checked 100% by production workers. Of these, 30% were sent back for reworking. Finally, from the pool of "satisfactory" items, a "random" sample of 15% was examined by the "quality inspection" team. Of these, 10% were still found to be defective in some fashion. Apparently, then, of the engines actually installed and shipped, the company must expect to be sending at least 10% defectives (by their own definition) into the market. In actuality, since the engine is only one component of a tractor, we would expect a high proportion of defective tractors generally. The actual number of defectives entering the market can only be a matter of conjecture, and highly dependent on the definition of "defective." However, we do know that the mean time between failures for their tractors was only between 80 and 150 hours, a figure far below that (260 hours) of tractors produced in the West. This kind of stasis of a high proportion of defectives is rather typical of the "quality inspection" paradigm wherever it has been the means of quality control. End "quality inspection" using preassigned tolerances does not provide the feedback mechanism required for stepwise improvement in the production process. The estimate of management of the total number of workers at the plant engaged in "quality control" was 4.3% (all figures taken in 1991). The educational level, intelligence and motivation of the workers at the Polish tractor factory were all excellent. The quality of the management was less wonderful. The workers in such a situation have an almost impossible task. Management tells them they are doing a bad job but gives them no clue as to how to improve the situation.

Following the fall of the Soviet control of Poland in 1989, the American experts had advised the Polish government to retire the top managers of factories (good idea). The experts might have suggested something really original, such as training production foremen in statistical process control and giving the management of the factories to them (good idea). Instead, they recommended simply going down the list of the current factory managers to younger members of the old managerial nomenklatura, sending these off to accelerated American MBA programs and promoting them to run the company. So, then, the tractor factory was given over to people who had learned naught about statistical process control either as members of the old regime or as newly baptized capitalist aprachki. Both their old training and that of the American MBA program had taught them about the importance of networking and self-interest, but little about how to make things. Of course they had learned the American scheme of increasing "productivity" by laying off employees. The knowledge capital of the tractor works was enormous in terms of its skilled workforce. Given some appropriate managerial initiatives in the forms of statistical process control and attempts to introduce maintenance training in service stations around Poland, the firm might have first recaptured their share of the Polish market (the Russians were dumping tractors onto the Polish market with some success) and then used their competitive advantage (in the form of low labor cost) to expand into European and overseas markets.

Instead, not knowing what to do, except believing they could increase productivity by laying off their highly skilled labor force, that is what they did, thus throwing away the company's most valuable asset. As is generally the case, those who suffer the greatest from poor management are not the managers.

The performance figures given are not untypical of production of many companies both in Poland and the United States. We notice a relatively high number of individuals engaged in "quality assurance." The number of person hours spent on rework is a harder to obtain figure, but is very high (note the fact that 30% of the engines are picked for rework, and this not by qa (quality assurance) people, but by the regular work force). Trying to assure quality by end inspection is an expensive and generally ineffective approach.

In fairness to the managers of the tractor works, it should be noted that theirs was a company which the Soviets had "poison pilled." That is to say that the Soviets had implemented a policy of requiring the company to receive many essential components from companies in other parts of the Soviet Empire. When the Empire fell, many of the suppliers went out of business, and the tractor works had not the capital readily at hand to create substitutes for the parts no longer available. The best thing the American advisors could have done for the Polish company would have been to create a new SPC trained managerial class from the old blue collar foreman class, and then figure out a way to provide capital for the retooling necessary to replace the parts no longer available from third parties. They did neither.

The willingness of advisors from the United States, the International Monetary Fund and the World Bank to let practically all the companies in the former satellites go bust is one of the great tragedies of the Nineties. Naturally, all this was done while chanting the mantra of "free enterprise." To note how well the American MBA advisors got along with the postcommunist managerial nomenklatura (who had been part of the old regime) and how they consistently avoided contact with the workers (whose blood and sacrifice had been largely responsible for bringing that regime down) says something. The greatest capital of the former satellites was the skill of their workers. By transforming skilled workers into an unemployed proletariat via bankruptcies and downsizings, the advisors from the West have caused a level of wasting of lives worthy of their Soviet predecessors. As a consequence of the dislocation of industrial workers in the former satellites, a great deal of entrepreneurship has been generated willy nilly. But it is hard to see why it is good for, say, a skilled tool and dye maker to be driven to selling vegetables in a clapboard stall.

A favorite analogy to the paradigm of improvement by harangue based on end inspection is that where we take an urn including a mixture of 800 white balls and 200 red balls and urge blindfolded workers to draw samples of, say 20 balls, in which no more than two balls are red. This is given simply by

$$\begin{aligned} P(X \leq 2) &= \sum_{j=0}^{2} \binom{20}{j} (.20)^j (.80)^{20-j} \quad (10.1) \\ &= \sum_{j=0}^{2} \frac{20!}{j!(20-j)!} (.20)^j (.80)^{20-j} \\ &= .206. \end{aligned}$$

Naturally, on the average, we would expect that 20% or four of the balls would be red. Sometimes, we will get lucky and find two or fewer balls, in this case around 21% of the time. But when we have achieved this paucity of red balls, it is simply a matter of luck, not improvement. When management demands the workers to reduce the number of failed items without showing how this is to be achieved and if they award those who achieve a lower than average number of failures and penalize those who do not, then they are rewarding good luck. Nothing has changed in the system unless and until we lower the proportion of red balls in the urn. To continue the analogy, in statistical process control, we use monitoring and modification to lower the proportion of red balls in the urn.

10.7 Flow Charting

Let us consider a well known example of the effect of a fix by Deming of a serious quality problem using rather skimpy data set as reviewed in *Quality, Productivity and Competitive Position.* The Nashua Corporation, was manufacturing carbonless paper for the Western European Market. Located in New Hampshire, Nashua had a ready source of wood pulp for paper; the expensive coating material for the paper was made completely from materials in the United States. Nashua had the very latest in equipment.

In the manufacture of carbonless paper, paper is coated with photosensitive material on a web 6 to 8 feet wide traveling at a speed of 1,100 linear feet/minute. A key part of the process is to coat the paper with the minimal amount of costly photosensitive material consistent with good quality of performance. Parts of the paper with too little material will not reproduce properly. In late 1979, Nashua was using 3.6 pounds per 3,000 square feet. It would appear that Nashua was in a strong competitive position indeed.

A Japanese competitor entered the Western European market. Ostensibly, this would seem to be no big problem. The Japanese were without domestic trees for paper and domestic minerals for the paper coating. They were far from Europe (shipping their product over the Trans-Siberian Railway). Yet the Japanese were able to sell carbonless paper to the Europeans for less cost than Nashua. Even worse, the quality of the Japanese paper was better (i.e., more uniform and hence less likely to jam and better at reproduction) than that of the Nashua product. Nashua was fortunate in that at the time the Europeans believed that the American product must be better than the Japanese product. But many of Nashua's customers quickly learned that was not the case. And they began to change to the Japanese product.

Any notion of imposing an American tariff on the Japanese product (a favored solution for many U.S. manufacturers) was, of course, out of the question, since the market was not in the United States. What was to be done?

The most likely option in late 1979 appeared to be to go into bankruptcy. Another was to buy a new coating head, at a cost of $700,000 plus loss of production during installation. The solution used by Nashua was try to find out what was going on in an orderly fashion. It is always a good idea, when a competitor, producing the same product with equipment and logistical support apparently inferior to our own, is able to best us both in terms of quality and price, to learn what he is doing better than are we.

At the time of the problem, there was not a great deal of monitoring information available on the Nashua product. There was end product information in terms of darkness tests carried out on test samples from the moving roll. We observe the sort of results obtained in Figure 10.5.

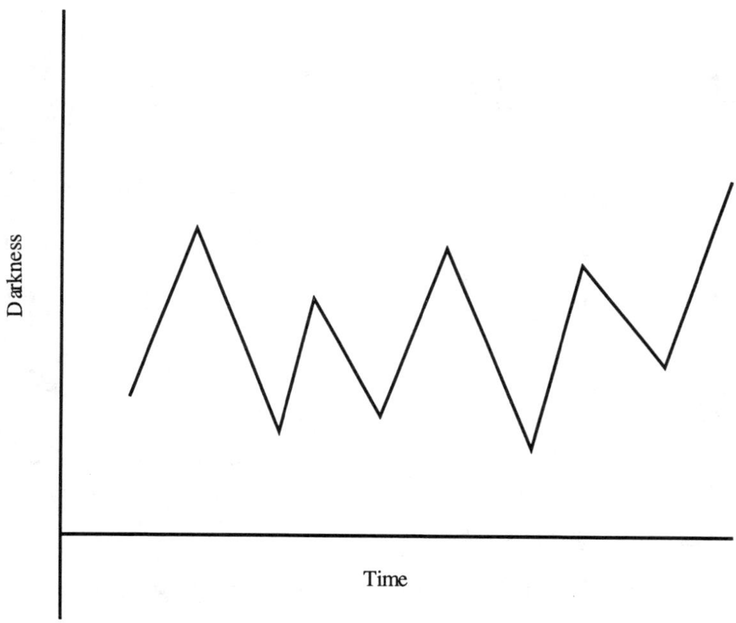

Figure 10.5. Darkness Measurements of Output.

The pathology shown in Figure 10.5 is one of the easiest to detect and correct. The zig-zag up and down graph is indicative of "over-control." The operators on the coating machine, noting the paper tested too dark, lowered the coating setting. Then, when the paper became too light, they increased it again. The operators had failed to note (for no one had told them) that it took the coating machine some minutes to implement the current setting. Thus, the operators were actually driving the machine into a state of constant instability. The solution here was relatively simple: set the coater and do not change the setting until we see the darkness under steady state conditions. In other words, don't fix something until you are confident it is really broken. The problem of "over-control" is one which is so easy to identify that no formal statistical analysis is necessary. In Figure 10.6, we note the sort of improvement obtained when the simple fix had been implemented.

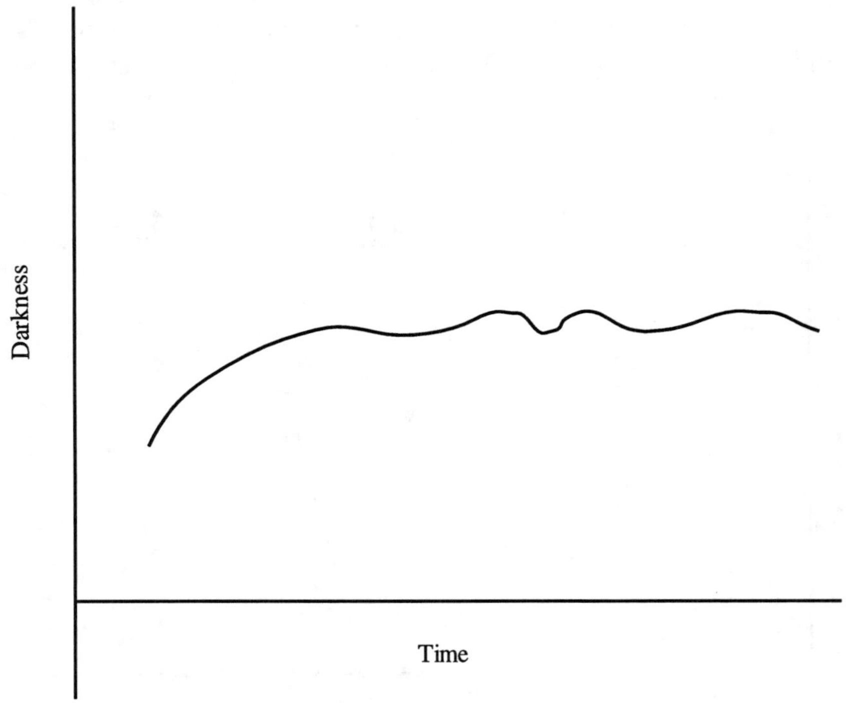

Figure 10.6. Darkness Measurements after Correction.

Letting the coating machine do its job produced immediate dividends. First of all, it was unnecessary to purchase a new coating head; hence a saving of $700,000 was made possible. More importantly, very quickly Nashua was able to produce a uniform product using a coating rate of 3.6 pounds per 3,000 square feet. This brought the Nashua product to being competitive. But this was not the end of the story. Quality control is a continuous evolutionary optimization process. Noting that the coating cost $100,000 per tenth of pound per year, Nashua began to take advantage of its high tech coating machine. In less than a year, they were able to reduce the coating rate to 2.8 pounds per 3,000 square feet, producing an annual savings of $800,000. By 1985, Nashua had adapted nicely to the SPC philosophy. The flow charts had become much more sophisticated and the data monitoring much more detailed. Improvements had reduced the coating level to 1.0 pounds per 3,000 square feet [4].

We should note, moreover, the utilization in statistical process control of a principle which stands in importance alongside that of Pareto's Maxim and is strongly connected to it. That principle is that a system, suffering from a defect, once the defect is corrected, will tend not to return to the old defect. In the current example, once we appreciate that we had a problem of overcontrol in too quickly making manual adjustments to settings on the coating machine, we are unlikely to repeat the old mistake again. Without such a principle, SPC would not be very effective. We would be condemned forever to the quality assurance paradigms.

Consider a man juggling balls. As he hurls a red ball upward, he notices that he must immediately turn his attention to the yellow ball which is falling. When he hurls the yellow ball upward, he notes that the green ball is falling. By the time he throws the green ball upward, he must deal with the red ball again. And so on. Systems tend not to behave like a juggler. To stretch the analogy, in dealing with systems, it is only necessary to throw the red ball one time.

The consequences of the above example are clear. An unprofitable American company escaped ruin and became a savvy enterprise which can stand up to competition from any quarter. No recrimination was taken against those who had overcontrolled the system. A superior, more profitable product benefited both the company and its customers. The price paid was not increased stress for the workers. Indeed, it eliminated a good deal of stress on the part of everyone involved. The company had simply engaged in that which Americans have typically done well: finding out problems, describing them and solving them.

The Nashua example is fairly typical, in that the initial problem presented was caused, not by a general malaise across the production line, but rather by a failure at one particular point of the process. It is not that everything else except overadjustment of the coating machine was perfect. But the other failings were relatively insignificant when compared to that of overadjustment. To get from the coating levels of 1979 to those of 1985 required numerous other optimizations. As big defects were eliminated, the company was able to detect smaller ones. Also, the Nashua example is typical of what happens when a company begins to use the statistical process control approach. Note that the flowchart used was rather similar to the crude noninformative flowchart in Figure 10.4. Still, enormous benefits were obtained quickly and easily. In the United States, it is fairly common for an SPC practitioner to be sought out when a problem similar to that of Nashua's is experienced. Frequently, examination of the data records will enable a finding of a defect whose elimination will solve the immediate problem. Unfortunately, that is generally the end of the company's interest in SPC until the next crisis occurs. The management of Nashua wisely decided to stay with SPC as a standard operating procedure. The company and its employees reaped the benefits. Perhaps the company was fortunate to have competition from a Japanese company which had itself implemented statistical process control. Nashua's management knew that they must continue to improve if they were to remain competitive.

The simple noninformative flowchart frequently has to be in the early stages of an SPC operation, since that is all that is available. (Indeed, it is frequently the case that there is no time indexed data base at all. We just know that the frequency of unsatisfactory product is "high".) It is better if we can make the flowchart more informative, as that shown in Figure 10.7. Each one of the outputs of a module is recorded in time. Let us suppose that we note something irregular in X_{14}. Tracing back in time, we notice appropriate time led irregularities in X_{13},X_{12}, X_{11}, but not in any output prior to X_{11}. In such a situation, we would look for a problem in module 11.

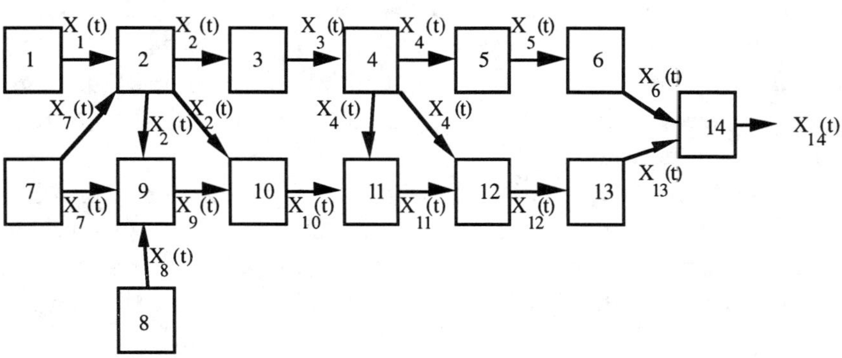

Figure 10.7. More Detailed Flow Chart of Simple Process.

The difficulty with just having output information such as X_{14}, is that it is then hard to pinpoint the source of problems. For example, a graduate student at Rice recently purchased a Hyundai Sonata. After 200 miles, the student found that, unless the airconditioning was turned on, the transmission of the car worked roughly, if at all. What are the possible causes of the problem? Perhaps an electrical short, perhaps a defect in the transmission, perhaps a defect in the airconditioning, perhaps .... If monitoring of parts and assembly had been taken stage by stage during the assembly, we might well have been able to have detected, say, a faulty insulation on a wire.

Note that it is *not* the function of statistical process control to detect an end product automobile with a flaky transmission. It is the function of SPC to find the problem in the system which can cause such defects and remove it from the system, so that it can no longer be responsible for the production of lemons. The SPC professional is not like the DEA cop trying to bust junkies one at a time. He is rather like the DEA person seeking out and destroying drug lords. One of the biggest misperceptions is that quality control is supposed to keep bad products off the market by inspecting the output. That is, in fact, the way most quality control operations are run (i.e., as "quality assurance"). In the early stages of an SPC operation, it will frequently be a good idea to carry on with 100% end inspection, for SPC does not monitor for faulty items *except insofar as they provide clues for fixing, permanently, the system problems which made them faulty.* But some time after the institution of a modern SPC paradigm, end product inspection begins naturally to atrophy. We recall that the manufacturers of the Japanese luxury car, the Lexus LS 400, spend fewer person hours on the construction of an average vehicle than some of its German competitors spend on rework of one of their average vehicles.

References

[1] Deming, W. E., *Quality, Productivity and Competitive Position*, Cambridge: MIT Center for Advanced Engineering Studies, 1982, pp. 16-17.

[2] Falcon, W. D., *Zero Defects: Doing It Right the First Time*, American Management Association, Inc., 1965.

[3] Ford, H., *My Life and Work*, Sydney: Cornstalk Press, 1926, p. 273.

[4] Mann, N. R.,*The Keys to Excellence: the Story of the Deming Philosophy*, Los Angeles: Prestwick Books, 1985.

[5] Sorin, Y., *On Quality and Reliability: Notes for Labor Union Activists.* , Moscow: Profizdat, 1963, p. 120.

[6] Thompson, J. R., "American quality control: what went wrong? What can we do to fix it?" *Proceedings of the 1985 Conference on Applied Analysis in Aerospace, Industry and Medical Sciences,* Chhikara, Raj, ed., Houston: University of Houston, 1985, pp. 247-255.

[7] Thompson, J.R. and J. Koronacki, J., *Statistical Process Control for Quality Improvement*, New York: Chapman & Hall, 1993.

[8] Todt, H. C., "Employee motivation: fact or fiction," in *Zero Defects: Doing It Right the First Time*, Falcon, William, ed., New York: American Management Association, Inc., 1965, pp. 3-9.

[9] Williams, E.E. and Thompson, J.R., *The Economics of Production and Productivity: A Modeling Approach*, Austin: Capital Book Company, 1996.

Problems

Problem 10.1 If the proportion of defectives in an assembly line is 5%, find the probability that a lot of 20 items will have (a) no defectives, (b) at least two defectives (c) more than three defectives.

Problem 10.2 In December of 1995, an American led NATO force moved into Bosnia to assist in a transition to a peaceful constitutional democracy. Use a fishbone diagram to delineate the problems which the NATO leaders might reasonably expect to confront.

Problem 10.3 Consider the following two run charts of diameters of bolts of nominal 10 inch diameter. Which of the two scenarios should be easier to correct?

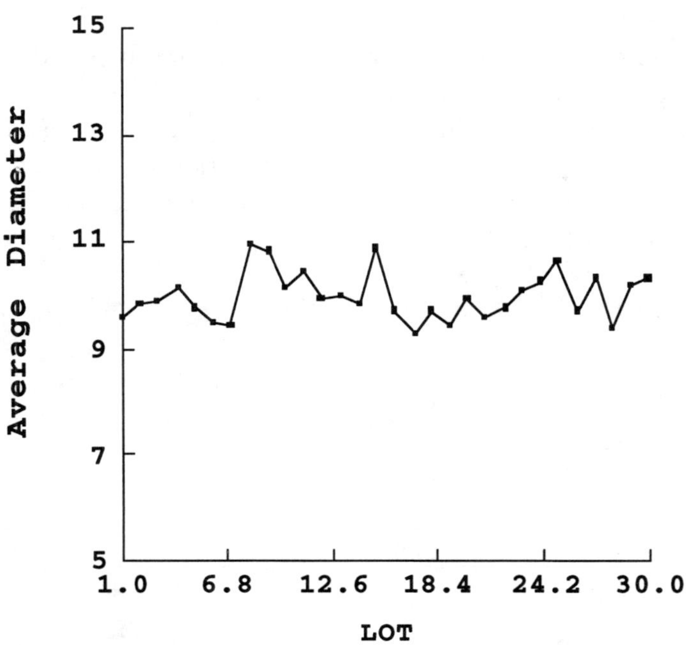

Bolt Diameters

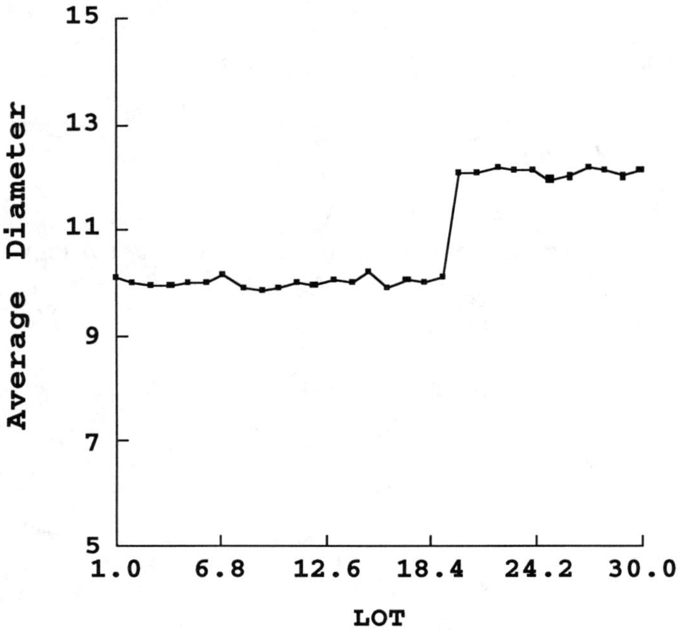

Bolt Diameters

Problem 10.4 The cost of inspecting an item is denoted by c_I. If a faulty item is defective and has been inspected, it is replaced (at no marginal cost). If a faulty item has not been inspected, the average cost of retrorepair is c_R. Assume that the proportion of defective items is p. Show that an optimal strategy is to inspect all items if $c_I > pc_R$ and none, otherwise.

Chapter 11

Control Charting: Some Case Studies

11.1 Introduction

As we have noted, Statistical Process Control does not seek for defective items. It seeks for readings at sensor points in the system which are significantly different from the average. When such a "Pareto glitch" is found, we go back and examine the system at that time (no, we do not have to "shut down the line" as soon as such a reading is found; we can use time indexed recordings of relevant inputs to the module(s) where the extraordinary reading was found). This is generally achieved by using control charts of samples taken at points within the system.

11.2 An Example With Open Ended Failure Counts

Let us proceed to examine an example using simple defect data from welds in the construction of a nuclear reactor. For such a reactor, government regulations demand 100% checking (by X-ray photography) of the integrity of the welds. Suppose we have two years of data from such a construction (carried out by a firm with extensive experience in the construction of nuclear power facilities). The data is presented in Table 11.1 and Figure 11.1 below:

Table 11.1. Weekly Failure Records.

Month	Number Faulty Welds Discovered
1	12
2	21
3	18
4	22
5	24
6	19
7	26
8	22
9	15
10	15
11	21
12	17
13	22
14	28
15	17
16	18
17	25
18	24
19	21
20	23
21	51
22	64
23	66
24	59

We note a dramatic increase in the number of bad welds discovered in month 21 and continuing for the remainder of the two year period. Could this have simply happened by chance or is it the result of some "assignable cause"? This sort of question is key in statistical process control. Without any statistical theory, most people would be inclined to think that the results in months 21 through 24 indicate that something is different about those four months from the preceding twenty months. Generally speaking, statistical process control is consistent with "common sense," so in this case, "most people" would probably be right.

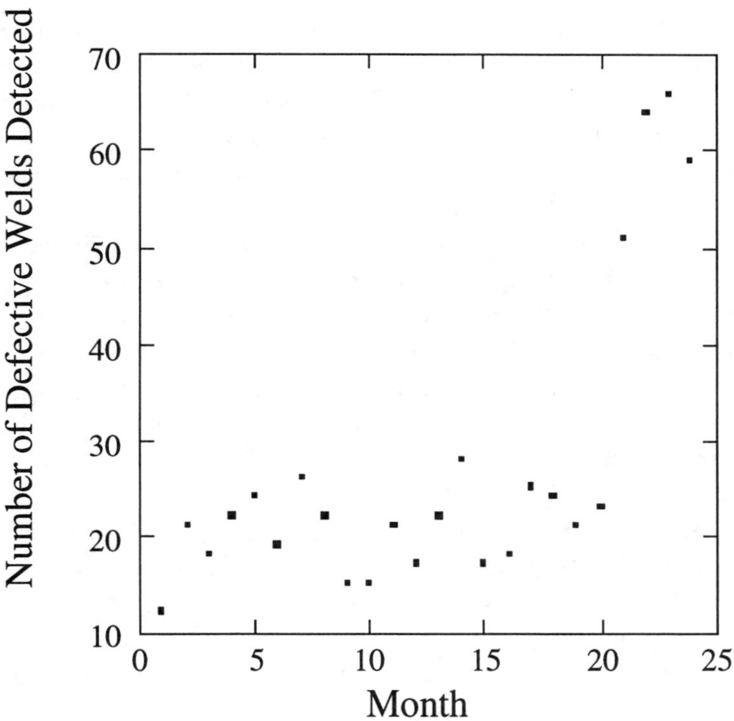

Figure 11.1. Faulty Welds Discovered.

It is, of course, possible to take the position that any perceived perturbation from normal behavior should cause us to believe that the system has taken a turn for the worse. Consider, for example, management which acts on the premise that there simply should never be a faulty weld. (Of course, such a standard of performance is desirable and generally, very nearly achievable over the long haul). Such an individual would be in a panic from that moment in the first month when the first bad weld was detected. But to what purpose will be this panic? Slogans, exhortations, threats, etc., etc. It is important to avoid such a common management mistake. Of course, we would hope to have no bad welds at all. We should be well aware that end product inspection is seldom hugely reliable. So, if we are told we have 20 bad welds; it is quite possible that we actually have 22. But we need to use our data stream to try to see what caused the jump in the numerosity of faulty welds in month 21. The indication that something dramatic happened in that month is the kind of information which drives SPC.

One possibility is that the inspection team changed to a better one in month 21 and that the higher numerosity of bad welds had actually been with us all along. Such information would not be very helpful from the standpoint of changing the system to lower the number of defective welds. But it would tell us that we must go back to the beginning and recheck all the welds.

On the other hand, we might find that in month 21 we had changed to a cheaper kind of welding equipment. In such a case, we would at the very least be able to return to earlier, smaller numerosity of failed welds. And, we might further consider that if the system was sensitive to moving to a cheaper set of welding hardware, perhaps we might improve the failure situation by investigating hardware alternative to that being used in the earlier epoch.

This, then, is the basic idea of statistical process control: use significant deviations from customary performance as clues which can be backtracked to find assignable causes which we then repair. Do not define "customary" as what we would like things to be, but rather things as they are.

We next address the technical and relatively minor matter of constructing a statistical test to make sure that the "glitch" we have observed when we go to month 21 is a "Pareto glitch," i.e, one which appears to be unlikely to have happened unless something noncustomary had happened to the system. The usual rule is that we would like to use tests which would claim that the system had changed, when it had in fact not changed, only two times out of a thousand. In the parlance of medical testing, we want to use a test which has a low chance of a "false positive." Clearly, such a procedure would not be appropriate if what we are aiming for is immediate "quality assurance." It would, for example, not be satisfactory if we were constructing a test to identify human cells as cancerous or not. But it is appropriate in a situation where we are dealing with a complex production system in which we are being besieged at all times by reams of data. We do not, in statistical process control, purport that we will be able to find all bad end product items. We, rather, purport that we are using information to improve the system itself and hence lower the likelihood that an unsatisfactory end product item will be produced. The probability of "Type 1 Error" (i.e., declaring a lot to be out of control when it is, in fact, in control) need not be set at .002, and it is not important that we know closely what the actual probability is. We will generally use the "rule of thumb" that rejects a lot as being atypical if it lies three standard deviations away from the overall sample mean. Seldom will it be the case that we can say that our sample is so close to the textbook ideal conditions that the plus or minus three standard deviations will correspond to a Type I Error of precisely 0.27%. Actual Type I Errors will range from one-tenth of one percent to two or three percent. And, in the SPC context, this range of Type I Errors will be quite acceptable. Our goal is to have an error detector which seldom falsely identifies as "nonstandard" a "standard" lot but which does detect a reasonable proportion of "nonstandard" lots. We recall that our task is not to find bad items or sets of items, but rather to correct the system which gave rise to them.

For "open ended" data, such as we have here, i.e., failures which could go upward to very high values, the usual rule of thumb for constructing a test, is to take the average $\bar{\bar{X}}$ of the failure counts for all the months (in this case 27.08). We then reject a month as being significantly unusual (a Pareto glitch) if its number of counts X lies outside the interval

$$\bar{\bar{X}} \pm 3\sqrt{(\bar{\bar{X}})}. \tag{11.1}$$

Here, our confidence interval extends from 11.47 to 42.69. The months numbered 21, 22, 23, and 24 clearly give, by this standard, unusual readings, worthy of further investigation for the cause of the high counts. (We note that in this case, ($\bar{\bar{X}}$ estimates both the mean and the variance of the number of failures

In summary, for failure data in epochs where it is reasonable to believe that the average number of failures should be approximately the same in each epoch, and where this average number of failures can be rather large (say 20 or more per epoch), the suggested procedure is as follows

1. Compute the average number of failures per epoch, called $\bar{\bar{X}} = \frac{1}{N}\sum_{i=1}^{N} X_i$, where X_i is the number of failures in the ith epoch.

2. Fix the interval $\bar{\bar{X}} \pm 3\sqrt{\bar{\bar{X}}}$.

3. Identify any X_i as "out of control" if it falls outside the interval.

4. Investigate the reasons why the out of control epoch occurred, i.e., find the "assignable cause" for the failures in the period being out of control.

5. Fix the problem.

11.3 An Example With Failure Proportions

Table 11.2. Infections Following Hip Replacement.

Month	Patients	Infections	Prop.
1	50	3	.060
2	42	2	.048
3	37	6	.162
4	71	5	.070
5	55	6	.109
6	44	6	.136
7	38	10	.263
8	33	2	.061
9	41	4	.098
10	27	1	.037
11	33	1	.03
12	49	3	.061
13	66	8	.121
14	49	5	.102
15	55	4	.073
16	41	2	.049
17	29	0	0
18	40	3	.075
19	41	2	.049
20	48	5	.104
21	52	4	.077
22	55	6	.109
23	49	5	.102
24	60	2	.033

Failure rate data is generally the crudest with which to work. Unfortunately, it is frequently the only kind we have. Let us consider an example considered by Thompson and Koronacki [7] concerning hip replacement infections in a metropolitan hospital. We show, in Table

11.2, the counts of operations performed and subsequent infections on a month to month basis over a two year period. This problem is not uncommon in that the charge from the hospital was to check whether there were any noticeable increases in infection rates at any time during the two year period. A casual examination of Figure 11.2 does not seem to indicate anything particularly out of the ordinary.

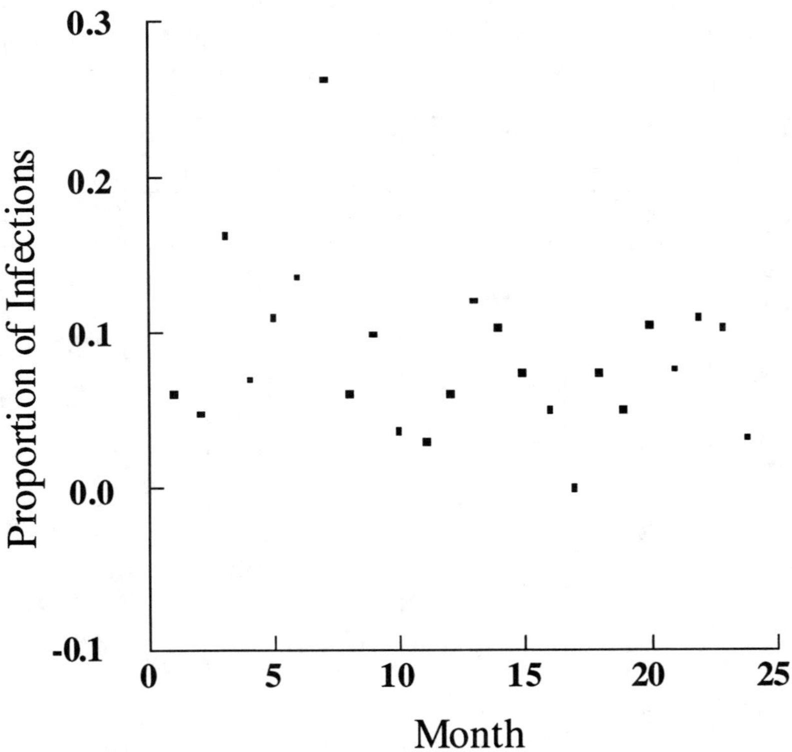

Figure 11.2. Proportion of Infections.

Let us again return to our "rule of thumb." We will reject a month as nontypical if the proportion of infections in that month falls outside three standard deviations from the overall proportion of infections. Suppose that over the entire two year period the proportion of infections is p $(= 95/1105 = .086)$. This gives us the upper control limit and lower control limit.

$$UCL = p + 3\sqrt{\frac{p(1-p)}{n}} \tag{11.2}$$

and

$$LCL = \max\{0, p - 3\sqrt{\frac{p(1-p)}{n}}\}, \tag{11.3}$$

where n is the number of infections in a particular month. Here, we shall probably be most concerned if the number of infections in a month goes over the the "upper control limit," i.e., if the proportion of infective hip replacements in that month divided by the upper control limit is greater than one. We show these augmenting columns in Table 11.3.

Table 11.3. Infections Following Hip Replacement.

Month	Patients	Infections	Prop.	UCL	Prop./UCL
1	50	3	.06	.205	.308
2	42	2	.048	.216	.232
3	37	6	.162	.224	.757
4	71	5	.070	.186	.399
5	55	6	.109	.199	.575
6	44	6	.136	.213	.673
7	38	10	.263	.222	1.241
8	33	2	.061	.232	.273
9	41	4	.098	.217	.471
10	27	1	.037	.248	.157
11	33	1	.030	.232	.137
12	49	3	.061	.206	.312
13	66	8	.121	.190	.673
14	49	5	.102	.206	.520
15	55	4	.073	.199	.383
16	41	2	.049	.217	.236
17	29	0	0	.242	0
18	40	3	.075	.219	.359
19	41	2	.049	.217	.236
20	48	5	.104	.207	.527
21	52	4	.077	.203	.399
22	55	6	.109	.199	.575
23	49	5	.102	.206	.520
24	60	2	.033	.195	.18

Looking at Figure 11.3, we note that month 7 is outside the limit of normalcy, since the proportion of infections divided by the upper control limit exceeds one. (Customary parlance here is to say that "month 7 is out of control.") At any rate, it seems as if there is enough indication of trouble to investigate further.

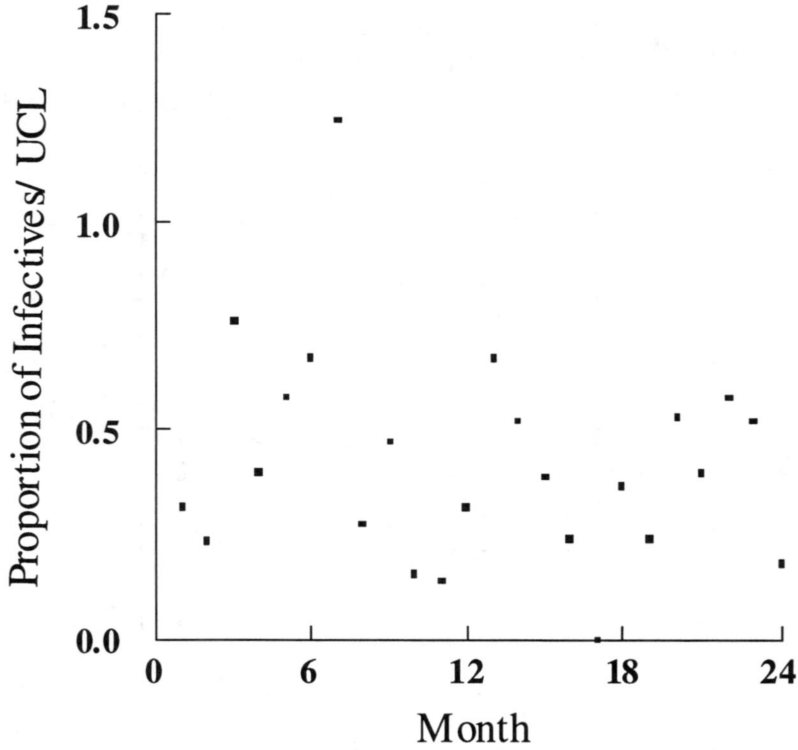

Figure 11.3. Proportion Infections Divided by UCL.

Upon further examination, it turns out that, as is the case with coronary by-pass operations, hip replacement is carried out by teams of physicians, nurses, etc. In this hospital, there were three teams, one of which only started operating in month 4. In Table 11.4, we show the records broken down by surgical team, where N denotes the total number of patients, and I denotes the number of infections.

As mentioned, Team C only began operation in month 4. In the start-up phase, Team C had a much higher rate of infections than did the other two teams. But from month 15 on, the performance record of Team C had essentially become the same as that of the other two teams. Clearly, Team C has learned from its mistakes (much good may it do the patients on whom these mistakes were effected).

Start-up difficulties are a problem with most systems. However, it is possible to minimize these by careful planning, design of system, and looking for discrepancies from the standards set by the established teams.

Table 11.4. Team Performance Data.

Month	N_A	I_B	N_B	I_B	N_C	I_C
1	20	1	30	2	0	0
2	22	2	20	0	0	0
3	20	2	17	4	0	0
4	30	2	35	1	6	2
5	17	2	25	2	13	2
6	20	1	15	2	9	3
7	15	2	10	2	13	6
8	21	1	9	0	3	1
9	19	1	19	2	3	1
10	10	0	15	0	2	1
11	15	1	15	0	3	0
12	25	1	20	1	4	1
13	31	2	20	2	15	4
14	19	1	20	1	10	3
15	25	1	20	2	10	1
16	19	2	15	0	7	0
17	10	0	9	0	10	0
18	14	1	16	1	10	1
19	10	1	10	1	21	0
20	15	1	10	2	23	2
21	20	1	20	2	12	1
22	19	2	17	2	19	2
23	14	1	15	2	20	2
24	20	1	20	1	20	0

The medical profession is thought by some to be beyond the notion of "system." "Every patient is different," they claim. This fails to note the many similarities of the steps taken in the management of a particular pathology. In the example given here, Team C learned from its mistakes. Statistical process control used in real time, as opposed to the retrospection here, would have minimized the start-up glitches. The kind of post-mortem quality control approach considered here is all too typical. In this case, we suspect it had to do with the danger of a lawsuit from one of the early operations performed by Team C.

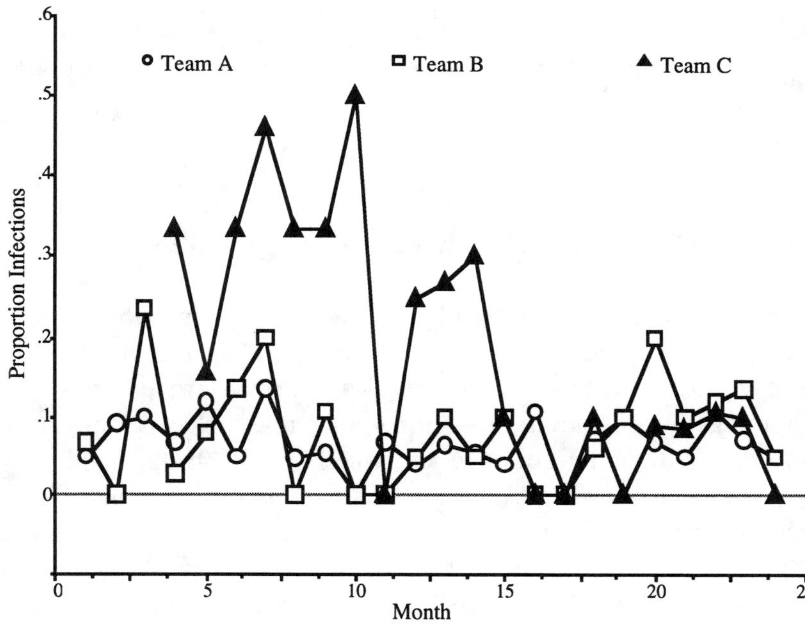

Figure 11.4. Comparison of Team Performances.

In summary, for failure data in epochs where it is reasonable to believe that the proportion of failures should be approximately the same in each epoch, and where this average number of failures can be rather modest (say 20 or fewer per epoch), the suggested procedure is as follows

1. Compute the average proportion of failures during the entire period called

   $p = \frac{1}{\sum_{j=1}^{N} n_j} \sum_{i=1}^{N} x_i$

   where n_j is the number of items produced in epoch j, x_i is the number of failures observed in period i, and N is the number of epochs considered.

2. Let $p_i = \frac{x_i}{n_i}$.

3. Let the upper control limit for the ith interval be given by

   $UCL_i = p + 3\sqrt{\frac{p(1-p)}{n_i}}$.

4. Reject the ith epoch as being out of control if

   $\frac{p_i}{UCL_i} > 1.$

5. Investigate the reasons why the out of control epoch occurred, i.e., find the "assignable cause" for the failures in the epoch being out of control.

6. Fix the problem.

11.4 SPC with Measurement Data

Since most systems are managed by people who simply count failures of end product results, it is such failure data which must be the beginning of most SPC studies. Nevertheless, once we are able to begin flowcharting the system, we can implement reasonable quantitative measurements at many nodes in the flowchart. Such data will generally be sampled. 100% inspection of all items produced is seldom utilized when we take quantitative measurements instead of simply classifying end items as satisfactory or unsatisfactory. We shall be working then with measurements from "lots" sampled at intervals of time.

Let us suppose that Figure 12.7 corresponds to the production of transmissions. In the course of an SPC operation, we will be sampling lots of each of the outputs shown. Each of these X_j can be multidimensional. Let us consider, without loss of generality, the measurement of one of the components of measurement X_{12} which happens to be the diameter Y of a plunger rod. Once again, we shall be employing a plus or minus three standard deviations rule. Our work will be based on sample lot mean and lot standard deviation information. Let us consider the data below of 20 lots of size 5 taken at 3 hour intervals.

Here, the lot mean of the first lot (of five items) is computed according to

$$\bar{Y}_1 = \frac{10.002 + 9.926 + 10.052 + 9.736 + 9.860}{5} = 9.915\ . \qquad (11.4)$$

The mean of all 20 lot means is given by

$$\bar{\bar{Y}} = \frac{10.030 + 9.930 + \ldots + 9.968}{20} = 9.979\ . \qquad (11.5)$$

Table 11.5. Rod Diameter Data.

i	Y_{1i}	Y_{2i}	Y_{3i}	Y_{4i}	Y_{5i}	$\overline{Y_i}$	s_i
1	10.002	9.926	10.052	9.736	9.860	9.915	0.124
2	9.908	9.933	9.936	9.751	9.910	9.888	0.078
3	9.971	10.024	10.047	10.080	10.030	10.030	0.040
4	10.073	9.839	9.849	9.897	9.992	9.930	0.100
5	10.004	10.031	9.989	9.988	10.051	10.012	0.028
6	10.183	9.930	10.012	9.847	10.036	10.002	0.126
7	10.135	9.946	10.060	9.960	9.940	10.008	0.086
8	9.945	10.041	9.993	9.820	10.006	9.961	0.086
9	10.090	9.828	10.163	9.913	10.095	10.018	0.141
10	9.956	10.063	9.975	10.018	10.029	10.008	0.043
11	10.023	10.121	10.001	10.037	9.890	10.014	0.083
12	9.781	10.103	9.980	9.795	10.092	9.950	0.156
13	9.960	10.093	10.036	9.900	10.012	10.000	0.073
14	10.029	10.090	10.041	9.800	10.037	9.999	0.114
15	10.139	10.134	9.966	10.001	9.910	10.030	0.102
16	9.976	9.969	9.912	9.940	9.908	9.941	0.032
17	10.086	9.792	9.974	9.917	10.009	9.956	0.110
18	9.990	9.811	10.095	10.136	9.875	9.981	0.139
19	9.913	9.976	10.064	10.042	9.856	9.970	0.087
20	10.026	9.992	10.034	9.888	9.901	9.968	0.069

The variance of the first lot is given by

$$s_1^2 = \frac{(10.002 - 9.915)^2 + \ldots + (9.860 - 9.915)^2}{4} = .01538 \ . \quad (11.6)$$

(Here we follow the convention, when computing the lot variance of dividing by one less than the lot size.) The lot standard deviation is simply the square root of the lot variance. Thus

$$s_1 = \sqrt{s_1^2} = \sqrt{.015376} = .124 \ . \quad (11.7)$$

The overall estimate of the variability is given by

$$\bar{s} = \frac{\sum_{i=1}^{N} s_i}{N} = .091 \ . \quad (11.8)$$

We shall continue with our basic strategy of declaring a lot out of control if it lies outside the "three sigma confidence interval." A lot may be out of control for two reasons. Its mean may be outside the confidence interval or the standard deviation may be outside the confidence interval. If the lot size is n, then we shall use Table 11.6 to obtain the confidence intervals.

Table 11.6.

n	$B_3(n)$	$B_4(n)$	$A_3(n)$
2	0	3.267	2.659
3	0	2.568	1.954
4	0	2.266	1.628
5	0	2.089	1.427
6	.030	1.970	1.287
7	.118	1.882	1.182
8	.185	1.815	1.099
9	.239	1.761	1.032
10	.284	1.716	.975
15	.428	1.572	.789
20	.510	1.490	.680
25	.565	1.435	.606

The confidence interval on the mean of diameters for a lot is given by

$$\bar{\bar{X}} \pm A_3(n)\bar{s} \tag{11.9}$$

Here, of course, n= 5, $\bar{\bar{X}}$= 9.979, and $\bar{s}$ = .091. So then, we have

$$UCL = \bar{\bar{X}} + A_3(5)\bar{s} = 9.979 + 1.427(.091) = 10.1089\ , \tag{11.10}$$

$$LCL = \bar{\bar{X}} - A_3(5)\bar{s} = 9.979 + 1.427(.091) = 9.8491\ . \tag{11.11}$$

We notice that none of the lot means falls outside the control limits for the sample mean. Let us now examine the control chart for the standard deviations. The formulae for the upper control and lower limits are given by

$$\text{Upper Control Limit} = B_4(n)\bar{s} = 2.089(.091) = .1900\ , \tag{11.12}$$

and

$$\text{Lower Control Limit} = B_3(n)\bar{s} = (0)(.091) = 0\ . \tag{11.13}$$

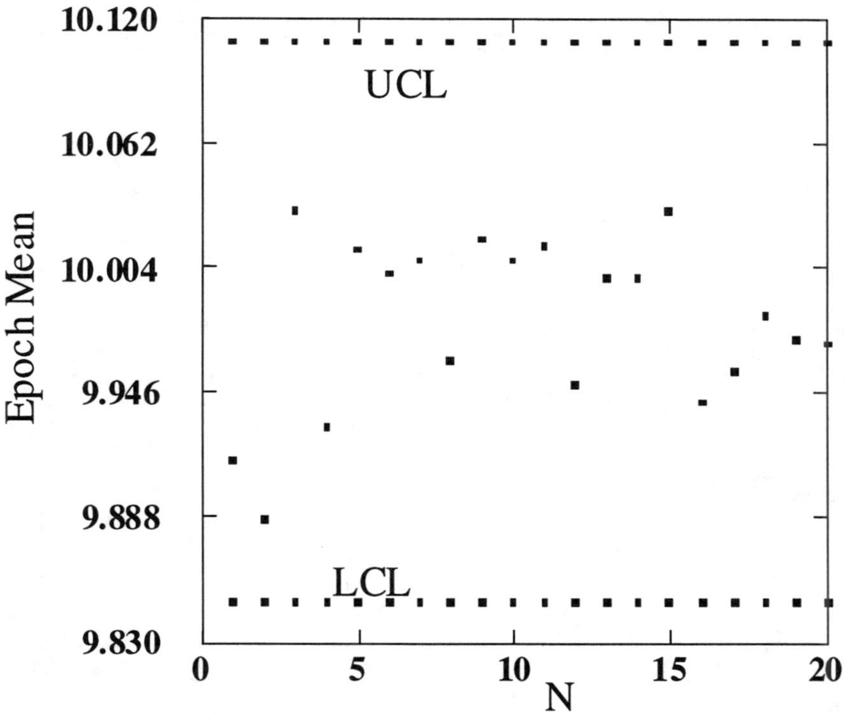

Figure 11.5. Diameter Means Control Chart.

The standard deviation control chart is given in Figure 11.6. We note that neither on the basis of lot means nor on the basis of lot standard deviations is any of the twenty lots "out of control." This is the sort of thing we should expect to see most of the time for all the variables measured coming out of the various modules in Figure 12.7. Any sort of quality control management which constantly declares the system to be out of control is doomed to failure. It is the classic example of the shepherd constantly crying "Wolf!'

Notice that the paradigm of statistical process control advocated by Deming does not declare a lot to be "out of control" because it fails to measure up to arbitrary standards. The benchmark for "in control" behavior comes from the performance record itself. We compare a lot not against arbitrary standards, but against the characteristics of other lots.

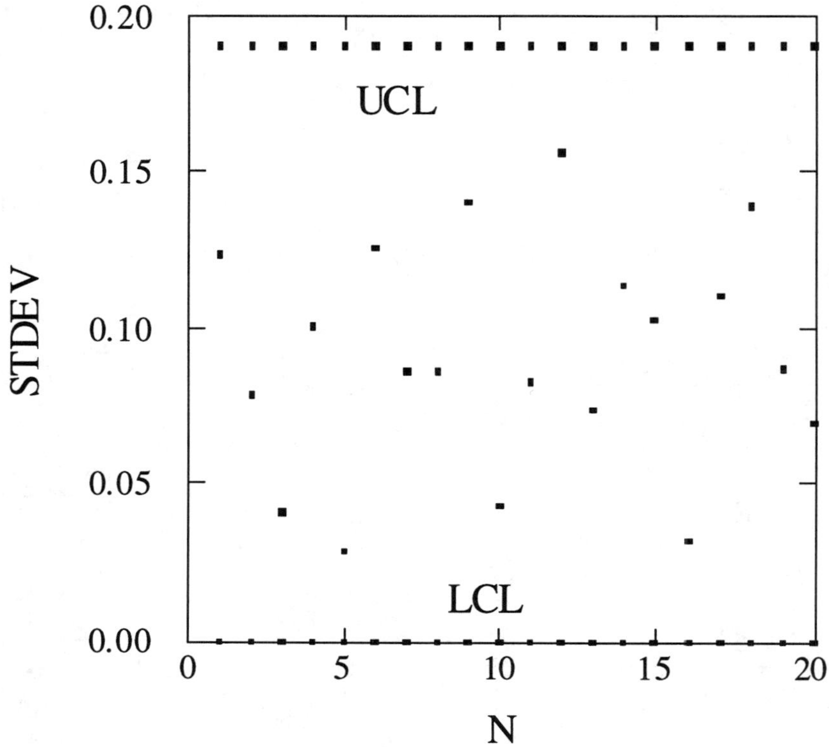

Figure 11.6.Standard Deviations Control Chart.

11.5 When Control Charts "Don't Work"

It is the basic task of control charting to find the "high frequency" Pareto glitch. Consequently, it might appear that the last thing we would want to consider in this context is smoothing, a device generally oriented to removing the high frequency wiggles in a time indexed data set. A concrete example [4, pp. 175-185] will show the importance of smoothing to the SPC investigator.

A manufacturer producing flexible construction material had a number of samples that were outside the tolerance limits on a particular strength index. (This was a manufacturer practicing "quality assurance" rather than statistical process control.) The manufacturer had originated the particular kind of flexible material. As is frequently the case, the federal government had invited the manufacturer to write the acceptable specifications for the material. On the face of it, it would appear this was a golden opportunity for the manufacturer to help the government present himself with a monopoloy.This can be achieved by writing the specifications to be tough where the manufacturer's product was excellent, lax where the manufacturer had difficulties. As is not uncommon, the manufacturer had his marketing department rather than his engineering or production department write up the specifications. Marketing was sensitive to the monopolistic opportunities, but had only vague ideas about the production capabilities. Accordingly, some of the requirements were written to be comparable to the best the manufacturer could produce.

Finally, there were about a dozen such measurement indices which were measured both by the manufacturer and his client. Not a great deal of attention was paid to these indices, which were perhaps only marginally related to performance of the sheets. Rather the manufacturing workers more or less identified good material visually. Nevertheless, the indices were a part of the state approved "code." Failure to comply with them on the part of the builder might expose him to subsequent lawsuits by an end user.

Some weeks after the material had been used, it was noted by a builder, who was the major client of the manufacturer, that a number of samples were outside stated tolerance levels for one of the strength indices. An on site task force was immediately dispatched to sites where the material had been used. Both the manufacturer and the builder agreed that the material was performing well. Extensive examination over a period of some months failed to find a problem. The head of the quality assurance section left the manufacturing firm "to pursue exciting opportunities elsewhere." Pressure from the builder increased. Veiled threats to changing suppliers were made.

The data in Table 11.7 reveals a situation where the lot size is one. From each of the 47 rolls a sample sheet is cut and tested. Consequently, our estimate for the overall mean is given simply by

$$\bar{x} = \frac{1}{47}\sum_{i=1}^{47} x_i = 144.398\ . \tag{11.14}$$

Similarly, the estimate for the overall variance is given by

$$s^2 = \frac{1}{46}\sum_{i=1}^{47}(x_i - 144.398)^2 = 6881.581 , \tag{11.15}$$

giving as our estimate for the standard deviation

$$s = \sqrt{s^2} = 82.955 . \tag{11.16}$$

Thus the upper and lower control limits for x are given by

$$UCL = \bar{x} + 3s = 144.398 + 3(82.955) = 393.26663 \tag{11.17}$$

and

$$LCL = Max\{0, \bar{x} + 3s)\} = Max\{0, 144.398 - 3(82.955)\} = 0. \tag{11.18}$$

As we note in Figure 11.17, all the data lie within the control limits. If one examines the graph cursorily, it seems to have two populations, one rather strong, one not.

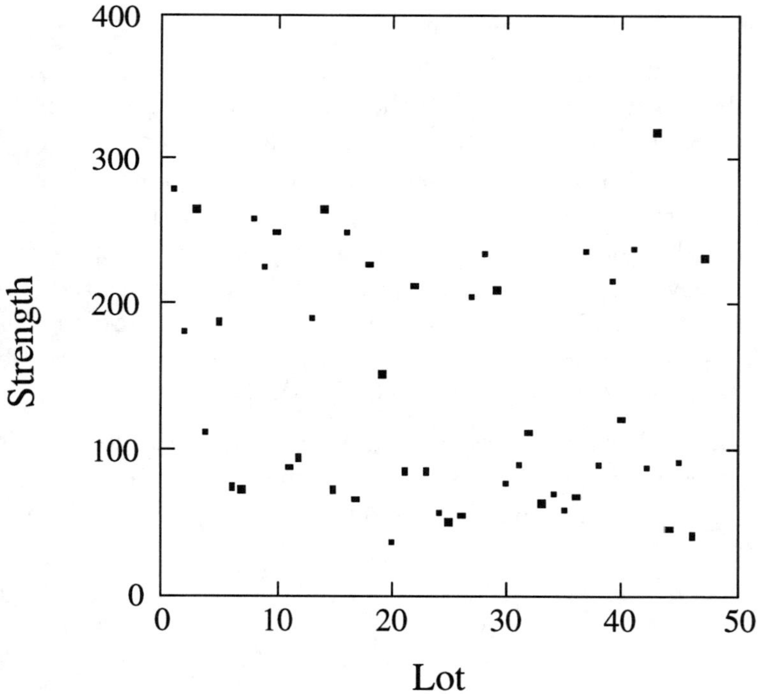

Figure 11.7. Chart of Strength Data.

Table 11.7.	
Roll Number	x = Strength
1	278.000
2	181.400
3	265.400
4	111.000
5	187.600
6	74.400
7	71.840
8	258.400
9	225.700
10	249.200
11	86.600
12	94.480
13	189.000
14	264.000
15	72.600
16	249.000
17	66.000
18	226.200
19	151.400
20	36.600
21	85.400
22	210.800
23	84.800
24	57.400
25	49.800
26	54.200
27	204.400
28	233.000
29	210.200
30	77.55
31	89.900
32	112.000
33	64.000
34	70.600
35	59.800
36	66.800
37	235.600
38	90.800
39	216.000
40	120.500
41	239.200
42	87.000
43	318.800
44	44.480
45	91.840
46	40.800
47	232.200

The split of the data into two groupings is made even more apparent by the histogram of the strength data in Figure 11.8. It turns out that the data appears to be dividing into a group with "strength" measurements in the proper range, and another very much on the low side. Such a data set is not untypical of the kind confronting statistical process control professionals as soon as they walk in the door. In the United States, in particular, SPC people seem to be called in by desperate managers more frequently than by managers who have cooly decided that this is the year when the company will get serious about quality control. The Deming analysis, which is generally excellent as a procedure once some degree of order has been introduced, frequently needs to be supplemented by nonstandard techniques in the first stages of an SPC implementation.

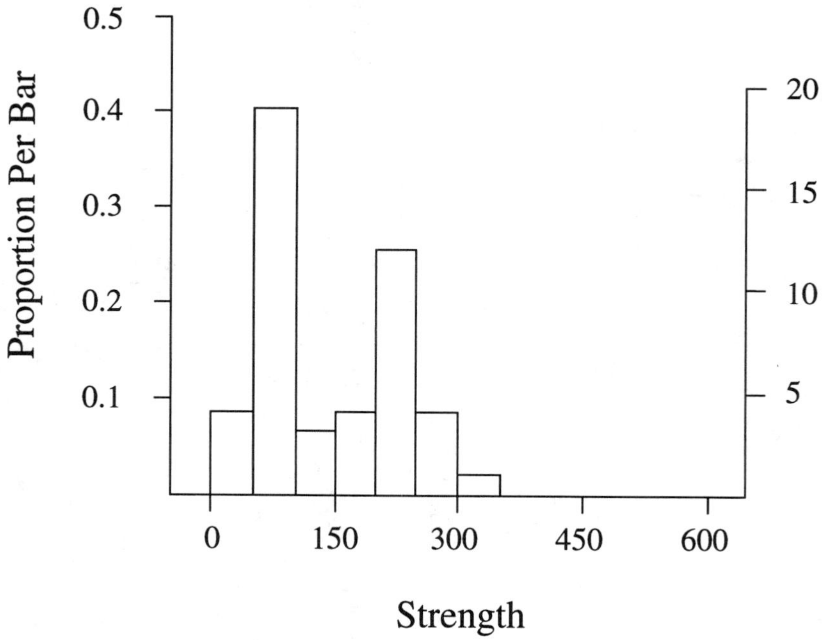

Figure11.8. Histogram of Strength Data

The anecdotal observations of field personnel to the effect that there seemed to be no discernible difference between the material from lots in which the "strength" index was low and those when it was in the satisfactory range could indicate many things. For example, the index could simply have nothing to do with anything.

In this situation, that seemed not to be the case. The company engineers were confident that suppressed values of the index should, in some cases, lead to material failures, of which there had, in fact, been none.

Perusing old records, we found cases in which the laboratory had inadvertently made two measurements from the same lot (naturally, they should have been replicating their tests always, but they had not purposely done so.) And, in some cases, it turned out that on the same testing machine, with the same material, normal range as well as low values had been found. So, then, one might suppose that the technicians obtaining the low readings were improperly trained or otherwise deficient. But still further investigation found that the same technician obtained normal and low readings for the same material on two different testing machines (there were 3 testing machines). So, then, perhaps there was a problem with one of the machines. But further investigation showed that low values had been observed on each of the machines, with approximately the same frequency.

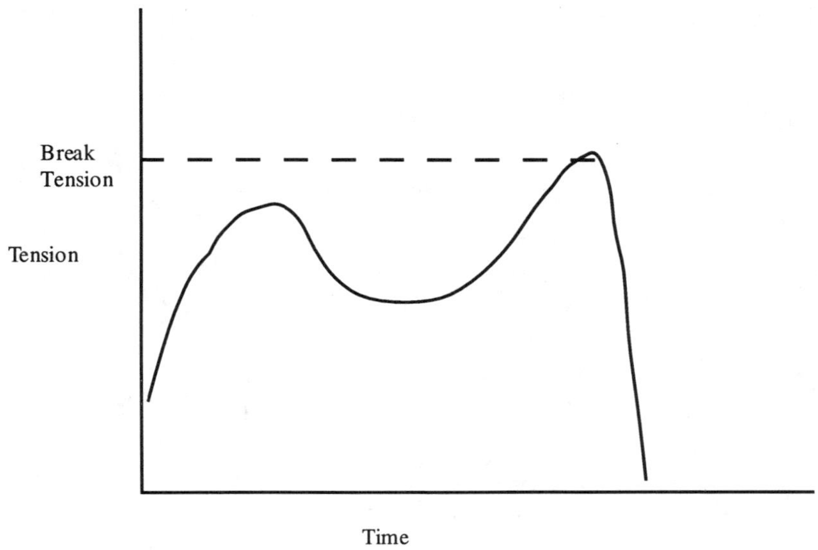

Figure 11.9. Tension Test of Material.

At this point, we arranged for the chief technician to take samples from three different lots and run them on each of the three machines, each lot replicated three times. For each set of material and for each machine, the technician observed both high and low measurements. A look at the testing curves (which had been automatically suppressed for observation, since an automated read-out software package bundled with the testing device was being utilized) revealed the difficulty.

In the case of this material, a sample was stretched by the machine until its elasticity was exceeded. At this time, the tension automatically dropped. But as the material was stretched further, the now deformed material actually increased in strength, until the material broke. The strength measurement which was being recorded was the tension at the time of break of the material. We show such a curve in Figure 11.10.

After retrieving the curves typical of the material under examination a possible candidate for the cause of the difficulty was apparent. Due to the special characteristics of the material, a high frequency jitter was present. If the software in the measuring instrument was not smoothing the data, and if it was attempting to find the "strength" (tension at failure) by looking for the tension the second time the tension began to decrease, then the kind of problem observed could well occur.

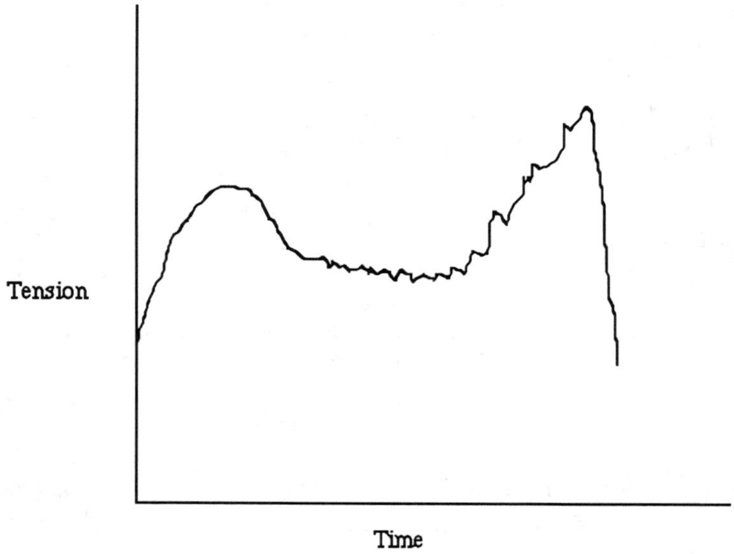

Figure 11.10. Tension Test of Nonstandard Material.

Table 11.8.

Time	Tension	Tension3	Tension33	Tension333
1	100	100	100	100
2	107	107	107	107
3	114	114	114	114
4	121	121	121	121
5	125	125	125	125
6	127	125	125	125
7	125	125	125	125
8	120	120	120	120
9	116	116	116	116
10	111	111	111	111
11	107	107	107	107
12	101	101	101	101
13	93	**98**	98	98
14	98	**93**	**96**	96
15	87	**96**	**93**	**96**
16	96	**91**	96	96
17	91	**96**	96	96
18	105	**100**	100	100
19	100	**105**	**102**	102
20	108	**102**	105	105
21	102	**108**	108	108
22	121	121	121	121
23	125	125	125	125
24	130	**128**	128	128
25	128	**130**	130	130
26	139	139	139	139
27	158	158	158	158
28	168	168	168	168
29	175	175	175	175
30	188	188	188	188
31	195	195	195	195
32	205	205	205	205
33	215	215	215	215
34	220	215	215	215
35	182	182	182	182
36	164	164	164	164
37	140	140	140	140

We immediately told the client to disconnect the "automatic yield finder" and reconnect the graphics terminal, so the technician could read the actual value as opposed to a bogus one. Then we called the instrumentation vendor to see if the conjecture about the way they wrote the software to find the "strength" could be substantiated. It was. Below, we indicate a quick fix for such a problem. Again, we rely on an Exploratory Data Analysis algorithm of Tukey's, namely the 3R smooth, where we replace each tension measurement by the median of the set formed by itself, and the measurement prior and the measurement subsequent.

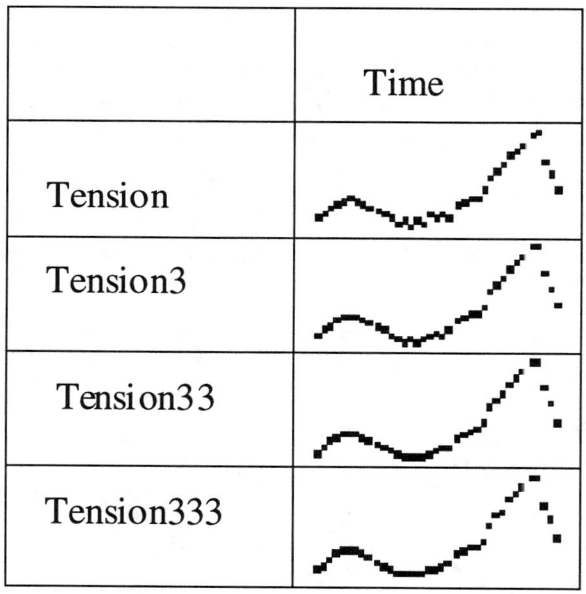

Figure 11.11. Tension Measurements with Smooths.

The "Tension" column shows the raw measurements (of the sort the software was using to find the second local maximum). In the second column, "Tension3," we have used the "3R" smooth. To show how this works, let us consider the 13'th Tension measurement, which is equal to 93. We look at the observation before and that after to see the triple {101,93,98}. We then replace the 13'th observation by the middle observation of the triple formed by the observation and the one just before and that just after. In other words, we write down 98 to replace 93. We start at the top of the list, and continue all the way through to the end (generally, the first and the last observations are not changed). We denote in bold face those values which have changed from the preceding iteration of the "3" smooth. In this case, three iterations brings us to point where there are no more changes. "3R" means "3 smooth repeated until no further changes take place." Accordingly, here, the "Tension333" column is the '3R" end result. In Figure 11.11, we denote the raw data and the evolution of smoothing as we proceed through the iterations. We note how the smooth tends to eliminate the perception of high frequency jitter as local maxima and minima.

The smoothing of the data solved the problem with the major client. The "fix" was incredibly easy, requiring only a few lines of computer code. The government approved sole source vendor of computing software for the measurement device was another matter, for they would neither allow access to their code so that it could be modified, nor did they seem to be able to effect the fix themselves. Six months after the fix had been presented them, gratis, they had not made the indicated modification. Therefore, it had to be carried out off line.

11.6 SPC versus Quality Assurance

In the "quality assurance" paradigm used by the Soviets (as well as by most American firms), the following evolution is common:

1. 100% inspection is implemented to see whether each end product item falls within acceptable levels set arbitrarily (i.e., external to the capabilities of the production system).

2. A large fraction of the items is found not to be within the acceptable levels. These are sent back for rework.

3. Management gets tired of the constant alarms and ignores them.

The Deming paradigm is quite different and follows the following evolution:

1. The characteristics of the modules of the production process are measured (generally time indexed), summarized in the mean and variance of each relevant data stream. These are by definition, "normalcy" for the process.

2. The mean and standard deviation of each lot are compared with confidence intervals from the overall process.

3. If a lot has a mean and/or standard deviation outside the confidence interval, it is deemed "out of control."

4. We then try and see whether this "Pareto glitch" can be used to identify a problem in the system.

5. We fix the problem.

There are many reasons why one might question the efficacy of the Deming paradigm for statistical process control. For example, it appears to be without standards. The system is essentially checked for consistency of performance. There would appear to be no help in finding items which are defective according to the specifications of the customer. That is a valid point. SPC does not address itself to the problem of finding defective items. SPC is oriented toward finding defects in the system itself which may lead to the production of defective items.

Next, suppose we find an "out of control" lot. Might not the cause simply be intermittent in nature? That is, we may be chasing a "will-o-the-wisp." Jugglers drop balls, after all, and to find that one has been dropped would appear to be no particularly useful discovery. The most important fact to be noted here is that systems do not generally behave like jugglers. A better analogy is that of a pack of wolves which largely lives off domestic sheep. The ranchers note that they are loosing stock regularly. But one night, the wolves make an all out assault leaving tracks back to their den. The ranchers follow the tracks back to the den and wipe out out the wolf pack, ending that particular problem once and for all.

Both the juggler analogy and the wolf pack analogy are simply plausible. It is experience which has shown that the wolf pack analogy is much the more accurate in practise.

11.7 Design and SPC

An early name for the automobile was "horseless carriage." Is it reasonable to suppose that it could have been developed by taking an ordinary horse carriage and making piecewise improvements according to the Deming paradigm? By no means. One can make the argument that SPC is simply work at the margin, since it is clear that without a good design for, say, a car, there is little hope that simple step-wise optimization will get us to a competitive product. That this argument is, in practise, false is clear if one observes that design modification is a natural part of the evolutionary optimization which makes up statistical process control. Anyone who observes the excellence of a Japanese luxury car, such as the LS 400, is impressed with similarities to German designs, particularly that of Mercedes. No doubt that a certain amount of "creative borrowing" of design at the beginning of the LS 400 was utilized. Yet, over the years, extensive use of SPC has enabled Toyota to find opportunities for improved design of its Lexus line. The resulting product looks similar to a Mercedes but is quite different, improved in many ways, and, thanks to the elimination of rework via SPC, sells for a fraction of its German near equivalent. To what does Toyota owe the success of the LS 400, to design or to SPC? No doubt, the management of Toyota would claim that the integration of SPC has been so thorough, it would be impossible to say where design stopped and SPC entered into the picture.

11.8 Design versus Tweaking the System

Over thirty years ago, one of us (Thompson) was working in the summer for a large paper company.

The company owned massive forests in central Florida, which were used for making paper. Since the forests were located in hot country, most of the wood fibers were produced under "summer" conditions. Summer wood fibers, examined under a microscope look rather like pencils. Wood fibers produced during cooler weather ("spring" wood) examined under a microscope look look like pieces of tape. The mix of wood was roughly 80% summer wood and 20% spring wood. Summer wood fibers are excellent for producing tough material, such as packing boxes, which resist damage from a punch from some object. (See Figure 11.7).

On the other hand, spring wood fibers, having larger surface area per unit volume (and the surface of wood fibers is covered with binding tendrils), produces a paper which is much harder to tear than summer wood. Such properties are desirable for, say, toilet paper. The company, which produced many kinds of paper, including toilet paper, was confronted by a competitor with massive Canadian forests, whose trees had roughly 20% summer wood and 80% spring wood fibers. It was hoped somehow to increase the proportion of spring wood fibers upon demand. Botanical strategies did not appear practical, i.e., it seemed there was no usable variety of tree which could be planted in the Florida climate giving a greatly enhanced proportion of spring wood fibers. What to do? For several years a strategy had been followed which would simply cut the fiber longitudinally, thus increasing the surface area per volume. This was to be done by passing aa laminar aqueous solution of fibers past a knife edge. The fix was not working. A little investigation by Thompson showed the reason: the thinnest practicable knife edge was not much thinner than a wood fiber, so that when the fiber hit the knife edge, it simply rotated, presenting a cut which was very much not longitudinal.

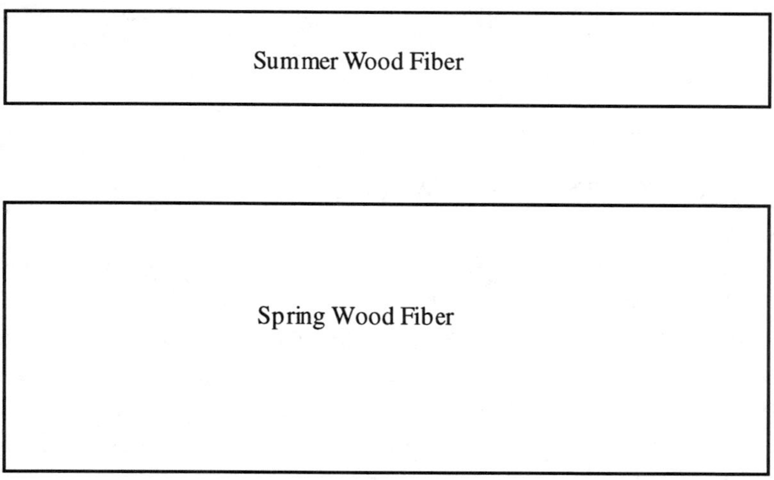

Figure 11.12. Wood Fibers.

It was observed by Thompson that the company regularly removed bits of gravel from the suspension of wood fibers by pumping it under high pressure through a conical cleaner. Clearly, summer wood is more like spring wood than it is like gravel. Nevertheless, the cleaner appears to work, in part, because of the differences in moments of inertia between wood fibers and gravel. It appeared worth a try to see whether the cleaner might be used to separate spring wood from summer wood. Upon one pass of the wood stream through the cleaner, it was very hard to tell whether the top stream was richer in spring fiber than the bottom one (at that time, fiber types were classified by technicians working with microscopes). However, taking the top stream and using it as the input into a second cleaner, and so on, for a series of twenty cleaners, it was possible to get to an output with more than 80% spring wood (remember, the input was 20% spring wood).

The use of a series of cleaners as a fractionator for obtaining virtually any desired proportion of spring and summer wood was extremely inexpensive. In one fell swoop, using equipment already at hand, the company had a new economically viable procedure for making specialty papers.

Admittedly, the procedure was not developed using any formalized SPC procedure, but it was carried out noting that something on the line already might be used for doing something else than its original purpose. Had the company, as a matter of course, monitored the input and output proportions of spring and summer wood fibers, the Thompson fractionator might have been discovered much earlier.

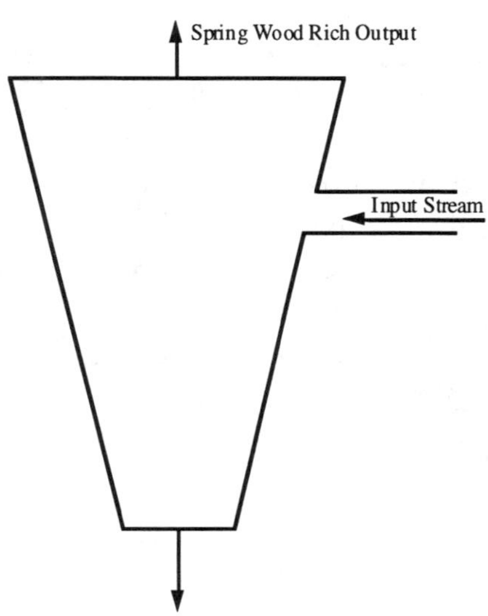

Figure 11.13. Cleaner as Fractionator.

A great deal of time and expense would have been saved.

So, was this a design or a tweak? Probably a tweak, if by a tweak we mean some improvement that can be effected more or less with the equipment at hand and using information readily at hand. In this case, the tweak had an enormous impact on the paper company. Thompson received his pay for the summer ($1,500) and a great deal of satisfaction and self confidence.

Take such tweaks, multiplied many fold, and you may well bring forth something like the LS 400. The SPC tweak is not appropriate for getting from a horse carriage to an automobile. For such a step, a quantum design leap is required. Once the quantum leap has been achieved, however, we may tweak a good ways before the next quantum leap is required.

In the case of high tech industries, some hold that design really is everything. Just come up with a good product and the production will take care of itself. The facts do not square with such a view. The enormous success of Motorolla in microchip production is credited, in large measure, to its use of SPC. And SPC is the rule rather than the exception throughout the Japanese semiconductor industry.

11.9 Some Final Thoughts

Henry Ford lived prior to the Deming SPC revolution. Ford's discovery that a machine, once a particular flaw has been repaired, is unlikely soon to experience the same difficulty is, of course, key to modern technology. Ford's Model T had approximately 5,000 parts, and the idea that such a complex system could function for very long without breaking down is, perhaps, Ford's greatest contribution. This notion of the inertia of reliability ranks with Pareto's Maxim as a pillar upon which the statistical process revolution could be constructed. Placed together, Pareto and Ford and Deming have given us the paradigm of enlightened industrial production:

1. Eliminate most potential problems at the design stage.

2. Use extensive pilot study testing to eliminate many remaining undiscovered problems.

3. Use testing at the production stage to improve constantly the system, always remembering that glitches in the outputs are

generally due to defects in a few submodules of the production process rather than a general malaise.

It is interesting to examine Ford's Four Principles of Industrial Production [2]:

1. An absence of fear of the future or veneration of the past. One who fears failure limits his activities. Failure is only the opportunity to begin again. There is no disgrace in honest failure; there is disgrace in fearing to fail. What is past is useful only as it suggests ways and means for progress.

2. A disregard of competition. Whoever does a thing best ought to be the one to do it. It is criminal to try to get business away from another man – criminal because one is then trying to lower for personal gain the condition of one's fellowmen – to rule by force instead of by intelligence.

3. The putting of service before profit. Without a profit, business cannot expand. There is nothing inherently wrong about making a profit. Well-conducted business enterprise cannot fail to return a profit, but profit must and inevitably will come as a reward for good service – it must be the result of service.

4. Manufacturing is not buying low and selling high. It is the process of buying materials fairly and, with the smallest possible addition of cost, transforming those materials into a consumable product and giving it to the consumer. Gambling, speculating and sharp dealing tend only to clog this progression.

These principles are hardly those of a complacent conservative. They are, rather, the thoughts of a true social revolutionary. In his plant, Ford introduced the 40 hour week, doubled the going wage, employed over 20% handicapped workers, instituted English language schools which were utilized by persons from over 150 linguistic and dialect groups. Ford's Model T, which he termed "the people's car" (a term shamelessly appropriated by Volkswagen) changed the structure of cities and of society as a whole.

Ford was no saint, to be sure. His eccenticities and prejudices are well known and were sufficiently "off the wall" to frustrate his ambitions to hold high public office. Indeed, Ford generally realized his limitations and always regarded his success as due to his tapping into an almost mystical natural force. To the "invisible hand" of Adam Smith, he added a level of technological progress of which Smith never dreamed. Having created such an engine of productivity, Ford felt that his success had been as irresitible as gravity.

There can be little doubt that governmental intervention in the economy has not always been helpful in nurturing increases in productivity, and hence, in the standard of material living. We harken back to the observation of Pareto that it is unrealistic to suppose that leaders in government act uniformly for the "common good" oblivious to their own personal interests. Taxation, regulation and the power to redistribute wealth give governmental leaders levers which enable them to network themselves into a "nomenklatura" of power and privilege. And a natural synergy exists between members of the private sector and government. Pareto's "circulation of the elites" between business and government is a longstanding reality.

But, increasingly, international competition appears to be acting as a force which limits totally unreasonable levels of taxation, subsidy and regulation. The Deming paradigm of management based on knowledge of systems of production (rather than the old boy networks) has given an enormous competitive edge to those who practice it. We do not forsee a time when governmental leaders and their legal and corporate allies will smilingly give up their power and privilege. Nevertheless, international competition is moving them to less influence, willy nilly. We have not written this book to prepare young managers for some libertarian utopia, which we, personally, might prefer. Rather, we have sought to give modeling insights which managers might use to good effect in the real world. The economy of this real world offers a myriad of imperfections, but also unlimited opportunities for translating technological progress into an improved life for all.

Throughout this book, we have attempted to use case studies where possible. Too much of a cavalier attitude is given in most business texts as to the fact that businesses exist to provide real goods and services. There really are no "widget" manufacturing companies. The entrepreneur must never fall into the trap of feeling that somehow he or she need only worry about marketing, finance and accounting. These are important, but as Ford observed 75 years ago, the real bottom line is the delivery to the public of goods expertly produced and for which there is a demand. The entrepreneur starting a new business will be more harried than the manager of a well established company. He or she will be tempted to brush aside notions of continuing improvement as advocated by Deming. These considerations will frequently be regarded as ones which the exigencies of day to day operation of a new company do not allow time for attention. That is unfortunate. The time to commit to a program of continuing improvement is at the stage of planning of the company, well before its doors have been opened. It is easy for us to say this, and to some our attention to continuing quality improvement may appear like an empty exhortation to perform good works. That would be unfortunate, for both of us have spent a fair amount of our professional lives helping companies which got into trouble because management put systematic quality improvement off till a future time when there would be the leisure to do it. Sometimes we can put out the fire. Sometimes nobody can.

We end this book with an amalgam of the first two of Deming's Fourteen Points:

> Create constancy of purpose toward improvement of product and service, with a plan to become competitive and to stay in business. ...Adopt the new philosophy. We are in a new economic age.

References

[1]Deming, W. E., *Quality, Productivity and Competitive Position*, Cambridge: MIT Center for Advanced Engineering Studies, 1982, pp. 16-17.

[2]Ford, H., *My Life and Work*, Sydney: Cornstalk Press, 1926, p. 273.

[3]Thompson, J. R., "American quality control: what went wrong? What can we do to fix it?" *Proceedings of the 1985 Conference on Applied Analysis in Aerospace, Industry and Medical Sciences*, Chhikara, Raj, ed., Houston: University of Houston, 1985, pp. 247-255.

[4]Thompson, J.R. and J. Koronacki, *Statistical Process Control for Quality Improvement*, New York: Chapman & Hall, 1993.

[5] Williams, E.E. and Thompson, J.R., *The Economics of Production and Productivity: A Modeling Approach*, Austin: Capital Book Company, 1996.

Problems

Problem 11.1 A company is producing bolts of 10 centimeters diameter. On each day a random sample of four bolts is taken. Using both mean and standard deviation control charts, comment as to whether the production system appears to be in control.

Diameter Measurements				
Day	X_1	X_2	X_3	X_4
1	10.36	9.21	9.67	9.75
2	10.31	9.25	10.27	9.84
3	10.28	10.24	10.03	10.07
4	10.27	9.69	10.11	10.17
5	10.40	9.96	9.73	10.39
6	9.91	9.54	9.72	9.82
7	9.38	9.88	10.03	10.18
8	9.43	9.46	9.62	9.62
9	9.93	9.74	9.57	10.14
10	9.98	10.05	9.70	10.19
11	10.35	10.31	9.96	10.33
12	9.81	9.38	9.90	10.23
13	10.14	9.70	9.93	9.84
14	9.55	9.40	10.10	9.79
15	9.97	10.00	9.84	10.05
16	10.04	9.82	9.69	10.01
17	10.18	9.75	9.67	10.47
18	9.98	10.41	10.57	9.64
19	10.49	10.13	10.50	9.44
20	9.92	9.66	10.10	9.58
21	10	9.58	10.25	10.02
22	9.94	9.73	9.95	9.75
23	10.11	10.09	9.98	10.11
24	10.12	9.97	9.89	9.97
25	9.90	10.15	10.53	10.68
26	9.73	10.11	9.84	9.57
27	9.92	9.82	9.56	10.07
28	10.28	10.02	9.84	9.90
29	10.19	10.28	9.68	10.37
30	10.10	10.09	9.95	10.16

Problem 11.2 In a statistical process control situation, let us consider items from N lots each of size M. The overall sample mean is given by

$$\overline{\overline{X}} = \frac{1}{MN}\sum_{i=1}^{N}\sum_{j=1}^{M} X_{i,j}$$

For the construction of control charts, one might be tempted to use as variance estimate

$$s^2 = \frac{1}{MN-1}\sum_{i=1}^{N}\sum_{j=1}^{M}(X_{i,j} - \overline{\overline{X}})^2$$

This is generally not appropriate. By the use of an appropriate mathematical model, show why this is the case. And give an appropriate estimator, using the model to show why your alternative estimator is appropriate for the in control population variance.

Problem 11.3 Comment on whether the following system is in control.

Profile of Defects			
TIME	SAMPLE SIZE	DEFECTIVES	%
MON.A	100	4	4
B	100	8	8
C	100	3	3
TUE.A	100	1	1
B	100	1	1
C	100	13	13
WED.A	100	5	5
B	100	5	5
C	100	2	2
THU.A	100	3	3
B	100	10	10
C	100	14	14
FRI.A	100	2	2
B	100	10	10
C	100	2	2
SAT.A	100	1	1
B	100	3	3
C	100	5	5

Problem 11.4 Use the tabulation of personal computers returned for defects during 30 consecutive months to see whether any month appears to be out of control.

Returned Computers	
Month	Number Returned
1	122
2	101
3	132
4	102
5	121
6	121
7	111
8	99
9	124
10	133
11	120
12	122
13	124
14	112
15	132
16	102
17	118
18	134
19	109
20	122
21	127
22	132
23	117
24	112
25	123
26	123
27	165
28	102
29	112
30	101